SIMPLE
BUT
NOT EASY

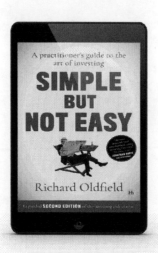

SIMPLE
BUT
NOT EASY

*An autobiographical and biased
book about investing*

2nd edition

RICHARD OLDFIELD

HARRIMAN HOUSE LTD
3 Viceroy Court
Bedford Road
Petersfield
Hampshire
GU32 3LJ
GREAT BRITAIN
Tel: +44 (0)1730 233870

Email: enquiries@harriman-house.com
Website: harriman.house

First published in Great Britain in June 2007 by Doddington Publishing. This second
edition published by Harriman House in 2021.

Paperback ISBN: 978-0-85719-800-6
eBook ISBN: 978-0-85719-801-3

British Library Cataloguing in Publication Data
A CIP catalogue record for this book can be obtained from the British Library.

Illustrations by James Burgess. Cover painting by Christopher Oldfield.

CONTENTS

PREFACE TO THE
SECOND EDITION

FOURTEEN years is a long time in investment. A lot has happened since the first edition of this book was published in 2007. Just to reprint did not seem, now, quite good enough. So this edition contains all of the 2007 book, but with this preface and a new afterword. So, to underline this point, pages 1–237 date from the 2007 edition unchanged (except for being re-typeset). The book has the same title as before; if I had to give it a new one, *Complicated and Extremely Difficult* might be it.

Nassim Nicholas Taleb writes about black swans: beings assumed not to exist, but which do. Thoroughly unpredictable things happen. Hurricanes just occasionally do happen in Hertford, Hereford and Hampshire. The 2008–09 global financial crisis was a black swan, a combination of events which was thought impossible. It was the last stage in a process described by another economist, Hyman Minsky. Because everything is going swimmingly, it is assumed that it will always go swimmingly, so that on the contrary when trouble starts – the Minsky moment – it is quickly calamitous: the result of a long period of low volatility is high volatility.

We have had high volatility in spades. The black swan of the financial crisis has been followed by the black swan of quantitative easing, with central banks pushing interest rates below zero and buying their own governments' bonds on a colossal scale. A third black swan, associated with near-zero interest rates, has been the appetite for mega-financing, and not just mega-financing but repeat mega-financing, of private companies with enormous losses stretching into the distant future. Now we have seen the blackest swan of them all, the Covid-19 crisis.

While these black swans have been flapping their menacing wings, investment has been at least as difficult as ever, and for many, including me, more difficult. Most books about investment by practitioners are written from hubristic heights. This is not. I began *Simple But Not Easy* with a chapter on howlers. To do justice to all the howlers committed since then would require a very long book.

Underlying individual howlers has been the nagging problem that the whole approach of value investing – that is to say, investing in companies with low valuations in terms of the usual measures such as price-earnings ratios, price-cash flow ratios, and price-book value ratios – has appeared to be a howler. It is certainly requiring immense patience. I am as convinced as ever of the merits of value investing.

The black swans have made much in the world of investment more complicated. The financial crisis revolved around hideously complex financial instruments which hardly anyone understood. They were a little like the Schleswig-Holstein question as described by Lord Palmerston: "only three men in Europe have ever understood it. One was Prince Albert, who is dead. The second was a German professor, who became mad. I am the third, and I have forgotten all about it." What followed the crisis – quantitative easing and negative interest rates – is novel and complicated in the sense that it is outside the experience of us all. But the basic lessons of *Simple But Not Easy* in 2007 are still lessons for 2021.

This edition of *Simple But Not Easy* is dedicated to the memory of two men who died within a few weeks of one another in 2019: Hans Rausing and Peter Stormonth Darling, both inspiring leaders.

Peter Stormonth Darling was chairman of Mercury Asset

Management when I worked there. He and I travelled from time to time to the US and Canada, and once to the Middle East. When he was held up at Immigration for the second night in a row because of a problem with his Canadian passport, his despairing plea reverberated across the terminal of Abu Dhabi airport to the distant corner in which I was chatting with a London banker: "Have I got to go through this all over again?" The banker wryly commented: "I don't think your chairman is constitutionally suited to travel in the Middle East."

But in fact Peter was constitutionally suited to travel anywhere: relaxed, curious, friendly to all, engaging with everyone. He was knowledgeable about all sorts of things and wore his knowledge lightly, never showing off, never grandstanding. He was utterly modest. His geniality and modesty made him the perfect chairman of an organisation which needed to hold together a number of individuals with a lot of ego, ambition and ability. It was impossible to have a bad-tempered meeting if he was chairing it. In investment crises he was a pillar of calm wisdom. His mantra, "do nothing", was much more right generally than the thing which would have been done if anything had been done. His book about S. G. Warburg and Mercury, *City Cinderella* (W&N, 1999), has all the best Warburg anecdotes. He wrote another book, about the Korean war in which he served in the Black Watch; this was privately published and had limited circulation. I suspect he found it too emotional a subject to present to public view. He wrote the foreword to the first edition of this book.

Hans Rausing, who built Tetra Pak, had that very special Rooseveltian gift of always making people feel better. Whatever news you brought him, good or bad, you went away feeling uplifted. That was one of several ways in which he was a great man. He dominated any room because of his enormous character as well as his height. He was an inventor and a pioneering engineer. He was a brilliant businessman. I was once with him at a meeting long after the Tetra Pak days, in Ukraine. Someone put forward a rather ambitious expansion proposition, not thoroughly thought through.

He was supported half-heartedly by his partner. Hans asked opinions, starting with me, and I burbled some management-speak about an interesting idea needing more research but no action for the time being. Everyone else was cautious about it too: too early to do anything, more research needed. "Good," said Hans, banging his fist on the table. "We go ahead." He and I left the meeting room together and he exclaimed happily: "That was an excellent meeting. It reminded me of meetings in the old days at Tetra Pak."

Post-Tetra Pak, he regarded ordinary investment in a portfolio of securities as very dull, just financial jiggery-pokery. Even so, to those like me who were doing it, he never failed to be inspiring, always optimistic and encouraging, never looking back and never blaming. He had some memorable aphorisms: "if it is not necessary to do it, it is necessary not to do it;" "all in the best of disorder;" "if unsure and full of doubt, run around and scream and shout." Another summed up his attitude to fame and fortune: "some people think it is important to be important. I have always thought it important to be unimportant." Many great men do not inspire much affection. He did.

RICHARD OLDFIELD
London
July 2021

INTRODUCTION

"AND what do you do?"
"I'm an investment manager."
"How nice." Pause. Slight embarrassment. "I'm afraid I don't know anything about investment."

The subject is a sure social conversation-stopper. The business of investment, said John Maynard Keynes, is intolerably boring for anyone free from an instinct for gambling. For many it is a no-go area.

A friend who looks after the money of one of Britain's wealthiest families told me that when members of that family come of age, and so into some money of their own, he has a chat with them. He tells them that they can either become actively involved in how their money is managed; or they can leave it to him and his colleagues in the family investment office. If they choose the latter, "Congratulations," he tells them, "you are normal."

Another person in the business has told me, "I have always thought that investing is something to do, rather than to talk about." Investment involves the fluctuating ownership from a sedentary position of what were once pieces of paper and have now been virtualised so that they are no more than entries in some computer records. It is an activity which can seem unreal.

Consequently, it is rather less normal to be interested in investment than in a dozen other potential enthusiasms. But most investment managers do what they do because they find it strangely captivating.

People outside the profession think it complicated. Generally speaking, it is not. One of the reasons that investment is, for the amateur, a rather obscure activity is that, like anything specialised, it is full of jargon, much of it devised to put off the amateur and to reassure professionals that what they are doing is scientific. But the rudiments of investing in equities and bonds can be expressed in fairly ordinary English, and picked up by anybody.

On the other hand, though not complicated, investment is difficult. People on the outside tend to think that anyone on the inside should be able to do better than the market indices purely by virtue of being a professional. Sadly not. Professional managers find it hard to beat the market over the long term. Fewer than half of professional investment managers outperform the market itself. All of them can be quite sure that they will not outperform the market in every year.

The fact that investment managers in aggregate are not producing anything useful does not mean that all investment managers are useless. How to decide who is likely to do a useful, outperforming, job is a fascinating challenge. To succeed in it the investor must first understand the paradox that investment is simple but not easy.

I should explain what this book is, and what it is not. It is not a stage-one primer. I have not provided a glossary of terms. If the reader wants to find out what an equity is or, more sophisticated, the definition of a Sharpe ratio, there are other places to look. It is not an academic book, and to avoid giving that sort of impression I have eschewed footnotes. Nor is it a detailed exposition of investment analysis. There is no discussion of how to look at a balance sheet or cash flow statement.

What it is meant to be is something in the middle: a commonsensical approach to investing, stripped of mystery and as far as possible of jargon. The aim is to make the subject of investment accessible to the many people who find it potentially interesting but baffling.

Simple But Not Easy has, I hope, plenty of snippets interesting to the experienced professional, but it is aimed also at the interested amateur investor with some money, possibly a hundred thousand pounds, maybe many millions – a broad spectrum.

The wealth management industry divides the well-off between four groups. Excluding the value of their homes, the 'mass affluent', about 4% of the UK population, each have more than £75,000 in assets to invest. 'High net worth', with up to £5 million, account for 0.7% of the population. 'Ultra high net worth', with more than £5m, are 0.3%. Finally, the 'super rich' are the top 1,000 richest, with more than £50m.

Any of these mass-affluent, high- or ultra-high-net-worth and super-rich individuals may be curious about investing. They might be quite happy to delegate to an investment manager, through one or more funds or portfolios, but want to make their choice without feeling alienated by a sense of ignorance and with a modicum of confidence, using criteria other than the colour of the manager's eyes and how good recent performance seems to have been.

The investor with millions will have the chance to scrutinise investment managers much more closely than the investor with a few hundred thousand; but even the latter, probably choosing a mutual fund or investment trust, has the right to understand what the manager of the chosen fund stands for, and what it is reasonable to expect and not to expect. The investor should have the means to understand as well as the right. This book is an attempt to provide some of the means.

Many investors, though happy to delegate to a manager, are also inclined to do a bit of direct investing themselves. For that, more than this book is needed. But I hope that it will provide some useful background for those who would like, at least to an extent, to DIY.

The advantage of some DIY is not only what it may achieve in itself, but the extra dimension of experience it then brings to judging others. Since investing is simple, those who want to manage their own money and are prepared to spend a bit of time (but not all their time) can do so. Besides having a decent chance of results as good as those of many professionals, they have the satisfaction of doing it themselves.

Having had the rare opportunity to observe other fund managers as well as to be one myself, what I aim to convey here are the fruits of that observation as well as of my own successes and failures. Failures first.

ONE

Howlers Galore

MY family motto used to be *vulnere viresco* – 'through my wound I grow strong'. This was a typical dog-Latin pun on our name: an old field, ploughed up and resown, grows a crop again and flourishes. But in India in the early 1800s an aggrieved employee tried to murder my great great grandfather with a sword. He was wounded in the back and lost two fingers. Thereafter, he could not bear the motto and changed it to something much duller.

Vulnere viresco is a perfect motto for an investment manager. That people learn from their mistakes is a truism. In investment management there are plenty of them to learn from. Mistakes are the things that make one fractionally better at it, at least as much as successes, and any manager who has only successes to talk about is a charlatan or a novice. Howlers, anyway, are much more interesting. That does not mean one should be constantly indulging in lachrymose retrospection. Sir Siegmund Warburg had a maxim, "Always cry over spilt milk." But if investors thought all the time about past mistakes, investment management would be a sorrowful business and so dispiriting that they would be far too depressed ever to invest with confidence; and confidence is vital to good investment. Nonetheless, one should at least, I feel, examine the spilt milk quite carefully, if not cry over it, because the experience of howlers can be instructive.

Howlers recur. A good investor still makes mistakes nearly, but not quite, half the time. The manager who makes asset allocation decisions correctly all the time, or who chooses shares all of which outperform the market, does not exist. The gap between the successful manager and the unsuccessful is between one who gets it right 55% or 60% of the time and another who gets it right 40–45% of the time.

Here are some of my howlers which I have found particularly illuminating.

1. Ethics matter

In 1982 I had been managing portfolios for about a year. I was interested in the US company Warner Communications. An experienced old hand told me there were ethical problems in the management. I brushed this aside and bought the shares.

One day in early December, the morning after my stag night, I groped my way into the office after little sleep and with a crushing hangover to find that the share price had halved overnight, only a few weeks after my purchase. I had to decide what on earth to do about it, a decision I was in no fit state to make. I staggered round the office, explaining myself to colleagues.

Investment managers have to learn early in their career that share prices can fall precipitously. This was the first time I appreciated what a complete fool one can make of oneself in investment management. Every manager should also learn not simply to abandon ship when such a disaster occurs, but to see whether anything can be salvaged. After such a share price fall, the right answer, emotionally difficult as it is, may be to go back for more.

*The author discussing recent events at
Warner Communications with colleagues*

With one exception, I did not experience quite such a savage collapse in the price of shares I owned for another 22 years. The exception was in the crash of October 1987, when the market indices fell by a third in a couple of days. But that was rather different because it was not specific to an individual company; it was a general market fall, which created a certain feeling of beleaguered companionship, a touch of Dunkirk spirit among investment managers.

The shocker for which I waited 22 years related to the US pharmaceutical company Merck. In October 2004 we held the shares. One day that month the price of Merck fell by 27% after the company announced that it was withdrawing one of its major drugs, Vioxx, because it had been found to increase the risk of heart attacks. I was out of the office at the time, and my colleague who told me the news on the telephone remembers me asking immediately, more hardened by then, "How much cash have we got?" We bought some more shares on the same day, at $31 per share.

There was another sharp fall ten months later, when the first court case resulting from Vioxx went badly against Merck. Immediately after this we made a further purchase at $27. This is generally, though not always, the right reaction to such traumatising falls, and with Merck it was the right reaction. Within six months the shares were at $35. We had thus rescued respectability from the jaws of disaster. A year or so later – after we had, prematurely, sold, and that is another story – the share price was $50.

The other lesson I learned from that dismal Warner Communications stag night aftermath was to pay some attention when people whose opinion you value say that there is some ethical issue. Ethics is not just a county to the east of London. Ethics matter, for material as well as ethical reasons. Markets are particularly intolerant of seriously unethical behaviour by managements, and the revelation of scandal is something which can be relied upon to cause a collapse in a share price.

2. Travel narrows the mind

In 1997 I was working for a family office and talked regularly with a group of experienced advisers. Early in the year I went to Russia for the first time. The Russian market had been booming and international investors were pouring in. I was one of those who poured. Russia seemed full of potential with its large and well-educated population and an economy which was being liberalised.

The visit confirmed my prejudices. At the next meeting of the family advisers (one of whom had employed several thousand people in Russia, spoke the language, and could quote passages of Pushkin; whereas I had spent two nights in the Baltschung Kempinski Hotel opposite the Kremlin and had jogged down the river as far as Gorky Park) I opined with the confidence of the newly expert: "I think investing in Russia is safer than investing in Coca-Cola."

A few months later the market started to go down. In August 1998 both the stock market and the currency collapsed. The economy crumbled. In US dollar terms, in a few months the Russian market fell in value by 90% – a collapse on the scale of the Great Crash in the US. My comparison of Russia and Coca-Cola haunted me as possibly the silliest thing about investment I had ever said.

It was, and it wasn't.

One lesson of this episode was that travel often narrows the mind.

My visit had confirmed my prejudices because visits nearly always do confirm prejudices. It takes more than a few days divided between aeroplanes, offices and hotel rooms, with the odd visit to a factory and time off to wander round a shop or two, to undermine a good solid prejudice. Visits make visitors think they really know something about the place, and then they are prepared to back the prejudice to an extent to which earlier they would not have dared.

The practicalities of life mean that quite often the visit comes at a fairly late stage in the particular market movement. Making time for the visit and planning it takes a while, and the planning only starts when the market has already been attracting attention for months or more. The investor therefore gets confirmation, and confidence to double the stakes, at what may be close to being the wrong time.

The first lesson, therefore, of "Russia is safer than Coca-Cola" is to keep one's distance.

The next few years provided more interesting lessons. Coca-Cola was a darling among growth stocks in 1997. It was the quintessential all-American company, with the most valuable brand in the world. It had limitless prospects for growth, if only it could persuade the people of China that they should all drink Coke and fulfil the hopes of one of its chairmen, Robert Goizueta, that Coke should be drunk as readily as tap water. In March 1997 its price-earnings ratio was 42. From 1997 to 2006 its earnings per share rose by 60%. But, no longer a darling, the market attributed to it a price-earnings ratio of 21. Consequently its share price at the end of 2006 was 20% lower than in May 1997 – and 48% below its peak in June 1998. Its fall was not spectacular, like that of the Russian market, but gradual and unremarkable.

From its bottom in October 1998 the Russian market doubled and redoubled and redoubled again, and the value of the rouble also doubled. By the end of 2005, the Russian market in US dollar terms was worth 18 times more than at the end of 1998. More to the point, it was worth 3.7 times more than in May 1997.

So, on the one hand, what I said to that group of advisers in May 1997 was memorably foolish. It was clearly safer in a sense to own Coca-Cola, which in any single year went down no more than 21%, than the Russian market, which in three months fell by 67%. The risk of apoplexy on opening one's newspaper was greater with Russia than with Coca-Cola. On the other hand, the investor who held tight in Russia would in the end, by 2005, have made 270%, about 16% per annum, while the investor in Coca-Cola would have lost 20%. So can it really be said that to own Coca-Cola was safer than to own Russia?

Safety is in the eye of the investor. It depends partly on time horizons. The nature of markets is that people are most enthusiastic about a market, and most sure of a quick buck, when the excesses are greatest. The Russian market had already had three extraordinary years following the collapse of Communism. I fell into the trap of enthusiasm at the peak, joining a crowded party when there was room for little disappointment.

In the event, disappointment is an understatement. Everything which could go wrong did go wrong in the next 18 months. Irrespective of what actually happened, it would have been silly of anyone to invest in a market as volatile as Russia expecting to cash in after a year or two. One should invest in equities, which are volatile, only with a long-term perspective, and in the most volatile of equities with an especially long-term perspective – five years or more – and only with money which one can be sure of not needing in the next few years.

It also matters a great deal how investors react after a 90% fall. Something so devastating can lead to completely the wrong decision. It is easy to say, when your $1,000 has turned into $100, "I can't take any more of this. I would rather be sure of my $100 than risk losing that too." Selling at the bottom is an unsurprisingly common fault, because the bottom in a share price is the moment of maximum fear. If the fall is 90%, the fear is acute.

Perhaps the best thing to be, after a 90% fall, is asleep. If Rip van Winkle were the investor in Russia, he would not have been subjected to the awful emotional pressure which a large share price or market fall exerts: he would have slept through it all.

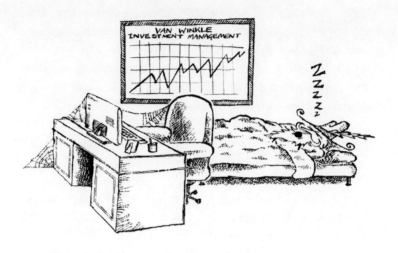

Later, on waking up to find that his Russian investments had made him 270% and his Coca-Cola had lost him 20%, there would have been no question that Russia had been the safer of the two. This shows the advantage of keeping your distance.

Safety, therefore, is not an absolute term. It is a function both of the investor's time horizon and of the investment's volatility. This Russia/Coca-Cola story is a demonstration, in an extreme way, of the different meanings of safety to different investors. For someone needing a lump of money in a year's time, the only safe investment is a cash deposit or a short-term government bond. For someone with no imminent need of the money and a desire to accumulate capital and increase purchasing power in the long term, it may be safer to invest in equities – volatile but with the historic and likely future characteristic of a high return after inflation – than to put money on deposit with the risk that over the years the real value of the investment will be eroded by inflation.

The other point which comes out of the Russia/Coca-Cola story is that the fall provided a wonderful opportunity to those of a disposition to take it. Anyone who added to Russian holdings after the 1998 debacle did much better than the 270% return between May 1997 and the end of 2005. We did in fact do this. We were not clever enough to add right at the bottom, by definition the moment when people are most afraid. But we did add after the market had begun to recover, still some 80% below its level in May 1997.

The fall of Russia and its subsequent recovery is a demonstration of the principle that a share price which has fallen is, *prima facie*, cheaper and more interesting than it was before it fell.

3. The unthinkable happens

Another influential howler, on the other hand, was a Russian example of an exception to this principle. A share price which has fallen is more interesting; except sometimes. (Every rule in investment has to have plenty of exceptions. If there were no exceptions, the circumstances in which the rule applied would cease to apply because everyone would instantly take advantage of them.) A share looks cheap; you buy it; it goes down and looks cheaper; you buy more; it goes down and down, getting cheaper and cheaper, until it reaches what practitioners call euphemistically the ultimate cheapness – zero. This is what is generally called the 'value trap'.

Roughly this happened with Yukos. Yukos, an oil and gas company, was at one time the largest Russian company by market capitalisation, so large that at its peak it accounted for more than a third of the total Russian market capitalisation. The company was one of many which sprang from the dismantling of the Soviet state when shares of state enterprises were sold to private buyers, and were accumulated overwhelmingly, by fair means and foul, by a small number of young businessmen who became known as the oligarchs.

After the market collapse in 1998, the shares were astonishingly cheap. The majority were in the hands of Mikhail Khodorkhovsky. At that time the share price of Exxon was such that the investor paid $8 for every barrel of Exxon's oil reserves. For Yukos, the comparable figure was well under $1.

Unlike Gazprom – the company with the largest energy reserves of any in the world – and Lukoil, both still essentially state-controlled companies, subject to political whim, Yukos was free of state control, a symbol of modern Western-style capitalism come to Russia. This image had been nurtured by Khodorkhovsky, originally regarded as a bandit. He accepted that if Yukos was to be given a valuation anywhere near that of Western companies, it had to behave like a Western company.

He involved highly regarded Western figures in charities and think tanks which he sponsored. Lord Rothschild was a mentor to Khodorkhovsky. American and British senior executives were hired. The company became, in the vogue term used to describe a high standard of corporate governance, transparent. There was no longer a perception, as there remained with a host of other Russian companies, that profits would be siphoned off to the benefit of controlling shareholders, so that ordinary public shareholders would get less than they should.

In the emerging markets portfolios which the firm I then worked for managed, we bought Yukos shares. We were not alone. Yukos had become, in its rehabilitated state, the darling of the Western financial media. Khodorkhovsky was treated accordingly. I saw him in person twice: once at a dinner given by the private equity firm Carlyle Group, when Khodorkhovsky sat at John Major's table, and once, a year or so later, at a conference in Moscow, in very different circumstances, when Yukos was already under severe pressure. On that occasion, Khodorkhovsky, clearly not at ease, arrived to give a speech, gave it in lacklustre fashion, and left immediately without answering any questions.

There were two clouds in what would otherwise have been the clearest blue sky. Sharp-minded observers saw these clouds early. The first was that President Putin was determined to ruin Khodorkhovsky. He had foolishly made himself extremely unpopular with Putin, who had done a deal with all the oligarchs. If they kept out of politics, he would not go after their ill-gotten gains. Most of them wisely kept their side of the bargain. But Khodorkhovsky had political ambitions. In the elections for the Duma, the Russian parliament, in 2003, he financed candidates who opposed the president. Most cynically, one of his senior colleagues stood as a communist candidate.

After a meeting of advisers I wrote a cheerful minute of the discussion about China, Russia and Khodorkhovsky.

Was China finer?
It appeared,
We feared,
When the dollars were counted,
The odds had mounted
That the markets discounted
The convincing prospect
Of the growth we expect.

Was Russia lusher?
It depended
We tended,
On how much imputing
To President Putin
Of a dubious motive
To increase his vote if,
As part of his prospectus,
He was seen by electors
To come out strong
When things done were wrong.

Too much faith in Khodorkhovsky
Could quite frankly be sort of costly.

It was not hard to grasp that too much faith in Khodorkhovsky was rash. He was playing with fire. The tax authorities started to impose enormous charges, relating to past years, on Yukos. Then, landing in his private plane in Siberia, Khodorkhovsky was arrested at gun point and charged with fraud and tax evasion. He was sentenced to eight years imprisonment.

Attracted by the cheapness of Yukos's shares in relation to the company's assets and profits, I did not think Khodorkhovsky's arrest was the end of the story. Even if Putin was determined to ruin Khodorkhovsky, rather than simply to get him out of politics, there could be some deal in which Khodorkhovsky sacrificed all his shares in Yukos in return for his liberty.

But, more fundamentally, Putin had decided Russia's energy was too important a strategic asset to leave in the hands of international investors. He wanted Yukos's assets back under state control. I was slow to appreciate this. The attack on Yukos emerged in time as part of a strategy by Putin to regain the control of the major energy companies which had been lost with privatisation.

The tax bills Yukos faced were followed by more of the same, on a gigantic scale, so that they would swallow up all of Yukos's assets. Yukos was forced to sell the major subsidiary, Yugansneftegaz. The auction for Yugansneftegaz was rigged. The successful bidder, paying a fraction of the real value, was a newly created company. Within days, Yugansneftegaz was sold on to another company, Rosneft, owned by the state.

Yukos still had important oil assets, but the rump of the company which survived continued to be pummelled by repeated tax demands. Finally, in 2006, the company declared bankruptcy.

The lesson of all this is that the unthinkable can happen. The unthinkable must be thought about. Investors must have convictions, but they should never be too convinced that their convictions are right, however apparently rational.

One of the things which had made me feel that Yukos would turn out all right was that it did not seem to be in Putin's interests to drive the company into ruin. He would alienate a great many foreign investors, and foreign investment was vital to Russia. But this was naïve. The foreign investors kept on coming. In 2006, only two years after this glaring example of state appropriation of assets, international investors were prepared to subscribe to shares in Rosneft when the Russian government decided to sell a portion of the company to the public in an initial public offering on the London Stock Exchange sponsored by Morgan Stanley – a good example of just how short the memory of the market is. Putin had got this right.

Although international investors now speak in a more jaundiced way about Putin's absolutism, the Russian market has continued to rise – far above the levels at which it stood when Yukos first began to bask in international affections.

Yukos was a typical value trap. Something looks cheap. But it is cheap for a reason which may not be apparent at the time to the optimist. Afterwards it always looks obvious. This is the most difficult thing to deal with, because really it *was* obvious: that is why the share price was as depressed as it was. There are many occasions on which the obvious is wrong, but there are also many on which the obvious is right, and the gloom apparent in the share price will have been well justified. To all those, the majority, who have recognised the obvious, the failure of a minority of clever dicks to see it too will seem especially obtuse.

There is no real defence against the value trap. Every situation can only be viewed on its merits. But the assessment of value is not a scientific one. The lesson of Yukos was not that better analysis would have led to a different conclusion, but simply that things do sometimes go just as wrong as the market seems to imply they are likely to. Investors have to work out what the probability of disaster is.

They will often get the probabilities wrong. A very experienced and successful manager, Dominic Caldecott, now retired from Morgan Stanley Asset Management, told me that he did not mind poor performance; what he could not stand was being wrong. I have always felt quite differently. I am quite happy to be right for the wrong reasons: if a share price goes up for reasons I had not expected, that is fine.

4. *When the going gets tough, the less-than-tough get going*

My Motorola howler is exactly the opposite sort of howler, and more scarring than any other investment mistake of the last ten years. Motorola in 2002 was a cheap stock. Its share price was little more than the book value of its assets, which usually implies undervaluation since the stated value of net assets in a company's accounts is normally less than their market or fair value. It had depressed earnings but it was not too great a leap of imagination to think that it could improve its operating margins significantly.

We bought the shares at a price of $15 in June 2002. The share price fell. We bought some more. We were patient. We waited. There was no improvement. We waited longer. Finally, when the share price reached $8.5, we gave up. We lost our bottle and sold.

Almost immediately, the share price recovered. In fact, its low during this whole period was $7.71, only just below the price at which we surrendered. There was no coincidence in this. The bottom in a share price cycle is the moment at which there is the greatest unhappiness of the greatest number. What this demonstrated is that we were rushing through the exit at more or less exactly the moment that most other people were.

Within a few months, the reasons for the share price recovery became apparent. The key to Motorola had become its mobile telephone handset business. It ranked third in this, behind Nokia and Samsung Electronics. At the time that we sold the holding, Motorola's share of the world handset market was around 12.5%. It then started to produce models which, in this intensely fashionable business, hit the spot. Even with my untutored eye, I could see that their clam-shell models (and later the extremely slim Razr models) were much cooler than the rather chunky things which Nokia continued to produce. Over the next four years, Motorola's share of the handset market rose to over 20%. At the end of 2006 the share price was $20.5, compared with the $15 at which we had bought and the $8.5 at which we sold.

This is an extreme and particularly depressing illustration of something which happens quite often. If people invest in shares which look cheap, in companies with essentially sound businesses but scope for improvement (which accounts for the moderate valuation), they have to be patient.

In such shares there is generally no catalyst immediately visible which will give a quick result. If there is such a catalyst – a major outside shareholder agitating for change, for example, or new radical management – the chances are that it is already reflected in the share price to some extent and the valuation will not be so moderate. But patience is tough. (After all, the original meaning of patience is suffering.) When the going gets tough, the less than tough get going. It is frustratingly easy to give up on a share after either dreary performance or downright awful performance, just at the point at which everyone else gives up, and just before finally it turns.

One day in the early 1980s, I had to go to Cambridge by train to talk to undergraduates about investment management as part of my employers' recruitment programme. Equipped with a first-class ticket, I wandered down the platform at Liverpool Street Station looking for a first-class compartment. There was none to be seen. I walked almost the whole length of the train. Just before the furthest carriage, I gave up, convinced that I must have missed it. I turned round and walked all the way back until I found a platform attendant, who told me that the compartment was in fact in the very last carriage – just after the point at which I had reversed.

This struck me instantly, and ever since, as a marvellous allegory of investment. So often investors are tempted to give up, and too often do, just before the thing for which they have been hoping happens.

5. *Keep your distance*

In October 1987 I was on holiday in Spain when my uncle rang to tell me about the storm which had annihilated woods and left an extraordinary chaos of fallen trees and branches over the roads of southern England. We had many trees, and many of them had fallen. In addition, a chimney had fallen through the roof of our house. We returned home a week early to deal with the carnage.

On Monday 19 October I was fully occupied in thinking how on earth we were to cope with the overwhelming task of clearing up the mess. Halfway through the afternoon, I was rung by someone in my office who told me that the Dow Jones Industrial Average was down 500 points, some 25%. I was then head of the US equity team at Mercury Asset Management, so this should have been important news.

A sense of perspective

Amidst all those fallen trees, which seemed to matter so much more, I thought it a question of supreme indifference. My reaction, far from the madding crowd of the City, was that shares were 25% cheaper than they had been, nothing much else had changed, and we should do some buying.

That was the reaction at a distance. I then made a terrible mistake. Still meant to be on holiday, I went back to work. Immediately, I discovered what I described in my diary as "a wall of gloom, a cloud of anxiety." Twenty years on, with the 1987 Crash no more than a blip in a long bull market, it is difficult to recapture the widespread feeling then that life had changed irreparably. A trader told me that he had seen people staring blankly, paralysed, at their trading screens, with sweat running down their faces.

The head strategist now wanted to sell shares, so as to hold 40% cash in the global portfolios we managed. Within a few hours, I swung from my distanced judgement that shares were cheap, to the consensus, almost uniform, view that the world had changed and that these shares, which had already fallen 25%, should be sold for fear of worse to come.

That is what we did. It was the worst mistake of my career – not one I was wholly or even primarily responsible for, but one in which I went along with the herd.

That episode carried several lessons. The first was the advantage of distance. Away from the City, the instinctive view was the right one. Back amidst the frenzy of a large investment management firm, in the thick of the action and assailed by an onslaught of opinion, I buckled. Distance brings dispassion.

The second lesson was to beware of circular arguments. The argument that the world had changed and that share prices would fall further was based on the fallacy of circular logic.

The thesis of the bears was that the fall in share prices which took place on Black Monday had destroyed the wealth of investors. As a result, it was argued, consumer spending would fall.

This was the so-called 'wealth effect'. If consumer spending fell, the economy as a whole would suffer, and in that case share prices would fall too.

But, simplified, the argument – the markets have fallen, therefore the economy will suffer, therefore the market will fall – had an obvious fallacy. It suggested share prices and the economy would fall in a spiral until shares were worth nothing at all. This could not really happen in a serious economy and stock market. However grave things were, shares would always be worth more than nothing.

In fact, things turned out very differently. There was no wealth effect resulting from the stock market crash. Consumers carried on spending. In time, not long in fact, markets realised this and rose. Those who bought in the face of the huge selling pressure in those days in the second half of October 1987 – and for every seller there has to be a buyer – bought wonderful bargains and made a great deal of money over the next few years.

The other lesson was to avoid single decisions on which investment performance depends too much. In any investment decision the chances of being right are 50–50. An investor who is lucky or good may be right perhaps 55% of the time. That still leaves a large possibility of being wrong. An investor who is wrong in one of these big decisions will be wrong in spades, and performance will be destroyed.

This is what happened to us after October 1987. The decision to hold 40% cash, during a period in which, as it turned out, markets rose reasonably strongly, created severe underperformance. Clients who initially, sharing in the consensus gloom, thought we were being prudent soon got bored of this explanation for underperformance. We lost business. In fact, the international business of Mercury Asset Management took several years to recover from the effects of this one decision.

So the third lesson I learned from this episode was that dogmatic large-scale views of prospects for the world, or for markets in general, are as unwise as betting all one's chips on a single number in roulette. This was the lesson also of howler six.

6. A portfolio needs a lot of little decisions, not one big decision

In my last year at Mercury, after a period of excellent performance in our global portfolios, we blew some of it because of a wrong currency decision.

The yen–dollar exchange rate in mid-1994 was ¥98 to the dollar. There were all sorts of fundamental reasons for the yen to weaken. The economy was weak, and interest rates in Japan were much lower than in the US.

We had plenty of exposure to Japanese shares. That meant, since these shares were denominated in yen, that we also had plenty of unwanted exposure to the Japanese yen in our US dollar-denominated portfolios.

Currency hedging is simple to execute and has an illusory appeal. Prospects for a particular equity market may look good when prospects for the currency of that market look poor. It then seems obvious sense to hold the equities concerned but to hedge the currency. This can most efficiently be done by selling the relevant currency in the forward markets. To hedge the yen currency exposure resulting from holding Japanese shares, the investor can agree – at an exchange rate determined now – to sell yen for US dollars at a point in the future, generally three months or six months.

At any time during the three or six months, the currency transaction, called a forward contract, can be closed by carrying out the opposite transaction: a purchase of yen against dollars. If the yen has fallen in relation to the dollar over that period, there is a realised gain. This gain is matched by the currency loss on the holdings of equities. If the equities have gone up, there is a gain on them. The use of the forward contract, with the gain there matching the currency loss on the equities, allows the benefit of the rise in share price to be preserved intact.

Even if the unexpected happens in the currency markets, and

the yen goes up instead of down, the resulting loss on the forward contract is still offset more or less exactly by the unexpected currency gain on the equity holdings. There is an opportunity cost – it would have been better not to have hedged through the forward contract, so that the currency gain on the equity holdings could have been added to any gain on the equity prices themselves. But an opportunity cost is not the same as a real cost. It does not really hurt.

That is the theory. What happened in 1994–5 was a good example that practice and theory can diverge. Instead of falling as I had expected, the yen appreciated strongly. By June 1995 the exchange rate was ¥86, so that the yen had gained 12%. Since we had hedged almost all of our Japanese equity exposure, around 40% of the portfolios concerned, we missed out on 5% (40% of 12%) of return which we would have had if we had not hedged the currency.

Opportunity cost may be different from real cost; but if it is big enough, and if all around have benefited from the opportunity which you have squandered, it seems to hurt after all.

We then compounded the error. When the exchange rate reached ¥82 to the dollar, we gave up, partially, and moved from hedging 40% of the portfolio to hedging some 15%. For a few days or weeks it looked sensible. The yen continued to strengthen, to ¥80 to the US dollar.

Then it stopped strengthening. Over the next year the yen fell from ¥80 to ¥120 to the US dollar. By reducing the hedging we had missed out on what we had intended in the first place to capture. This was just like giving up in the search for the first-class carriage of the train to Cambridge immediately before getting to it.

It was true that too much had depended on the hedging. The effect of this one decision, good or bad, could overwhelm many other decisions about individual holdings and exposure to the different equity markets. That was the first lesson: a portfolio should depend on a lot of little decisions, not on one big decision. But the time to pay attention to this was before embarking on the whole hedging exercise, rather than after it had all gone wrong. In investment, too late a right is a wrong.

The second lesson is a highly subjective one. Currency decisions and equity decisions do not, in my view, mix well. People who are good at dealing with exchange rates are not usually the same people as those who are good at investing in equities. The dynamics of all markets have much in common, but they also differ.

Dealing in currency markets is, I think, for traders, and not for those who argue the fundamentals. There is one purely technical reason why this is so. An equity can be held for ever. A currency contract has a finite term, usually no more than six months and more generally three months. This means that at the end of the three months investors are obliged to close the existing, maturing, contract, and, if they want, to replace it with a new one.

If the maturing contract has been profitable this is quite an easy path to take. But if the maturing contract realises a loss it gets psychologically more complicated.

After three months, the investor takes the loss on the existing contract, and says, 'Never mind; the loss we have taken on this contract is matched by the unexpected currency gain we have had on the equity holdings. The fundamental reasons for doing this are unchanged. On we go.' The investor takes out a new contract for three months.

At the end of that period, there may again be a loss. Once more the investor justifies renewal: the fundamentals are just the same. Another three months go by. Still the currency marches in the wrong direction.

The time comes to close the latest contract. At this point, the investor says, 'I've had enough. To hell with this,' and closes the contract without taking out a new one. Before very long the currency movement expected all the time starts to happen, but the investor no longer has the forward contract to benefit from it – having turned round before getting to the first-class compartment.

The awkwardness of currency hedging is that the instruments with which it is carried out are short-term. Equities sit in a portfolio, perhaps not behaving well but at least not nagging. Currency forwards nag, because every three months they demand to be looked after. They tug insistently at the investor's skirts.

When currency contracts are going badly, they play the same role as a difficult client homing in on errors, putting investment managers off their stride and on the defensive. That is why, I think, currency hedging is more suited to traders who are better at disposing of the baggage of the past: they start each day as though it were their first. They look at each position entirely afresh, unburdened by the detailed arguments for one course or another.

There is another important point about currencies, and that is that the world currency market is in aggregate a zero-sum game. This is not true of world equity markets. In the long run those holding an international portfolio of equities can hope to make a decent real return, which may be increased or reduced by their investment manager. Those holding an international portfolio of currencies can, over time, expect to make a real return of zero, because all that currencies can do is go up and down in relation to one another.

––––––––––––

That is quite enough howlers to leave the general, correct, impression that I have made plenty of them. It is partly because of the lessons I have learned from them that I venture to write this book.

TWO

Types of Investments

M UCH the most important decision in investment management
is what sort of assets to invest in.

Most types of investments are straightforward. There are exceptions.

Derivatives – such as options to buy or sell shares, futures on
stock market and bond market indices, and forward foreign exchange
contracts – are complicated. They are not suited to amateur
involvement.

Structured products, themselves involving derivatives, add
several layers of complexity. They can be utterly impenetrable. The
impenetrability allows those who do the structuring to charge
high fees, which are hard for the investor to get a grip of. In this
book we will leave these aside, which is where the private investor
should leave them.

Fred Schwed, in his book *Where Are the Customers' Yachts?* (Simon
& Schuster, 1940), posed this celebrated question when the moored
yachts of a number of Wall Street geniuses were pointed out to
him by an enthusiastic friend. The customer/supplier yacht ratio
probably touches rock bottom when it consists of those who invest
in structured products and those who supply them.

Apart from structured products, built upon an inscrutable pyramid of derivatives, the characteristics of investment assets can usually be described without too much confusion.

Some practitioners produce formulae with Greek letters which demonstrate cleverness and expertise. Warren Buffett, immensely quotable as well as in the top tier of all-time greats, says that equations with Greek letters should be avoided. Investment management can and should be kept simple. To invest successfully it is not necessary to have a clue what this stockbroking analyst is on about (though no doubt it is all quite right):

For a Cobb-Douglas utility function, the amount of money needed to achieve a given level of utility depends on a price index that is identical in form to the utility function itself. For example, if the utility function is $U=x^{\alpha}y^{1-\alpha}$, then the amount of money needed to achieve a given level of utility $(U^{\star})$ is $M^{\star}=U^{\star}[(P_{x})^{\alpha}(P_{y})^{1-\alpha}]$. The term in brackets is nothing but a price index.

Nor is it necessary to adopt a special language, as in this stockbroker's advice:

Taiwan Semiconductor Corporation will have better than normal seasonality in the first quarter of 2007. We believe the stock market may be ignoring the optionality for better growth and/ or higher return on equity and dividends from TSMC. In our view, the company is not adverse to growing inorganically to augment its growth.

(Translation: In the first quarter of 2007 Taiwan Semiconductor Corporation will do better than usual at that time of year. TSMC's growth, dividends, and return on equity may be higher than the stock market thinks. The company might want to grow faster by buying another company.)

The main categories of investment assets are equities, bonds and cash. Equities behave in a radically different way from cash. The returns of these two asset types are rarely the same. Bonds are different from either.

In recent years a new broad category of investments has become popular: 'alternatives'. Ironically, the focus of discussion in investment forums these days is usually on alternatives, which, as the name suggests, one might expect to be the gravy and horseradish sauce of a balanced portfolio, rather than the roast beef and potatoes.

Alternatives include hedge funds (or absolute return funds), which are not really an asset class at all, and private equity. They also include real estate, gold, commodities, and art. The special popularity of hedge funds, and their particular characteristics, deserve special treatment.

Property

This book is mainly about investing in securities, principally equities, and I am not therefore going to discuss in any detail property, an immensely broad and diverse subject.

The rule of thumb is that in the long term the investor should expect from property, if bought without any borrowing, a rate of return above inflation, better than bonds and cash and not as good as equities. In 2006, and in the three, five and ten years to the end of 2006, global property (as measured by the Datastream World Property Index) outperformed equities, but this outperformance is not a normal state of affairs and should not be relied on. The party in property in most parts of the world has been too good to last.

Investors, whether especially acquainted with the London residential market or the Tokyo office market, hardly need reminding of two aspects of property investment.

First, there are ferocious cycles. Second, location, location, location.

The cycle is far from global. It is not even national or regional. In the US some cities may be in feast and others in (relative) famine. The same is true in the UK. One part of London may be stagnating while another is flourishing. Birmingham may boom while Burnley busts. The London top end residential market is a phenomenon which stands alone.

Investors can get exposure to property in a number of ways. They can buy property itself. They can buy units in a fund which invests in property, and which will give a diversified exposure to a range of properties, which may include offices, retail, and industrial. They may invest in a more aggressive property fund, managed on private equity lines – private equity is discussed below. They may buy shares in property companies or their more tax-efficient equivalents, real estate investment trusts.

All of these have advantages and disadvantages. Apart from direct investment, in which case investors make their own decision about how much to finance through borrowing, the private equity approach to property probably provides the prospect of the highest return and also has the highest risk. The risk comes partly or mainly from the fact that, as in other private equity investments, the manager is likely to make use of a good deal of borrowing in order to increase the fund's return on the cash invested.

Property shares tend to move in line, to a lesser or greater extent, with the equity market, though they have phases of sharp outperformance or underperformance. In the four years from its low point in March 2003 the FTSE All Share Real Estate Index – quoted property companies – rose 220%, outperforming the FTSE All Share Index by 75%.

In general, these quoted property companies provide some of the attributes of property, enhanced (or mitigated) by the skill of the company's management in four respects: in reducing or increasing exposure to property assets and to borrowings at the right time, in choosing the right properties, in property development, and in managing the property investments to get the best return from them. Property shares can be assessed like any other shares.

Investment in an ordinary property fund gives pure undiluted property exposure, but the returns may not be as exciting, after fees, as those of private equity alternatives. There may well be worthwhile benefits in that the property cycle can be quite different from the stock market cycle so that in times of, say, high inflation when equities are performing badly property prices could be shooting up.

The historian John Adamson makes a special case for property as the thing which has preserved British families' fortunes better than their continental counterparts. He points out that the same five families who owned all of Westminster and central (as it then was) London in 1580 still own 85% of the land freeholds today. The French aristocracy devoted to land a proportion of their fortunes – around 20% – which the British, he says, would have regarded as recklessly small.

The great advantage of the property-centred policy was that in a panic property was very difficult to sell. The British kept their property because they could not do otherwise, and prices always recovered. They were prevented by the illiquidity of property from selling at the bottom.

This is an interesting line, though British primogeniture also had something to do with it. Moreover, the English rich paid attention to John Dryden's maxim, "all heiresses are beautiful." One of the early Dukes of Norfolk married a woman much older than himself who had three stepdaughters, each with a fortune. He married his three sons to these three. Late 19th-century aristocrats went to the US making no bones about the fact that they were after a rich wife. John Adamson also makes the point that English families took on financial advisers, not just lawyers. These advisers were highly respected until their status seemed to be demoted in the 19th century. Sir John Thynne, whose descendant became the first Marquess of Bath in 1789, was a supreme example. As steward to the Earl of Hertford in the mid-1500s, he amassed sufficient reward to build Longleat. This is an encouraging precedent for those who manage family offices nowadays.

Equities, bonds and cash

Property aside, by far the most important single decision the investor can make is how much to hold in equities. The reason for this is that equities are both the most volatile of the four main categories (including property), going up and down most, and probably the category most likely, over the long term, to provide the highest return. Bonds and cash are reasonably predictable; equities are the least predictable but the most promising.

The case for equities over the long term is very strong. Since records began, which roughly speaking means around 1850, equities have given a real return – that is to say, a return after inflation – of about 6% per annum plus or minus a percentage point in most countries. There are exceptions, such as Germany, Argentina, and Russia, where over the long term returns have been much lower. But for most developed markets this statistic is true.

Studies of the long-term returns of different asset classes have made use of different periods of time, but they all come to pretty much the same conclusion. An Ibbotson Associates study (1925–1997) shows the return of US equities to have been 11% per annum, of long-term government bonds 5.2%, short-term US Treasury bills 3.8%. Inflation was 3.1%, so to put it another way the real return of equities was 7.9%, of bonds 2.1% and of short-term Treasury bills 0.9%.

A study by CSFB looks all the way back to 1849 and concludes that between then and December 2003 the real return of equities was 6.4%. For the UK markets, Barclays Capital calculates the average annual return between 1900 and 2005 to be 9.2% for equities, 5.2% for government bonds, 5% for cash, and 4% for inflation – so real returns of 5.2% for equities, 1.2% for bonds, 1% for cash.

According to Jeremy Siegel in *Stocks for the Long Run*, between 1871 and 1996 US equities outperformed bonds in 72.1% of five-year periods, 82.1% of ten-year periods, and 94.4% of 20-year periods.

Looking at the UK experience from 1918 onwards, Oxford Investment Partners found that equities gave a real return of more than 5% per annum over five-year periods two-thirds of the time. In other markets the details vary but the essentials are the same: provided you are looking at a long enough period, equities provide a much higher return than bonds, bonds higher than cash, cash a little higher than inflation.

This outperformance of equities over bonds is not surprising.

Equities are a stake in the assets and profits of companies. Bonds are merely loans, in the form of securities, to be repaid at some point, and in the mean time paying some interest. There is more risk in equities than in bonds or cash. Governments almost never go bust: they repay the money they have borrowed through bonds and bills. Banks rarely go bust, and if they do it is even rarer for depositors to lose their money. But companies, in which equities are the investor's stake, do occasionally get it totally wrong, so that their equities become worthless; or they simply perform disappointingly, failing to grow revenues and profits much or at all, as a result of which the price of the equities goes down.

In aggregate, however, companies increase their revenues over time and, with a bit of luck, increase their profits faster than their revenues by doing their job, year by year, a little more cost-efficiently, through use of technology and other ways of improving productivity. In return for the extra risk of occasional failure by a particular company, and of frequent short-term poor performance, equities give extra long-term return.

In nearly all countries, bonds have done better than cash. The main exception has been Germany, because of the hyperinflation of the 1920s.

When I started in the City, I used to go to the after-hours classes in investment given by a formidable US stockbroker, George Hacker of Bear Stearns. "Bonds are death; equities life," he barked. Although there have been frequent periods when bonds have outperformed equities, I have always been prejudiced in favour of equities, sometimes wrongly.

In the end the balance on offer is quite simple: a high long-term return from equities, with plenty of hard knocks on the way; a lower return from bonds, with fewer nasty surprises; or a still lower return, probably just ahead of inflation, from cash on deposit at the bank or short-term Treasury bills, and no surprises.

The potential difference is huge. The table below shows what the investor ends up with after investing £1,000 in equities, government bonds, and cash, assuming returns in the future are in line with the

Barclays long-term figures for UK asset classes. The final figure is in constant pound terms – in other words, after allowing for inflation, hence showing the purchasing power in today's terms of what the investor is left with.

£1,000 invested	Real return per annum	Real value after 20 years	Change
Equities	5.2%	£2,756	£1,756
Bonds	1.2%	£1,269	£269
Cash	1.0%	£1,220	£220

It seems quite likely that equities will go on giving bigger returns than bonds or cash or anything else, with, as in the past, periods of exception.

In the last few years, the case for equities has been questioned. In the three years 2000–2002 the return of the MSCI World Index was -44%, and of the FTSE All-Share Index -42%. NASDAQ, the US index with an emphasis on technology companies, gave a return of -52%. I went to a meeting of family office managers in early 2003 when one of the subjects on the agenda was 'Are equities a proper asset class for private investors?' The question was not wholly rhetorical. People were wondering. That meeting coincided, within a month, with the bottom of the bear market. In the following 12 months most markets were up by 40%. This kind of questioning is typical in that it is only after something has given a rotten return that people generally begin to wonder whether they should hold it.

In a note in December 2006 entitled 'What rate of return can you reasonably expect: an update' – referring to his earlier article in the *Financial Analysts Journal* in 1997 – the respected stock market commentator Peter Bernstein showed the total returns of US equities in a variety of separate periods beginning when valuation levels were identical. He found that there had been four dates in the past – in 1935, 1959, 1966 and 1969 – when the valuation (in price-earnings ratio) of the Standard & Poor's Index for US equities had been at the same level as in October 2006. The total return from each of these four dates to October 2006 had varied between 10.4% per annum and 11.1%, and between 5.8% and 7.2% after deducting inflation.

Over the next 20 years or so returns could well be lower than in the past. The valuations of stock markets now are higher than their long-term averages. Part of the strong return in the past was attributable to the improvement in the level of valuation. If a price-earnings ratio, for example, increases from 10 to 12.5 over ten years, that alone accounts for a 25% return, or 2.3% per annum.

Given that current levels of valuation are higher than average, it is reasonable to assume that there will be no such increase in the level of valuation over the next 20 years. Looking forward, therefore, it is sensible to expect something more like a 5% after-inflation return from equities in the future. This makes sense if economies grow at around 3% in real terms and productivity improvements allow profits to increase by more than the rate of economic growth.

Doomsters predict something much worse. They may be right. Nobody knows. But it is not really reasonable to predict that equities will give, say, a nil after-inflation return over the next 20 years. Most of the doomsters are biased by the recent past. There were few who in 1999 were expecting returns to be nil or negative over the next ten or 20 years. It was only in the midst of, or even after, the calamitous three years 2000–2002 that most such commentators became so depressed about the future, and many have still not recovered their enthusiasm, in spite of the strong markets since 2003.

There are honourable exceptions. The tremendously rigorous Jeremy Grantham, founder of the US investment management firm GMO, has long expected low equity returns on the basis that all returns eventually revert to the mean – in other words, if, as had been the case up to 2000, equity returns in the immediate past were outlandishly high, they were likely to be much lower, even negative, looking ahead. But most forecasters just extrapolate. When something has been going well, they assume, with glorious optimism, that it will go on going well; and when something has been going badly, they assume just as pessimistically that it will go on going badly.

Gary Steinberg, then of Wellcome Trust, made an interesting calculation at the end of 2002. He took to heart the multifarious woe-laden mutterings at that time that the glory days of equities were over. He made the assumption that the ten years beginning 1 January 2000 would be the worst ten years in recorded history for the UK stock market – equal therefore to the period 1929–1938, when the market fell by 29%.

He then calculated what return was necessary for the remaining years of the decade, given that the returns for the first three years were already known – -16% per annum, or -42% altogether. The answer was +8% per annum, not a bad figure. The investing world, conditioned by the immediate past, shakes its gloomy head about the future when it is merely extrapolating recent history.

The point of this is that the long-term attributes of equities should not be deemed to have vanished just because in some recent years they have not been displayed. An investor should assume that over the long term equities will provide a higher return than property, bonds or cash, because in the past, over long periods, this has been a reliable expectation.

International diversification

If equities are to be a big part of the investor's portfolio, what sort of equities? In the four or five decades up to the 1980s there were few large economies in which equity investors invested much outside their home market. This was for historic reasons. In other words, that is what they were used to. Originally, this was because it was difficult to get up-to-date information on shares outside the home market; and in many countries, there were special disincentives, tax or otherwise, to investing overseas.

The UK had a much greater tradition, in the more distant past, of international trade and investment than any other major country. It had the combination of a sophisticated financial industry, and a small economy compared with those of the United States or Japan so that its investors needed to look outwards. Its history of internationalism included much of the US railway boom in the 19th century being financed from London (and Edinburgh). In 1900, the *Financial Times* had at least as much coverage of what was going on in Lima and Shanghai as of what was happening in the UK.

The UK's surviving internationalism in investment was in spite of restrictions in the form of foreign exchange controls, which meant that there were special, more expensive, exchange rates for the purchase of overseas shares – the dollar premium.

Mrs Thatcher swept these restrictions away when she came to power in 1979. As better communication made it easier to invest abroad, the proportion of investors' portfolios outside the home market rose.

The US was slower on the international scene. American investors were parochial. They had a very big parish. The large multinationals listed in the US, like IBM, Coca-Cola and Esso, in any case gave plenty of international exposure. In the 1970s (before Mrs Thatcher liberated UK investors), British investment houses started to make the case to US pension funds that a bit of international investment, alongside their US equity holdings, would do them good: potentially a higher return, but also lower volatility for the portfolio as a whole, because of the lack of correlation between the overseas markets and the US market.

I spent two years based in New York working for the merchant bank, Warburgs, in a subsidiary called Warburg Investment Management International (WIMI), pounding the pavements of the US pension fund world to try to persuade them to invest 5% or 10% outside the US. My friend and colleague Norman Bachop, an accomplished songwriter, summarised the arguments in a song to the tune of *Thoroughly Modern Millie*:

> There are ways
> Nowadays
> To ensure
> All that your
> Funds' returns
> Could possibly need.

When your local market rates are quite deplorable
Foreign markets then no longer are ignorable.
For the fact is

International diversification
Lowers your volatility,
Raises your internal rate of return,
Improves your liquidity.
Invest
Just 10%
Outside the US.
If New York markets fall
Then your results may well impress
With their relative success.

If domestic price inflation should increase
Unanticipatedly
And the currency should start to decline
Even if belatedly,
Your foreign stocks
Will counter shocks
And stem that decline.
So split your fund
And give some money
To us at WIMI now.
We'll show you how.

The argument for international diversification was not only that it gave the opportunity to increase returns, but also the strong likelihood that it would lower the volatility of the overall portfolio.

The latter is now less certain. In the early days of large-scale international investment the markets of the US, Japan, UK, the rest of Europe, and the Pacific tended not to move closely together because they were each dominated by their domestic investors with local economic, political, and other concerns.

Some markets which are now serious and large were then more or less unexplored. The markets of Spain and Italy were as obscure as, say, those of Ghana and Morocco now. In 1978 a note went round the small international investment department at Warburgs urging investment in Italy under the title *Fiat investor ut forum stet* (in dog Latin, let the investor have confidence that the market will remain firm), Fiat and Stet being among the two largest Italian companies. Nowadays there are few unexploited markets. The flows of funds around the world are so huge that just about all markets correlate pretty closely, with the US tending to set the tone.

Investing internationally now makes sense not particularly to reduce volatility but simply to take advantage of the full range of opportunities. For a UK investor, not to invest outside the UK would seem rather short-sighted and self-denying.

Emerging markets

Not to have something sometimes in emerging markets with high growth rates, such as Brazil, Russia, India and China – the so-called BRICs – and Taiwan and South Korea, is especially self-denying.

Emerging markets are the markets of the so-called developing, or less-developed, world. One definition of an emerging market is a market in an economy where the average income per head is less than about $10,000 per annum.

The term 'emerging markets' was coined by Antoine van Agtmael, then at the World Bank and later co-founder of the firm Emerging Markets Management. It is a phrase less disparaging than its precursors – third world, lesser-developed countries. But there is still an implication of juniority. There is nothing junior about some emerging markets now. Many of them have come of age and many of the leading multinational companies are based in emerging markets, succeeding not just because of lower wages but because of entrepreneurial flair and what van Agtmael calls creative adaptation.

Emerging markets should not be a postscript to any investment strategy. They should be a big part of it.

Emerging markets do not always go up. There are periods when they earn the weary title of 'submerging markets'. Another cynical view is that emerging markets are markets from which it is impossible to emerge in an emergency. There can be big shocks. Many such markets have greater political risk than is normal in the developed world, and also corporate governance risk: there is generally more corruption in emerging markets, according to those who measure such things, like Transparency International.

Until 1995, for many years the returns of emerging markets in aggregate had been higher than those of developed markets. This led many investment advisers to conclude that investors should hold a chunk in emerging markets, since by doing so they would both lower the overall risk (through diversification) and increase the overall return of their portfolios.

From 1997 to 2002, emerging markets were a disaster. Some of the same advisers then concluded that there was no evidence that emerging markets increased return, and they reversed their advice to invest in them.

This approach was wholly backward-looking. Most emerging markets do not, because of their special risks, deserve quite the same level of valuation as developed markets. But they usually have higher population growth, and higher economic and profit growth because they are starting from a lower base and have lower wage costs. The process of globalisation brings production to the parts of the world where costs are lowest. In some countries there are first class companies.

Van Agtmael reminded a recent interlocutor "you are talking to someone who has lost half his clients' money twice in the last 20 years during the Mexican and Asian crises of the 1990s." That is a reminder that equities are volatile, and emerging market equities more volatile than most. But it is also a reminder that to the long-term investor volatility does not really matter, because even those who invested in emerging markets at the most unpropitious times in the end have done well, and those who invested with van Agtmael's firm have done very well.

So most equity investors would want to have a fairly international portfolio, with a large slice of emerging market exposure, rather than one limited to, or even overwhelmingly biased towards, the home market.

Volatility and the importance of long-termism

Apart from a return higher over the long term than that of bonds or cash, the key attribute of equities is their volatility: their prices go up and down much more than property or bonds, and very much more than cash which in effect has zero volatility: the return you get from cash, reliably, is the interest rate you are told about when you make the deposit for the particular period.

Volatility is usually measured by the standard deviation of returns. A standard deviation of annual returns of 15%, for instance, means that in any one year there is a two-thirds possibility that the return will be in a range between 15% more than, and 15% less than, the long-term average return.

Since US equities do have a standard deviation of roughly 15%, this means that, taking the long-term average return to be about 10%, there is a two-thirds probability that the return will be between −5% and +25% in any single year.

A two-thirds probability is not much to write home about. With a standard deviation of 15%, there is theoretically a 95% probability that the return in a single year will be in a range between 30% more than and 30% less than the long-term average — so wide a range as to be just about useless.

Since talking in terms of standard deviations has its limitations, a better way for investors to examine their tolerance for volatility is to look at the worst possible case. From the beginning to the end of the Great Crash in 1929–32, the US stock market fell by 90%. By comparison both the 1973–4 and 2000–02 crashes were mild. The

Standard & Poor's index fell 48% from peak to trough in the first and 49% in the second; the MSCI World Index for developed markets (as opposed to emerging markets) 46% and 51%. But in the UK, the stock market fell by 70% in 1974–5. It then rose by 136% in 1976.

Another way to look at it is to see how long you might have to wait to make money if it turned out that the moment at which you chose to invest was the worst possible moment. Those who invested in the US NASDAQ index (smaller companies, mainly technology) at the peak in 2000 would have had a portfolio, six years later, worth half as much as what they started with. Those who bought the leading US shares in 1929 (as measured by the Dow Jones Industrial Average) or the leading Japanese shares in 1989 (as measured by the Nikkei index) were still waiting to be above water 15 years later.

Time is all-important. Richard Bernstein of Merrill Lynch, looking at the period 1985–2006, calculated that the probability of losing money by investing in the US stock market is 46% if the investment is just for one day, 42% for one week, 35% for one month, 27% for one quarter, 18% for one year, 14% for three years, and 0% for ten years.

Investors need to take seriously the chance of catastrophe. But they should cheer themselves up with the thought that markets in due course tend to rebound to resume the long-term trend rate of return.

This always has been the magic of equities. The magic may cease to work. The future may for some reason turn out to be utterly different from the past, and from whole series of samples of past periods. The chances are, however, that the long-term future of equity market returns will be something like the long-term past of their returns.

But because of their volatility, any money which an investor earmarks for equities must be regarded as a long-term investment.

A long-term temperament as well as long-term circumstances

A Japanese man went into a bank to change some Japanese notes into sterling. He was surprised at how little he got.

"Please explain," he said to the cashier. "Yesterday I was changing some yen for sterling and I received many more sterling. Why is this?"

The cashier shrugged his shoulders. "Fluctuations," he explained.

The Japanese man was aghast. "And fluck you bloody Europeans too," he responded, grabbed the notes, and walked out.

Fluctuations matter if the money could be needed soon. Money invested in equities must not be money which will be wanted in a year or two, or might be urgently wanted at any time, because there is a fair chance that the moment when it is needed will be a bad one for the stock market and the investor will therefore be selling at low prices. If investors think they might need the money soon, the message is clearly stay away: the chance of a minus return is just too great.

Even if investors are in a position to allocate a fair amount to equities, they should not necessarily do so. It is not enough that the circumstances are right. Investors need to be temperamentally inclined to the sort of long-term investment which equities are.

Long-termness must be subjective as well as objective. The fact that the circumstances of a particular investor might objectively lead to a certain viewpoint does not mean that he or she necessarily has that viewpoint. A baby is in an objective position to take a long-term view, but will not actually look beyond the next feeding-time.

A long-term investor?

A subjective long-term outlook, as well as objective long-term circumstances, must be tested. Two wealthy families can take opposite views of their wealth.

One family might say that, since there is a large fortune, they can afford to maximise returns. They might even feel that they have a sort of moral obligation to do so, in line with the New Testament parable of the talents. It might not be clear immediately what the moral purpose of a huge fortune is; but a purpose is likely to emerge possibly over some generations. Some of the biggest American philanthropists have decided ultimately to devote the great majority of their money to good causes but first to make the amount as big as possible before they give it away.

Another family may take the line that, having made money, what they want above all is not to lose it, and capital preservation should be emphasised more than maximisation. Many exceedingly rich people, who could invest a large fortune overwhelmingly in equities, should not do so, because volatility does not suit them. This is particularly true of many industrialists who have sold their operating companies. They have taken, in their time as entrepreneurs, enormous risks. They may be determined above all to hang on to what they have made rather than to maximise. They may dislike the feeling of disempowerment which ownership of a portfolio of shares, without control of any of the underlying companies, gives. They may also be suspicious of financial markets, as many industrialists are. For them, quoted equities are not the thing.

Nor for boxers: I met Chris Eubank, former world middle-weight champion, in a hotel in Monte Carlo and he asked me what I did. I told him. "Far too risky for me," he said. "I take enough risk in the ring."

One of the family trusts which I used to advise had a Protector who asked me once whether the reason that I advocated a lot of equities was that the trust concerned was so big that it really did not matter how much was lost. I said that in fact I had exactly the same policy for myself. Having a decent income, I had no need for the funds I invested in the foreseeable future, so could afford to try to maximise for the long term.

Perma-bears

Equities are also not the thing for the perpetual pessimist. An old lady I knew delighted in the vagaries of the English weather. If it was a horrible day, she said with great relish, "It's a horrible day today." If it was a nice day she said, "It's not going to stay like this", with lugubrious satisfaction.

My former chairman, Peter Stormonth Darling, recalls one of his first colleagues, a man of great experience and seniority, who used every day to prophesy a disaster for the Dow Jones Industrial Average. Throughout much of the 1960s, when he made these quotidian predictions of impending doom, the Dow Jones Industrial Average rose to new heights. One day it fell quite sharply, a trifle compared with its rise over the preceding years. "There you are," the Cassandra exclaimed. "I told you so!"

There are always some very convincing reasons to be seriously worried about prospects for the world and by extension for equity markets. Some people specialise in deflation-phobia or inflation-phobia. Some worry about Iran and nuclear weapons, or about China and Taiwan.

A recent mega-worry has been bird flu. It may well turn out that bird flu will have a catastrophic effect on economic activity. I was asked in early 2006 by the chairman of an investment committee of which I am a member what action, if any, we were taking to recognise the risk, and what would lead us to take action. I answered:

"We have not reduced risk, do not believe the situation as it stands merits reducing risk, and do not have in mind any trigger event which would lead us to reduce risk.

It is unlikely that on such a matter we will be cleverer than the market. Therefore it is unlikely that it will help to decide on trigger events which would lead us to shift policy, because the market is likely to have reacted to and discounted such an event before we get there.

I do not feel that anything I have read so far justifies a shift in policy. The number of deaths is small. There is no evidence that the virus mutates so that it moves from human to human. But needless to say I am not an expert.

Kiril Sokoloff of 13D has highlighted avian flu since April 2005. He has been right to worry about it in a social sense but if the early reader had reacted by shifting investment policy that would have been wrong.

I remember reading the word AIDS for the first time in an article by Harriet Sergeant in *Harpers & Queen* (essential investment research) in 1982. Over the next few years the worries about AIDS became huge, and generally speaking rightly. But it would have been wrong to shift investment policy.

More generally, re your reminder that the family are keen for the Investment Committee to help the investment team preserve capital: that sounds a good idea. What we all know about equities is that (1) they (tend to) provide higher returns than other things over the long term (2) they are volatile and sometimes go down. They would not do the first without also doing the second. But no one to my knowledge has been able to predict when they go down with more than 60% accuracy. If the committee is brilliant (and a brilliant committee must be an oxymoron!) it might be able to clock up a 60% success record in avoiding downturns, but no better. It follows, therefore, that if avoidance of downturns is of paramount importance to the family they should avoid equities altogether, and forego the probable long-term advantage – a perfectly reasonable stance to take, but not the current one."

Those temperamentally unsuited to equity investment should rest content with the lower returns, but fewer nasty surprises, provided by other assets, notably bonds and cash. Or at least they should have less in equities, more in bonds and cash, than those of a sunnier disposition.

But for those who are in the appropriate, long-term, circumstances, and also have the temperament to accept volatility, equities are the thing.

In an equity portfolio, the risk of having too much in a single country or sector or stock, and too much therefore resting on one or two decisions which may be wrong, can be reduced through diversification, but the portfolio remains an equity portfolio. The chances are that if equities are lousy, the return of the great majority of equity portfolios will be lousy too.

Investors should not think that dividing a portfolio among lots of equities, or among several equity managers, takes away their risk of exposure to the equity markets. The only way to be sure that part of a portfolio is not exposed to equity market risk is to invest in something other than equities – and equity hedge funds and private equity are not something other than equities.

Correlations

Experts who advise on asset allocation sometimes use asset-liability models and portfolio optimisers. These take the past volatilities and correlations (the latter a measure of the extent to which different assets tend to move in the same direction), and either past or expected returns, to produce a theoretically perfect portfolio, or most efficient portfolio, in terms of the balance of risk and return. The trouble with these models and optimisers is that they are only as good as the data which is fed into them. Past correlations and volatilities do not always hold good.

An alternative measure of correlation is the beta, the percentage by which an asset may be expected to change in value if another asset changes by 1%. If a share has a beta of 0.9 based on the Standard & Poor's Composite Index for US equities, this means that on average it will rise or fall by 9% when the S&P rises or falls by 10%. Fulcrum Asset Management calculate that the beta of hedge funds relative to the Standard & Poor's Index of US equities is 0.41 for the period from 1995–2006, but 0.69 for the shorter period since 2004. The beta for multi-strategy hedge funds – those which do anything, not restricted to equities but including activity in currencies, commodities, and bonds – has gone from 0.03, completely insignificant, to 0.27.

The correlation between emerging market equities and developed market equities has also increased, and likewise commodities and gold have recently correlated much more closely with equities than in the past. The only major investments not correlated with equities, according to a Merrill Lynch study in 2006, were bonds and cash.

Early 2006 gave a good example of the tendency of assets to correlate when the correlation is least desirable – when their prices are falling. Between 2001 and 2005 the correlation between oil and US equities was zero, between oil and gold 0.09, very low, and between gold and US equities it was negative (-0.09) so that the two tended to move in opposite directions. In the first six months of 2006, oil and US equities had a 0.26 correlation, oil and gold 0.58, and gold and US equities 0.43. In May and June 2006 share prices and commodity prices fell sharply, temporarily. Diversification had not helped. Hedge funds fell, on average, just as sharply as equity indices.

So assumptions based on past correlations are often wrong. The correlation between different asset classes can change dramatically over short periods. Everything, or almost everything, can go down at once. The only truly safe investment is money on deposit in a bank – and even that depends on the bank not going bust.

As Philip Coggan wrote in the *Financial Times*, "this looks like a clear example of how the markets are a complex adaptive system." Investors move into new asset classes (like commodities and hedge funds) because these have shown little correlation with the ones they have already. But as soon as investors are in, in quantity, the new asset classes start to correlate with the old, and especially when a wave of caution sweeps through markets.

Diversification works best when the thing being diversified into is neglected or unfashionable. Just as tourists get most pleasure from places which other tourists have not discovered, so the assets which genuinely provide not only low correlation but the reasonable likelihood of high returns are above all those in which no one is much interested. As soon as the asset class is truly fashionable, two things are likely to happen: first, the correlation with other assets rises, so having some of it does less to lower the volatility of the overall portfolio; second, the probable future return falls.

Investors should be sceptical about metaphorical resorts where before breakfast the Germans have already bagged the best investment sun-beds by the swimming-pool. Such investment resorts are unlikely to do much good.

Of course, everyone is in search of undiscovered investment islands and there cannot be many left. But the happy characteristic of the investment world, unlike the real tourist world, is that a resort overrun with investment tourists can become, after a time, neglected and overlooked.

An interesting example, in early 2007, is within emerging markets. While the correlation between most asset classes has grown as everyone, in searching for diversification, has undermined its effect, paradoxically the correlation between different emerging markets has actually fallen. This is principally because a few large emerging markets are under a cloud, and cheap (mainly for reasons of political uncertainty): Korea, Taiwan, Thailand. A global investor could not go entirely overboard here, but those who invest something in these markets not only probably lower the volatility of their overall portfolio, if that is something which bothers them, but are buying cheap assets with the prospect of a decent return at a time when this has become more difficult.

Why not 100% equities?

A study of assets and liabilities which takes into account that the investor is wholly unconcerned about volatility and is interested only in maximising returns will come to the conclusion that the investor ought to have everything in equities.

Why not? In practice, all advisers shy away from such a draconian solution for simple practical reasons. It is just too aggressive. Equities can go down, sometimes drastically. Even those who think they have nerves of steel, very long time horizons, no need for liquidity, and no need for a high income, would be ill-advised to put everything in equities.

The reason for this is above all psychological. Let us say the investor starts with £1m. The worst that can realistically happen to equity markets is a decline in value of around 90%. This happened in the US in the 1920s/30s, in Thailand and Indonesia and Russia as recently as the last ten years, and it came close to happening in Japan in the 1990s.

One million pounds wholly invested in a diversified pure equity portfolio could therefore become £100,000. The investor, contemplating such a fall, and still wholly vulnerable to the vagaries of equity markets which already will have done something scarcely imaginable, could be tempted to take cover by selling. If so, the sale might be at the bottom, locking in a loss, with no possibility of ever regaining any significant portion of that loss.

If the £1m were invested 80% in equities and 20% in, for example, bonds and cash, then at the worst point for equity markets the investor would still have at least £280,000 – or more, because bond prices are quite likely to have risen. The investor is not likely to be unperturbed, but at least can take comfort from the fact that, irrespective of what equities do next, £200,000 is safe from the whimsies of the stock market.

Conversely, 80% in equities is likely to provide enough upside for most people. During a prolonged consideration of long-term asset allocation in 1998 I spoke to Robert H. Jeffrey, veteran head of a family holding company, on the introduction of Professor Jay Light, now Dean of the Harvard Business School. Jeffrey's approach struck me as such eminently good sense that I wrote it down verbatim:

"We had a coal mining machinery business which we sold in 1974 and the money has been in stocks and bonds ever since then. For the first few years we had the ubiquitous 60% equities, 40% bonds type of portfolio that everyone has with no particular intellectual basis, subject to the occasional movement of 5% in the percentages based on what the most articulate member of our board of directors said at the last meeting.

In 1980, I asked my very good friend Peter Bernstein why we held any bonds. He said, "you need to have some protection against the volatility, sometimes stocks go in the tank." So I said, "but Peter, you know we have no economic reason to be concerned about short-term volatility."

Then he said this: "Maybe you don't care about volatility in stock prices, but what about the dividend stream from corporations? In the Great Depression it wasn't just prices which went down, but dividends too."

So we looked at what happened in the Great Depression. Prices fell, from top to bottom, by around 92%. Dividends fell by around 55%. That gave us something to go on, and we asked how much we needed to put in the rainy day piggy bank to keep income coming at the same rate as at the start of the Depression. We assumed that we would put the piggy bank money in high-quality tax-exempt municipals.

We came up with a number, and proposed it at the next directors' meeting. They liked the logic. That gave us an asset mix of 92% equities, 8% bonds. Everybody swallowed hard at this because it was a big jump from 60% equities, 40% bonds. One of the directors said, why not double the piggy bank number? That will give you an extra layer of comfort. So we agreed on that, and the consensus is important because no one can say afterwards that they didn't really agree with the decision. Ever since then we've been between 81% and 87% in equities."

Jeffrey wrote an article in the 1984 *Journal of Portfolio Management,* called 'New Paradigm for Portfolio Risk', in which he asserted that volatility was a poor measure of risk, and he defined risk as "the likelihood of not having enough cash to buy something important." The article was reprinted in *Classics* by Charles D. Ellis, like Peter Bernstein an acknowledged investment guru.

Gold and commodities

Gold and commodities have become fashionable in the last four or five years, which is good reason to hesitate about them.

Gold bugs assert that gold is a monetary asset. Anti-gold bugs say this is nonsense. It was once the case, when the US dollar and other currencies were linked to gold by means of the gold standard, but now, they say, it is no longer. On the contrary, the central banks around the world have been falling over themselves in the last decade or two to get rid of the large reserves they have held. The Bank of England distinguished itself in 2001, under instruction from Gordon Brown, by selling 60% of its gold reserves at a price of $275 per ounce, close to the lowest price gold has touched in recent years. By the end of 2006 it had more than doubled.

However, this is only part of the story. While many central banks have reduced their reserves, none has eliminated them entirely. They still seem to think there is something special about gold. Others have built up their gold reserves, including the central bank of China. There is still therefore a perception by the authorities that gold is in some sense a monetary asset.

And it is not just the authorities. The chairman of an advisory group used to dole out gold coins to each participant, as a partial reward. Did the recipients immediately go off to the bank and convert the gold into cash to spend? Without exception they did not. They kept the coins. They did not, of course, put them on their mantelpieces. They shut them away in a safe place. In some cases they gave them to children or godchildren as Christmas presents. The godchildren's parents did not sell them either. They hid them away somewhere.

This seems to me to demonstrate empirically that gold is regarded as a monetary asset and as a store of value by individuals as well as by authorities. Why else would one keep the coins?

At the beginning of my time in running a family office, in 1997, we put a small percentage in gold mining shares, in a fund managed by experts in that field, the successors to probably the most famous gold share investor, Julian Baring. I had sat at the bank of desks next door to that of Julian Baring for three years in the early 1990s.

The author learning from Julian Baring

Julian Baring was a remarkable man. He invented the Savoy dinner measure of the value of gold. Every year he would go off to dinner at the Savoy Hotel to test whether gold was holding on to its purchasing power by seeing what fraction of an ounce was needed to pay his bill. He was not only a formidable fund manager but a wonderful teacher. He taught me by accident, because he also had a very loud voice. I heard him booming his nuggets of wisdom to his colleagues every day.

He paid little attention to the recommendations of stockbrokers (having been one himself) but made use of their information. Above all though, the information he depended on was provided by the companies he was investing in. He was interested primarily in cash flow – the surplus profit which a gold mining company is able to generate at different levels of the price of gold – and in the value of the reserves of gold mining companies. He detested the frequent practice by managements of hedging – locking in the current price of gold by contracting now to sell future production. This, he averred, destroyed the operating leverage of the company, the ability to benefit from future rises in the price of gold. He took the view that anyone who invested in gold shares, and in the fund which he ran, was looking to benefit from this operating leverage.

1992 was a terrible time for gold shares. In January 1993 he came to a morning meeting at which 30 or so of the Mercury Asset Management managers were gathered together and proclaimed that his fund had been the worst performing of all UK unit trusts in the previous year and that he expected it to be the best performing in 1993. This was a bold claim, and untypical for a fund manager to make. Usually, when the going has been disastrous, fund managers lie low, with their heads below the parapet. To make such a prediction showed great courage and confidence. Sure enough, in 1993 his fund rose by 400%.

The money put into gold shares in 1997 by the family office which I managed had a rotten time over the next couple of years, and the investment fell in value by 50%. I ceased to talk about it specifically: it was a small enough part of the total portfolio not to need to be singled out for mention, so I hid it away, for reporting purposes, in a bucket of assets called 'other'. 'Other' is often a convenient bucket.

The years passed. Between 1999 and 2006 the price of gold rose from $250 to $650, and the value of the gold share investment first doubled from its low point, then doubled again, then again, and then again; so that by 2006 its value was several times the original purchase cost and, in spite of the hapless first couple of years, it had proven to be an excellent investment. By this time I had dug our clients' gold shares out of their reporting bucket of 'other' and had come out of the closet as a gold investor.

This experience has been, to me, testimony to the attractiveness of gold as a long-term investment, to be tucked away, not fussed over. It appeals to a Rip van Winkle style of investing where no attempt is made to time exactly when to be in and when to be out. With the notable exception of Julian Baring in that remarkable pronouncement in 1993, I have not found that gold managers are any better than the rest of us at predicting when gold will do well and when it will do badly.

At different times, strength in gold has been said to be associated with different things. It was linked with inflation in the 1970s, and yet in the early 2000s, when inflation was still falling, gold had a resurgence. It is linked generally with war and disaster, yet during the Gulf War in 1990–1 and after 9/11 it did very little. It is linked with US dollar weakness, but then, in 2005, its strength coincided with a large rise in the US dollar against other currencies.

I asked a gold manager recently whether in all his years of investing in gold he had ever figured out what it was that made gold move. He had not. What is reasonably for sure is that gold usually behaves in a way quite different from that in which ordinary equities, or bonds, or cash, or property, behave. There is a good chance that when other markets, and in particular the ordinary equity markets, are doing badly, and when investors may well be rattled by this, a cushion of gold will give them comfort.

Gold is a case for benign neglect. A chunk of gold or gold shares in the portfolio will provide some help when it is most needed.

Unlike the chunk in cash or bonds, it cannot be relied on not to go down (or not to go down much); but it can be relied on, generally, to move independently from equities, and therefore not to go down disastrously when equities go down disastrously. And generally it will be a cushion of comfort with more oomph than bonds or cash.

The anti-gold bugs frequently quote John Maynard Keynes on the subject of gold. "Barbarous relic", they exclaim dismissively, and usually that is enough. But Katherine Pulvermacher of the World Gold Council pointed out to me that this in fact is a quotation out of context. What Keynes said was not that gold was a barbarous relic but that the gold standard which tied currencies to gold reserves was a barbarous relic. Gold, I think, is a relic of days when the convertibility of money gave it a unique status; but it is not barbarous.

I am not so sure about other commodities. They have been much recommended by investment consultants and asset allocators in the last few years for their diversification merits – in other words, their tendency not to correlate with equities. A study by Professor Harry Kat of the Cass Business School in 2006 concludes, though, that commodities do not provide a consistent risk premium – a return to justify their level of volatility.

A funny thing about diversification is that people tend to get keen on the thing being diversified into only after it has gone up a lot. Goldman Sachs calculate that the amount invested in commodity indices increased from less than $20bn in 2003 to more than $110bn in 2006.

In early 2007, the commodities indices have just had a bigger rise than ever before, which makes me reluctant to enthuse. Most commodities over the long term have given a negative real rate of return – their prices have not kept up with the rate of inflation – because producers have got better and better at producing them. Miners and farmers, with technology, have cut their costs of production. Moreover, commodities do not generate any income, unlike profitable companies which provide cash flow and dividends. Gold likewise provides no income; but then it does have that peculiar monetary asset characteristic which copper, zinc, metal, grain and sugar do not.

Art

Art is questionable as a serious investment asset. The British Rail pension fund invested in art during the 1970s and emerged with a creditable rate of return. Almost no one else has succeeded in institutionalising investment in art. Several funds started in the last several years. The Fine Art Fund, launched by Philip Hoffman, formerly of Christie's, is one of the very few to survive, and meritoriously.

Works of art have to be stored or shown somewhere. They have to be insured. They may be fakes. They may get damaged. In 2006, an unlucky billionaire, not an oxymoron, from Texas put his elbow through his Picasso just before his planned sale of it. Works of art may deteriorate. If they are dissected cows by Damien Hirst they will certainly deteriorate. One of the most expensive bottles of wine in the world came to grief when, exhibited under a strong spotlight, its cork popped out.

People may want to collect pictures and may do well financially out of them, but whether they should be regarded as part of their investment portfolio is another matter. Pictures are for looking at.

Private equity

Private equity completes the roll-call of the main types of investment asset. Private signifies unquoted. Private equity sub-divides into leveraged buy-outs and venture capital.

Individual investors are ill-advised to invest directly in unquoted companies unless they have some expert knowledge of the industry or company involved. Otherwise the best course is to invest through funds of private equity put together by those who are indeed expert in this medium. The best private equity practitioners are both expert in the financial engineering of investment in an unquoted company and get extremely actively involved in directing the companies in which they invest. They may be adept not only in controlling costs – for which they have recently become controversial especially amongst trade unions – but in planning a long-term strategy, and in merging with or taking over other companies in the same sector.

Some purport to do all these things but really only do the first, the financial engineering. With buy-outs, what financial engineering mainly means is leverage: investing partly with borrowed money to begin with and then, as soon as cash flow allows, paying back the debt and returning some of the initial investment to the investors.

Jeremy Greenhalgh of Charterhouse, a leading European private equity manager, describes the change in private equity opportunities. In the 1980s and 1990s the qualities required were faith in leverage, a hopeful management, and charitable sellers; but the greatest of these was the charity of the sellers. Investments typically, he says, were in low growth companies where the attributes for a successful investment were a low original cost of purchase and plenty of leverage through borrowings. Provided the business had good cash flow, the borrowings could be repaid. With a bit of luck the multiple to earnings at which the business could then be sold would be higher than the charitable multiple at which it had been bought.

But now, Greenhalgh says, with huge private equity funds in search of investments, and much more savvy sellers, that game is over. Managers need really to do something useful with the businesses they buy.

While quoted equities can be sold at any time, in private equity the investor is locked in for years. There are two levels of illiquidity: first the investor commits capital to a private equity fund. The capital will be drawn down by the managers as and when they find investments – usually over a period of several years. Second, the investments the managers make are not liquid.

The aim for the manager in every investment is in due course to sell it either to a single buyer – a trade buyer operating in the same industry, or another financial investor such as another private equity manager – or on a stock exchange through a public flotation. Only when this is done – when the investment has been realised – is the manager able to return the investor's capital, plus, with luck, profit. In the last several years an increasing proportion of sales has been to other private equity managers – 70%, roughly, in 2005, an element of pass-the-parcel.

Most private equity managers charge a management fee or commitment fee on the whole amount of the commitment even though not all of it is invested. That fee is usually 2% per annum of the total amount committed. On top of this comes a share in profit – usually 20% of the profit, once investments are realised.

The idea of this combination is, as with hedge funds, that the management fee covers costs and the performance fee is the reward for doing really well. These things evolve. A few years ago a leading manager raised a private equity fund of $700m on which they charged a management fee of 1.5%, to cover costs. In their next fund they said that they would raise $1.4bn and charge 2% (though their cost base had not changed much). In the event, they raised $3.3bn and still charged 2%. Recent funds have been much bigger, still with the same 2% management fee.

The illiquidity suggests that private equity should give a return several per cent higher than quoted equities. Most people believe that the difference should be not much less than 5% per annum. This is a tall order, and most private equity managers fall well short of meeting it – in part because of the very high fee burden.

To the extent that private equity managers have in the past come up to scratch, the use of borrowings has had much to do with it. One of the longest standing, largest and best known private equity managers is KKR – Kohlberg Kravis Roberts, named after its three founders. The firm dazzled the investing world with the notorious acquisition of RJR Nabisco in 1988, for a long time the largest leveraged buy-out ever until KKR broke its own record with a bid for HCA for $33bn in 2006.

KKR is deemed to have been among the most successful private equity managers, with a return after all costs of 15% per annum to its investors over the long term. A study has shown that they used 70% leverage – borrowings of $70 for every $30 of equity capital invested. If the same degree of leverage were applied to the Standard & Poor's index for quoted US equities, the return would have been 50% per annum.

Citigroup in 2006 conducted a similar analysis. Going back ten years, they put together a notional portfolio of UK public companies with characteristics attractive to private equity firms – reasonably consistent revenues, high cash flow. They then applied leverage to this portfolio – three parts debt for every one part cash, this being a typical private equity mixture. The return on the cash theoretically invested worked out at 38% per annum over the ten years, compared with the average return of actual private equity buy-out funds of 14% per annum. Even the first quartile buy-out fund in the period – the fund which did better than three-quarters of its competitors – had a return of 36%, lower than the theoretical leveraged portfolio of publicly quoted companies.

So even the most successful of buy-out firms, which certainly get thoroughly involved in the management of companies, may still do no better than ordinary investors would do if they chose, instead of putting $100 of their own money in quoted equities, to put in $25 or $30 of their own and another $70 or $75 borrowed from the bank.

There is a flaw in this sort of critique. Borrowing heavily to finance quoted equity investment is fine in rising markets, and a poisonous mixture when markets fall. In 2000–02 the FTSE All Share Index return was -42%. An equity portfolio bought with three parts debt, one part cash, at the beginning of 2000 would before long have been worth less than the debt alone. The investor would have needed a remarkably accommodating bank to stay in the game. The fact that private equity funds do not lose all their money suggests that their managers have some skill in managing the degree of leverage at different times, and in maximising the cash flow from their investments.

Venture capital has similarities with buy-outs but it is investment in fairly new unquoted companies, with a product and business which may or may not succeed. Most will not. But one or two successes can be sensational.

Investors need to spread their money around so that there is a decent chance of a winner amidst all the inevitable losers. Different venture capital and buy-out firms have vastly different results. Small exposures to the best funds, if only one can be sure about what a best fund is, are worth pursuing energetically. For example, a $5m commitment to one venture capital fund gave investors a profit of over $125m because the fund was one of the early investors in eBay. Yale University invested, through a fund, $300,000 in Google and had $75m of gains when the company went public in 2004.

Private equity and venture capital have made a tremendous impact on the returns of both Yale and Harvard, two extremely successful endowment funds. An analysis by Frontier Asset Management (not confirmed by Harvard or Yale) shows the possible effect of private equity (including venture capital):

1997–2005

	Harvard	Yale
Average private equity exposure	10.7%	18.4%
Annualised return including private equity	15.1%	16.6%
Annualised return excluding private equity	11.8%	7.6%

Over this period a portfolio consisting half of US equities and half of fixed income would have given a return of 8.1%. For the (not quite the same) period 1996–2005 the return Harvard got from its private equity portfolio was 32% and Yale 39.5%. In 2000 alone, the year when the technology bubble was at its biggest and then burst, the return from private equity and venture capital for Harvard was 155% and for Yale 169%.

Harvard and Yale, and many others, have shown remarkable skill in persistently picking winners among private equity and venture capital managers. But new investors, however rich, are unlikely to get access to the managers who have been most successful and who are regarded as best. New investors are in the position of Groucho

Marx, only wanting to join clubs which would not be prepared to have them.

Summary

Asset allocation appears to have become immensely more complicated in the last twenty years because of the emergence of apparently new asset classes to sit alongside equities, bonds, property, and cash.

Private equity and venture capital are specialist areas. There is a vast difference between the performance of the top quartile (top 25%) and bottom quartile in private equity and venture capital, much wider than the difference between the quartiles in quoted equities. The average moneyed investor will find it difficult to get access to what he or she wants in these areas. To worry much about getting exposure to private equity and venture capital is, therefore, to worry about something which may in reality be rather academic. This means that the essential choices, for the great majority of investors, are the same as they have always been: how much to have respectively in equities, bonds, property and cash; and who should look after each of these.

But we must not forget about hedge funds.

THREE

Hedge Funds

M ANY definitions for hedge fund have been tried. None has quite done the trick. The former chairman of the SEC, William Donaldson, said: "The term hedge fund is undefined, including in the federal securities laws. Indeed, there is no accepted universal meaning. Basically, many so-called hedge funds are not actually hedged and the term has become a misnomer in many cases."

The best definition probably is that of the sceptic who said that hedge funds are not an asset class but a compensation system. Their typical management fee is 1.5% or 2%, and there is a fairly standard 20% performance fee, sometimes more and rarely less. The importance of fees is discussed in the next chapter.

The first hedge fund was started by Alfred Winslow Jones, a Time Inc. journalist, in 1949 with $100,000, of which $40,000 was his own money. His successors in managing hedge funds were lucky that he happened to fix on a performance fee of 20% of profits, which set the precedent.

The second common factor in all hedge funds is that they allow short positions, or short-selling (or 'shorting'). The Jones hedge fund was a fund which allowed him not only to buy shares (or in the vernacular to own long positions) but to sell shares he did not own, the practice known as short-selling.

The third common factor is that they employ leverage, or borrowing. The exposure which a hedge fund has to investments other than cash is therefore much greater, often, than its asset value. Some hedge funds use little borrowing, but it is rare to find one which uses none.

Hedge funds operate in all sorts of asset classes – fixed income and currencies as well as equities – and are therefore not themselves an asset class but more a means of investing. By far the largest single category, accounting for roughly half of the total of about $1,300bn which is estimated to be invested in hedge funds, is equity funds of one type or another.

This is a big part of the investment world. According to the management consultants McKinsey & Co. in a paper published in January 2007 ('Mapping the global capital markets'), the value of all investment markets is around $102,000bn, so hedge funds account for more than 1%.

They punch above their weight. In terms of investment activity they are a bigger part of the investment world, because they typically buy and sell securities much more frequently than long-only portfolios – though not invariably: some equity hedge funds are notably long-term and focussed in their investment policy. According to Baupost Group in 2005, hedge funds then accounted for close to 25% of daily US stock market volume. A European stockbroker estimates that hedge funds have annual turnover on average roughly 12 times the value of their assets. According to Greenwich Associates, hedge funds pay approximately 30% of all equity trading commissions in the US and account for more than half of the trading activity in certain US fixed income markets.

Some equity hedge funds specialise in merger arbitrage, where the manager estimates the odds of a likely merger or takeover (either announced or rumoured) actually being completed, and accordingly invests in the company to be acquired and short-sells the stock of the acquiring company – or the other way round.

Another category of hedge funds is 'pairs trading' where the manager invests in one company and short-sells the shares of another company in the same industrial sector. It does not matter how well the sector as a whole does: what matters is the relative performance of the share bought compared with the share sold.

Some equity funds are market neutral – they try to neutralise the effect of overall market movements entirely, so that again the only thing which matters is the relative performance of the things bought compared with the things sold.

Despite all these intricacies, equity hedge funds have become, at least in aggregate, increasingly correlated with equity markets. Part of the object of the hedge fund exercise is to get something close to the same return that equity markets offer but without the downside, and to do all right in phases when equities are doing badly. Correlation with equity markets defeats that object.

Bridgewater Associates in 2006 found that "emerging market hedge funds are more than 80% correlated to a simple 50:50 mix of emerging market equities and bonds, and are failing to outperform this basic combination." Based on this research, McKinsey reported in their *Asset Management Industry in 2010*: "increasing transparency with respect to performance is beginning to expose many players that have been selling beta products disguised as alpha, with alpha packaging and pricing" – beta being shorthand for the return which exposure to the stock market alone produces, and alpha the element of outperformance.

Nobody minds a high correlation with equities when equities are going up but disconcertingly the correlation appears to rise particularly when equities are going down sharply. This seems to have been the case in recent years, notably in September 1998 (the Russian crisis and the collapse of Long-Term Capital Management), early 2000 (the end of the tech boom), and April/May 2006 (nothing in particular). Increasingly hedge funds have failed to bale out the investor at a time when equities do badly.

The process of short-selling

The objective of short-selling a share is to profit from a fall in the share price. Short-sellers are then able to buy back the stock at a lower price and pocket as profit the difference between the price at which they sold and the price at which they bought.

The way to accomplish this is first to borrow the shares from someone who does own them, paying a small fee to the owner, and collateralising the loan with cash or some other asset such as Treasury bonds. If the investor were for some reason not able to return the shares to the lender the lender can rely on the collateral. The circumstances in which this can happen are, for example, if the share price rises so dramatically – for instance because of a takeover bid – and the short-sellers are so financially unsound that they cannot afford to buy back the shares and then return them to the borrower, but instead go bust.

The business of selling what you do not own is unusual in life. It does not happen with houses or pictures or furniture. Grocers do not sell fruit or flowers which they do not have. Short-selling of stocks may be seen puristically as fundamentally flaky, but it is big business.

Great expectations

The key attractions of hedge funds are said to be that they have a lower volatility than long-only portfolios, and that especially talented people manage them. The reason for the latter is the high fees which by custom they command.

These propositions are bound to be true of some hedge funds. However, in aggregate, hedge funds are a con. That is not to say that individual hedge fund managers are con artists. But in aggregate hedge funds cannot offer the advantages which are claimed for them. Only a tiny minority can fulfil expectations – a much tinier proportion than can be expected to fulfil expectations among ordinary (long-only) equity managers, though there too it is only a minority who can succeed.

It is more or less accepted in the long-only world that, since professional investment managers effectively constitute the market, the average manager will perform in line with the index, or a little worse reflecting fees and costs which the index does not bear. Charles D. Ellis of Greenwich Associates called the business of active investment management "the loser's game" for that reason.

By contrast, when people start considering hedge funds, they often talk about the exceptional pool of talent involved in this corner of the investment world. Much of the starry-eyed discussion of hedge funds seems to assume that their game is different and that hedge fund managers have in aggregate a systematic ability to beat benchmarks.

But if there is a loser's game in long-only management, there is the same game for hedge funds. Even if once – when the hedge fund arena was sparsely populated by an arguably select breed of talented people – this was not so, it must be true now when the field is crowded with 8,000 hedge fund managers. The average hedge fund manager is unlikely, therefore, over a sustained period, to outperform the relevant indices.

Hedge fund managers are disdainful of indices. They generally would not claim to be aiming to outperform an index overall. Implicitly, though, equity hedge fund managers are in fact trying to outperform an index with their long portfolios, by picking companies to own which do better than average; and they are trying to outperform an index with their short portfolios, by short-selling shares which do worse than average.

The typical equity hedge fund might these days have total long positions – holdings in shares as a percentage of the overall net assets of the fund – of around 100%. It might have total short exposure – stocks short-sold as a percentage of total net assets – of around 40%. This means that the net long exposure is 60% (100% less 40%). The gross exposure is 140% (100% plus 40%).

If the average manager can do no better than achieve an index return, the overall return of that average manager will be 60% of the return of equity markets, plus the cash return on the sale proceeds of the short-sold shares, less the cost of borrowing shares to short-sell and dealing costs. From this has to be deducted the management fee (say 2%), and the performance fee (20%).

This return does not amount to very much unless the index return is excellent. Assuming that in the future the return of the index is pretty much in line with returns over the very long-term past (which some will think a generous assumption), that might be 10% per annum. The sum is then:

	%
Index return (10%) × 60%:	6.0
Interest on cash less short-selling costs (say 3%) × 40%	1.2
Return before fees	7.2
Management fee	(2.0)
Return before performance fee	5.2
Performance fee (20%)	(1.0)
Net return to investor	**4.2**

4.2%, I submit, is the reasonable expected return of the average hedge fund manager if markets provide a return of 10%.

Good managers: hedge fund vs. long-only

Hedge fund enthusiasts may argue that hedge funds generally will get more invested in strong markets and less invested in weak markets. This implies that there is no loser's game in market timing. There is, of course. The average manager does not succeed in making asset allocation decisions which improve performance; on the contrary.

Some hedge funds will do very much better than the average. When I made roughly these points at a family office conference an irritated hedge fund manager pointed out that all the family offices present were in the business of choosing managers who do better than average. There were around 60 family offices represented, and if all of them did better than the average that would be marvellous.

Of course each of us expects to do better than average. An article in *Lingua Franca* found that 95% of British car drivers think they are better drivers than the average. To exceptionally good drivers like myself, it is always a puzzle that so many other drivers think they drive well. It must be because of their over-confident driving that my car seems to have such a lot of bumps.

But even if our self-confidence about the picking of managers is justified, it is still likely to be hard to do better with a really good hedge fund manager than with a really good long-only fund manager.

This applies in poor stock market conditions as well as good. Suppose that the future for stock markets, over the next several years, is lack-lustre, and that the indices give a return well below their historic averages, say only 3% a year – perhaps close to a zero return after inflation.

Now suppose that we have picked two really good managers, one of a long-only equity portfolio and the other of a long-short equity hedge fund. Suppose that both are able to outperform the equity market by 3% with the shares that they own and, in the case of the hedge fund manager, also with the shares short-sold. That would be impressive because over the long term outperformance by 3% a year is a rare achievement.

Now suppose the hedge fund manager has a long portfolio of 100% of net assets and a short portfolio 40% of net assets; and that the long-only manager charges fees of 1.25% and the hedge fund manager a management fee of 2% and a performance fee of 20%.

The long-only manager gives a return, net of fees, of 4.75% (3% market return and 3% outperformance less 1.25% management fee). For the hedge fund manager the calculation is more complicated:

	%
Long portfolio 100% of (3% + 3%)	6.0
Short portfolio 40% of (-3% +3%)	0
Interest on cash less short-selling costs (say 3%) × 40%	1.2
Return before fees	7.2
Less management fee	(2.0)
Return before performance fee	5.2
Less 20% performance fee	(1.0)
Net return to investor	**4.2**

So even if the stock market gives a poor return – 3% before inflation, or close to a zero return in real terms – the good long-only manager still does better for investors than the good hedge fund manager.

In a report in February 2007 the investment bank Dresdner Kleinwort carried out a similar analysis, based on returns in 2005 and 2006 only. They included another element of cost which takes account of the huge amount of trading done by most hedge funds, and they estimated that this cost, paid to investment banks, prime brokers and trading counterparties, amounted to around 4% in each of these years. These are their figures for the average of all hedge funds:

	2005	2006
	%	%
Gross performance before trading costs	17.0	22.5
Trading costs paid to investment banks	3.8	4.3
Gross performance after trading costs	13.1	18.3
Fees paid to hedge fund managers	4.3	5.3
Net performance to investors	**8.8**	**13.0**

The hedge fund industry was estimated to have assets under management of around $1,300bn at the end of 2006. Calling it a round trillion, this means that investment banks and hedge fund managers received $81bn in fees and commissions in 2005 and $96bn in 2006.

Any questioning observer has to wonder whether the total pie of available return is big enough to allow the professionals who get between the owners of money and their investments to take such an enormous slice of it without leaving, over the long run, too small a slice for the owners – even if, in years such as 2005 and 2006 when markets generally were very strong, the slice for owners looks all right.

Investors must be confident that they have got a good hedge fund manager who is much better than a competing good long-only manager to make the game worthwhile.

Hedge fund optimism, equity scepticism

Not every hedge fund investor is being sold a pup. But there are plenty of pups to go round. For every hedge fund manager who does much better than average, there will be one who does much worse. The fact that investors have wholly unrealistic expectations of what hedge funds will in aggregate do is demonstrated by survey after survey. At a family office conference in 2005, the collective view of those attending was that over the next five years equity markets would give a return (before inflation) of 6% – remarkably low, and evidence that since the great bear market of 2000–02, in spite of strong markets since then, investors had never really recovered their poise. They remained, at least in 2005, in aggregate notably lacking in enthusiasm for equities.

The same group of family office people expected a return of 9% from hedge funds. This is a completely unrealistic combination of expectations. If equities were to give a return of 6%, then (with the same assumptions about exposure as above) the expected return of the average equity hedge fund would be around 2.3%.

Maybe habitual hedge fund investors are almost obliged to

have this Doctor Doom attitude to equity market returns. Their expectations are self-reinforcing. They are determined always to see the dark side because they need to, in order to support their hedge fund investment philosophy rather than a philosophy of investing in equities in a more old-fashioned way. But despite their equity gloom, inconsistently they become unduly optimistic about the capability of hedge fund managers to do what they want.

The optimism of a hedge fund investor

Expecting a higher return from hedge funds than from equities is the equivalent, in weather terms, of saying not just, "I am carrying this umbrella so that when it rains I won't get wet", but also "under this umbrella it will always be sunny."

This unreasonable expectation about returns is the first reason for caution. It does not mean that investors should avoid all hedge funds. It does mean that they should be realistic about what hedge funds as a whole are likely to achieve, and therefore ultra-cautious in choosing a manager.

It would be salutary if, in any asset allocation table, in place of the usual line marked 'hedge funds' was substituted 'funds with very high fees'. This would be a bracing reminder of what investors are up against. It should not deter them from any hedge fund action at all. It would just make them think twice.

The trouble with short-selling

Another reason to be twice as careful about investing in a hedge fund as in a long-only fund is that there is a fundamental difficulty about short-selling. In a long-only fund, if the manager makes a mistake, the mistake has the attractive attribute that it gets smaller. In a sense the manager can worry about it less. If shares in a position which is 5% of the portfolio halve, and nothing else changes, they will now account for roughly 2.5% of the portfolio, and thenceforth have less of an impact on overall performance than they did.

With short-selling the opposite is the case. If a manager sells something without owning it, and the price doubles, the exposure in the portfolio has doubled. If initially the short position was 2.5% of assets then, other things being equal, it is now roughly 5%. If the share price were to double again, the investor would lose close to a further 5% of the portfolio – and be at risk for four times as much as at the start.

Since share prices can go up without limit, the investor has an open-ended liability, akin to what investors in the Lloyds insurance market used to have. As Warren Buffett beautifully put it, Lloyds investors accepted this liability, down to their cufflinks, because of "300 years of retained cufflinks." A whole fund can in theory (and occasionally in practice) be wiped out because the fund can no longer afford to buy back short-sold shares whose prices have gone up unexpectedly, and especially strongly.

This is a horrible characteristic with horrible consequences. It forces managers to adopt disciplines which prevent their exposure rising to an uncomfortably high level. These risk control disciplines are known as stop losses. Managers might, for example, limit any short position to 2.5% of total assets. This means that, if they start by short-selling a stock with 2% of the portfolio, they can tolerate a rise of 25% in the share price. But if the share price goes up by more than 25% so that the exposure is then more than 2.5%, they are forced to take action.

The forced action is to start to buy the shares which the managers have sold and do not own. They are obliged to buy shares which they are quite likely to think are valued in the market even more unjustifiably than when they first started to sell them.

Proponents of stop loss disciplines say that they are simply an essential element of risk control. Many investors recognise the illogicality of these disciplines, and have a softer version of them. One hedge fund manager – call him Fred – told me how this tended to work in practice. Murphy's law rules. For example, Fred has a 2% short position in ABC Corporation. Instead of going down as he expects, the shares go up by 25%. Never mind, Fred says: we are as sure as ever that these shares are overvalued. We will stick with our position, which is now 2.5%.

There is a lot of chat in the hedge fund community and hedge fund managers frequently seem to have the same ideas. Unfortunately, some of Fred's friends happen to be short-selling the same shares and they have harder versions of the stop loss discipline: they started with a 2% position, but when the share price goes up, their increased exposure obliges them to buy shares to reduce the position back to 2%. This helps to put buying pressure on the stock which goes up further, say another 25%.

Fred now has exposure of 3.1%. This is more than his soft stop loss discipline will allow. He is as sure as ever that the shares are overvalued, but prudence dictates that he reduce exposure by buying at least some shares.

This buying, by him and by like-minded investors, adds to the buying pressure. The shares go up again. At this point doubts set in, the normal doubts that all of us have when something is going in the wrong direction. Events always provide some rationale which allows commentators to suggest that the shares deserve the price move they have had.

Fred gives up. He declares that something fundamental in the outlook for the company has changed, and closes the entire position by buying back all the shares of which he is short, taking a large loss. Short-selling is full of pitfalls.

The risk delusion

The third major difficulty about hedge funds stems from their investors' expectations for volatility.

Many investors are looking for a free lunch. They want 'absolute return': quite high returns, with low risk. In looking at a particular hedge fund they focus especially on monthly drawdowns – falls in value over a month – and on the maximum drawdown, the largest fall that the hedge fund has suffered in any period, or that can be expected.

Hedge funds can turn out to be an extremely expensive lunch in more ways than one. They are expensive undeniably in terms of fees. The lunch may be delicious and it may even be regarded as good value, but it certainly costs a lot.

They can also be expensive in that, taking big risks, they may incur big losses. But current experience – with notable exceptions, of which Amaranth in 2006 was a high profile example – suggests that there is more risk of hedge funds taking insufficient risk than of their taking too much. This is partly because of the universe of investors that they have come to serve.

In mid-2004 a hedge fund in which my clients were invested had two rotten months, down about 5% in both May and July. Early in August I rang the management firm and asked if I could speak to the manager. An assistant rang me back to arrange a conference call the following morning at 9.30. Why conference, I wondered?

I rang. I realised at once that in addition to the fund manager there were two or three minders gathered round the speaker phone at the other end.

"I just wanted to have a very quick word. I've seen the last couple of months have been rotten, and I wanted to say keep bashing on with what you do."

There was an audible exhalation of breath at the other end of the phone.

"Don't you want an explanation of what has gone wrong?"

I did not. I could see it pretty clearly from the performance of the largest positions shown in the manager's newsletter.

It had become evident that this scheduled conference call was one of a series of several, maybe many, which the manager's minders had organised to explain a couple of months of bad performance. It demonstrated the intolerance either of some of the fund's investors for poor short-term performance, or of the manager's colleagues and bosses, or both.

This manager did keep bashing on, without changing investment style, and has done well since this incident. But faced with this kind of short-term expectation it is not surprising that most hedge fund managers have sharply reduced their risk, and therefore reduced also their scope for really strong performance as well as their vulnerability to really bad performance. Expectation quickly becomes pressure, and pressure becomes requirement. Such pressure seldom comes after strong performance. It comes after weak performance.

The tolerance for consistently high returns, on the part of investors, is limitless. Only when a manager falters do the doubts set in. One fund in which we were invested had had a brilliant past, with very high annual returns in both good and bad markets over several years. It was volatile. There were many individual months, in some years the majority, in which the return was either better than +4% or worse than −4%. It then stumbled for three or four years in a row.

Thereafter the pattern changed. In the most recent two years there were hardly any months in which the return was more than +2% or worse than −2%. The investment style changed, whether because of internal pressures from colleagues or the manager himself, or external pressures. The focus shifted from obtaining a high return and putting up with volatility, to not losing money over more than a few months, and not losing much money in any single month. Because there is no free lunch, this meant that the manager would never make much money for clients either – especially after all the costs.

The tendency to lower risk after a few poor results is not limited to hedge funds. But the tendency is more acute in hedge funds than in long-only funds because of the nature of the client base. Many clients will have been attracted to hedge funds because of the expectation of a free lunch. They want to do well in the good times but are not prepared to do badly in the bad times. They do not have the philosophy of investors in high risk assets, likely to get good returns over the long term, but implicitly accepting that in the short run they can suffer hard knocks.

Managers realise that the risk with such investors is asymmetric: the dissatisfaction these investors feel when their return is minus is bigger than their pleasure when their return is plus by the same amount. The manager is forced therefore to aim low: never to disappoint too much, in the same way that in another context institutional managers cling to the index because they feel that the sort of clients who measure their portfolio carefully relative to the index will not be disappointed as long as their return is more or less in line with it.

Judging hedge funds

In spite of all these cautionary comments, investors need not be polemically opposed to hedge funds. Their one unifying characteristic, high fees, has a predictable effect: investment managers like managing them. Only those who are thought to be good can get away with charging hedge fund fees. Some of those thought to be good really are good. Their speciality may be finding companies the prices of which are too low in relation to prospects, or in spotting grossly overvalued companies to short-sell, or in hedging market exposure ahead of stormy times.

This discussion is limited to equities: there are managers who trade currencies or interest rate movements brilliantly, or arbitrage between different types of securities of the same company. There are managers who burrow forensically through loan documents of companies close to or in bankruptcy and are willing to go to court to exploit some hidden value. All of these are likely to be drawn to the higher fees which hedge funds offer.

Some hedge fund managers are not so good – or may be good but have an unlucky patch ahead of them. The average hedge fund manager is no better than an average manager; and an average manager is no better than the comparable index or combination of indices would be. Then the hedge fund fees have to be deducted to leave potentially slim pickings for the owners. To set out to choose the average hedge fund manager makes no sense at all, yet some investment banks now offer a vehicle designed to provide exactly that – average hedge fund performance.

Aiming to find an individual hedge fund manager who is much better than average is another matter. At least it makes sense, though it is hard. It is always difficult to judge managers, but with hedge funds it is particularly difficult, for several reasons.

1. Often hedge fund managers are offering their wares in this form for the first time. The typical career path of hedge fund managers is to have spent a number of years in a more conventional institutional investment management firm, running long-only portfolios. Performance will have been good: otherwise they would not stand a chance of attracting money from new clients for their hedge fund.

    They may be drawn to running a hedge fund not only by the fees but by the freedom to short-sell. All fund managers see shares which they think unduly expensive, or due to fall for some other reason. The long-only manager simply avoids them, but cannot profit from their avoidance.

    The hedge fund manager can profit by short-selling. But short-selling is, because of the unhelpful attribute that a mistake becomes a bigger part of the portfolio rather than a smaller part, emotionally and in time hugely more consuming than long-only activity.

New hedge fund managers may thus be starting to do something which they have never done before. It is really an entirely different sort of job from running a long-only portfolio. They have limited experience by which a client is able to judge their abilities, and they need a different mindset. That makes the decision for the client difficult.

2. Another common career path is that the manager will have spent some years with one of the major investment banks, generally as a trader. Investment banking traders are in an environment very different from that of a new hedge fund manager. They are surrounded by other clever traders, and have privileged access to information about the flows of funds in markets – where the buying is, where the selling is. Much of this may make their life more complicated. There may be information overload, and too much noise. It is certainly stressful. But, whatever it is, it is different from life in a much smaller firm as a hedge fund manager. It is hard to tell what effect the change in environment will have on a manager.

3. Some new hedge fund managers, coming from investment banks, have tried to get round this problem by immediately putting together a big team of people also from a trading, investment bank, background. They need a reputation and credibility to afford to do this, so not many can. But this itself brings problems and unpredictabilities. One hedge fund was able to raise over $2bn on day one of its operation, with a team of 32 people many of whom had never worked with each other before. However brilliant the principal one or two, and however brilliant the other 30, it would be hard to know how well such a team would work together.

4. Many hedge fund managers will not tell the client in detail what they do. The reasons for this secretiveness are not all good ones.

The managers sometimes argue that they do not want to reveal their positions for fear that others will copy them.

Short positions are extremely vulnerable to what is known as a short squeeze. This is not something nice but perfunctory that happens between long-married couples. It is nasty. In order to throw the short-sellers into confusion and alarm, some investors start buying a stock which has been heavily short-sold and push the price up, forcing the short-sellers to cover their positions at losses. It is possible to get a fairly good handle on the overall volume of short positions in a particular stock through the securities lending figures: in order to short-sell a stock a manager must first borrow it, and there are services which give aggregate figures for the securities which are on loan.

Shares are lent for one of two reasons: either so that the lenders avoid taking the dividend because they are taxed on it while a tax-exempt borrower can share the benefit of the saved tax with the lenders; or for short-selling.

It is usually fairly easy to tell for any given stock whether dividend avoidance or short-selling is the major influence at work. Since figures are thus available at the aggregate level which give a reasonable guide to short-selling activity, the only reason apart from secretiveness that individual managers might be reluctant to give details of short positions is that they fear being targeted by other managers who, if they know the short positions, might try a short squeeze.

Inscrutability in much that hedge fund managers do is the norm. They may, in their monthly or quarterly reports, mention a few positions, and perhaps list their largest five long positions, but they are typically extremely reticent about the short side and about much else, and in the absence of information about what they actually do it is difficult to judge them.

Some describe their investment approach in grandiose and inscrutable terminology. In early 2007 one major hedge fund management firm, launching a hedge fund on the London Stock Exchange, described what it did:

"The underlying philosophy is to construct strategies, often contingent in nature, with superior risk/return profiles, whose outcome will often be crystallised by an expected event occurring within a pre-determined period of time."

What this seems to say is that the managers decide what they think is going to happen and invest accordingly.

5. Hedge funds can make use of leverage: they borrow. Few long-only funds borrow. The purpose of borrowing is of course to increase the overall rate of return, but this makes it necessary to borrow at the right time and not at the wrong time.

Large scale borrowing is not normally a problem with equity long-short funds. Some funds might have as much as 300% gross exposure but these are exceptions. This leverage means that the total value of all long positions and all short positions, added together, is three times the value of net assets. The manager will be trying to achieve a balance so that if the markets are weak the long side may not do all that well but the short side will: the share prices of the shares sold without being owned will go down a good deal, balancing the losses on the shares owned.

However, there may be freak moments when a manager manages to lose heavily on both the long and the short side. If the manager has, for example, taken a highly negative view of prospects for the US and a highly positive view of prospects for Japan, and turns out to be diametrically wrong, there is trouble on both sides. Managers tend naturally to balance their risks so that they are not too exposed to a combination of circumstances such as this which, though improbable, would result in heavy losses if it occurred. But with high leverage the risks are compounded.

A combination of high leverage, and of long and short positions which each went in the opposite way to that expected, was the undoing of Long-Term Capital Management, the leading light in the most famous hedge fund debacle. In 1998, after years in which, guided by two economics Nobel Prize winners and a bevy of intelligent and experienced managers, Long-Term Capital Management's fund had scored steady successes with little volatility, the fund went bust. It did so because it had huge leverage. At the beginning of 1998, the firm had equity of $4.72bn. This was not a little company on the fringes. It was a huge hedge fund, much trusted, with some of the most keen-sighted and experienced clients. Compared with this equity position, the firm had borrowed over $124bn. It had off-balance sheet derivative exposure amounting to $1,250bn – mostly interest rate derivatives such as interest rate swaps, also equity options.

LTCM were happy with their positions because their painstaking analysis had provided ample evidence that there would never be a combination of circumstances in which their long positions went down at the same time as their short positions went up; but then there was.

One hedge fund manager I met had a simple strategy: he invested, fairly passively, in long-term Danish mortgage bonds, leveraged four times with borrowing in Swiss francs. The return depended on the Danish bond market not going down too much, and on the Swiss franc not going up too much. The manager charged a management fee of 1.5% and a performance fee of 25%. I asked why investors interested in this strategy would not simply buy Danish bonds themselves and borrow Swiss francs. "They would not dare." (In the two or three years since our meeting, this strategy will have been stupendously successful.)

If a fund is truly inscrutable the investor cannot be sure what the manager is doing about leverage, though as discussed earlier the greater problem with most equity long-short hedge fund managers is too little risk, in an effort to avoid monthly drawdowns, rather than too much.

6. As with private equity, the concept of 'access' is much talked about. Those who perform best become inaccessible except to those investors who have been with them before. With 20% performance fees, hedge fund managers do not need to maximise

the amount of assets under their management, and they often conclude that they are more likely to be able to provide good performance if they limit the amount of assets they manage and close their funds to new entrants. This means that the services of the truly talented – certainly those perceived as truly talented – are just not available.

7. Hedge funds are often illiquid. Investors are tied in, prevented from selling their holdings, for periods which vary from a few months to several years. To give them even greater control of the funds at their disposal they often provide lock-ups so that the investor cannot sell for some years.

   The regulators have taken increasing interest in what hedge funds are up to. The Securities and Exchange Commission decided that, with effect from February 2006, hedge fund managers should be registered if they had US investors, just like other funds. There were a few let-outs, and one was that if investors were committed to the fund for at least two years, the manager did not have to register.

   Ironically, given that the SEC was trying to improve the position of the investor by regulating, hedge fund managers were able to use this let-out to make the investors' terms of investment worse. Twenty-six of the largest 100 hedge fund managers failed to register with the US, in many cases introducing for the first time lock-up arrangements so that investors, if they wanted to stay invested, had to consent to stay in for at least two years.

   The US courts then decided, in June 2006, that the SEC had no right to compel registration by hedge fund managers, so it was not necessary to find ways to avoid registering. Nonetheless, the new lock-up terms, which many firms had introduced to avoid registering, remained.

Despite the disadvantages of hedge funds, the investor should not be put off totally. Although the prospect of high fees attracts many managers who may turn out to have been merely lucky in the past and to be less successful, through bad luck or lack of skill, in the future, the same prospect also attracts the really good, some of whom luck will not desert in the future and some of whose funds may not be closed to new investors.

The trickiness of telling the difference between the lucky and the good should make the investor reluctant to commit too much to hedge funds. The investor is looking for a prodigious talent to overcome the handicaps posed by the hurdles of high fees, inscrutability, the intrinsic difficulty of shorting, and illiquidity.

Bangs and whimpers

Occasionally people worry about whether there is a hedge fund bubble and if so whether and when it will burst. Hedge funds represent a hugely diverse set of management styles. Even though there is a tendency for some hedge fund managers to flock together – lots of them investing in the same companies in which for some reason there is a catalyst for something to happen – they are not all facing in the same direction at the same time. It seems unlikely that, if there is a bubble, it is the sort of bubble which will burst. It is more likely that the fad will dissipate with several whimpers rather than a single bang. The whimpers will be whimpers of disappointment with results.

There may be the occasional drama. The regulators will probably probe a bit harder than they have done. Hedge funds which act with too much bravado have come under attack from governments. The German foreign minister talked about the "locusts" who descended on German companies after several hedge funds managed to secure the resignation of the chief executive of Deutsche Boerse in 2005. Hedge fund managers will be more anxious than in the past not to give any appearance of acting in concert with other managers.

If there is a nightmare scenario for hedge funds in aggregate it is probably something to do with the dominance of the prime brokers who often help put together and launch the funds, execute all their transactions, lend them money, provide valuations and other administrative services, and carry out their securities borrowing. Goldman Sachs, Morgan Stanley and Deutsche Bank dominate this market, and for each of them prime broking is a major source of profit.

Individual hedge funds come and go with remarkable alacrity. The average shelf life of a hedge fund is about 2.5 years. Managing a hedge fund, with the tendency to ferocious activity and the sensitivity to getting it wrong on the short-selling side, is exhausting. That is one reason for the low figure for average life. The other is that investors are so intolerant of short-term poor performance.

The present vogue in hedge funds has lasted so far about ten years, and it looks like lasting for years to come. Big institutions are continuing to pour money into hedge funds and such institutions find it as difficult to reverse as the Queen Mary.

This is not the first time hedge funds have been hugely fashionable. The first such phase was in the 1960s, a follow-up to A.W. Jones's pioneering of the concept in the 1950s. It came to an end in the 1970 bear market. The magazine *Fortune* in May 1971 recounted what had happened to the assets managed by the leading hedge funds as, after a period of bad performance, investors took their money out.

	Total assets ($m)	
	December 1968	September 1970
A.W. Jones & Co.	220	31
City Associates	107	18
Fleschner Becker	75	15
Fairfield Partners	63	28
Cerberus	51	23
Steinhardt Fine Berkowitz	47	50
Strand	37	13
Lincoln Partners	34	33
Hawthorn Partners	29	8
Boxwood	27	12

Investors in hedge funds should first consider the advice of Peter Fletcher, who runs a successful family office:

Hang them first and try them later: if he senses any trouble at all, he is out.

Not so Sharpe ratio. (The Sharpe ratio is a quantitative measure of risk.) Fletcher does not have much faith in quant data. Qualitative factors are much more important.

Leverage and illiquidity are the kiss of death.

Be cynical.

FOUR

Fees

O H *how dull. Fees. This is really the cart before the horse, isn't it? Who cares about fees? All that investors should care about is the net return – the return they get after all fees and costs.*

This is an understandable but naïve view. It is quite true that all that matters in the end is the net return, but the net return is, after all, the gross return less fees. Fees make a difference.

When in 1992 a colleague and I sat in a Melbourne meeting room staring out of the window while we waited for a client, my companion passed the time, as he later told me, by thinking about how much his share options in the firm for which we worked were now worth. The shares of our firm had gone up a great deal because the economics of investment management are wonderful, and the firm had done especially well.

The great beauty of the investment management business is that it is not at all capital intensive – beyond some computer systems and the overhead involved in ever increasing compliance with regulatory requirements it consumes little capital – and that the revenues take the form of low percentage figures attached to large amounts of assets.

The cost of managing an account of, say, $50m is not much

greater than the cost of running an account of $5m. This means that, once the break-even level is past, nearly every penny of extra revenue goes to the bottom line of profit.

Moreover, in normal circumstances an investment management business with a large proportion of its activities in equity markets is likely to have strong growth. The reason for this is that equity markets can be expected to provide a real return, after inflation, of 5% or more, and revenues based on asset values will have the same growth rate. If the increase in costs can be constrained to this rate, the business's profits will also grow at this rate, and if costs grow only at the rate of inflation it will be even better.

This combination – little requirement for profits to be put back into the business in the form of capital investment, the ability to charge fees which result in high profit margins, and strong long-term growth characteristics – easily compensates for one other facet of investment management, which is that it is extremely cyclical. Markets go sharply up and down, and fees tied to the value of assets also go sharply up and down.

Clients need not feel too sorry for investment managers. Investment management fees provide profits to investment managers except where the business concerned is failing so badly that it falls below the fairly low threshold of its overheads.

The pie and its slices

To a capitalistically minded investor, there is nothing wrong in itself with providing profit to an investment manager. But the pie of total return is not infinite. If the manager has too big a slice of the pie, the investor has too small a slice.

Some people have no objection to high fees, and even seem positively to revel in them, on the theory that you get what you pay for. If you pay peanuts you get a monkey. Their practical justification is that they are only interested in the net return, after fees, and could not care less about the money the manager makes. This sounds like sensibly enlightened capitalism. But it is all very well looking at past net returns and concluding that they would have been satisfactory. It is quite another matter to look forward and conclude that the level of fees is irrelevant to the net return.

Alistair Blair in *Investors Chronicle* gives a simple illustration of why fees matter. If you invest £10,000 and achieve a return of 7.2% a year for 40 years, you end up with £160,000. If you invest the same £10,000 and earn 5.5% a year (only 1.7% less – which he suggests, possibly understating, is the typical performance drag from fees, dealing costs, and other expenses in a retail investment fund) you end up with £85,000. So if the market index gives a return just above 7.2%, this is the difference between buying an index fund with low investment management fees and almost no dealing on the one hand, and buying an actively managed fund which happens to perform in line with the market (before costs) on the other.

In this illustration the hapless investor invests in a fund which provided, before costs, the same return as the market. Obviously investors choosing a manager hope that, both before and after fees, they will do better than the index. Suppose that Adam and Eve are two such investors. They each have £10,000. They each choose a manager of a UK equity portfolio. They choose well, and times are good. The UK market gives a return of 9% per annum over the next ten years, and the portfolios of Adam's manager and Eve's manager each outperform, before fees, by 6% a year – by the way, sensational performance.

Eve's manager charges 1% per annum. Adam's manager charges 1.5% per annum, plus a performance fee of 20% of the return, quite a common pattern of fees – the norm, or slightly below, in the hedge fund world, but high fees are contagious and many long-only managers also charge this sort of fee. At the end of ten years, Adam's £10,000 has turned into £28,591. Eve's £10,000 has turned into £37,072. Adam's manager has taken £6,583 in fees. Eve's manager has taken £2,204.

Of course, Adam only appointed his manager because he was confident his choice would do better than Eve's manager. If he had turned out to be right – and right by a large margin – that would have been fine. But for one manager to outperform another by the difference between Adam's and Eve's net return is quite an achievement. In retrospect it will always seem to have been obvious and easy. It is not.

The devil's advocate counter-argument is that low fees may encourage a manager to take on too much business. Investors must expect managers to want to run profitable businesses. If the managers' speciality is, for example, investing in small companies, then they cannot take on too many assets without having an impact on the way in which they can invest. A small cap manager merits higher fees, therefore. It may be better to pay 2% per annum to a manager who promises not to take on more than $500m than 0.75% to a manager who takes on $2bn.

The big investment management firms allowed the big pension funds, aided by the pressure of investment consultants, to drive fees to apparently very low levels – for example 0.15% of assets. 0.15% on, say, a £1bn pension fund portfolio is still handsome incremental revenue. But acceptance of this sort of business suggests that the object for these firms had become asset accumulation and retention, with incremental fees dropping to the bottom line, rather than strong performance.

Low fees can therefore be damaging, in a roundabout way, to net returns. Disenchantment with the big firms which were prepared to charge low fees made it much easier for hedge funds to charge very much higher – not just slightly higher – fees. In extreme cases the fees are much higher than the typical 1.5% or 2% of the asset value, plus 20% of the return. James Simons of Renaissance Technologies, a manager with a superb record, charges 5% plus 44% of the profit. Such fees make the odds of the investor doing well low – which is not to say impossible.

The attraction of the standard fees lured a great many fund managers into the hedge fund world. The first hedge fund manager, A. W. Jones, charged a performance fee of 20% of profits, but unlike his successors he did not also charge a management fee. The brilliant manager Seth Klarman of Baupost comments: "Twenty percent was the share of profit the captain of a merchant vessel traditionally received from his patrons upon a successful return. That Jones established fees in this manner was fortuitous for today's hedge fund managers, who obviously do not have to undertake the same personal risk as a 17th-century captain and who would still do quite well for themselves at appreciably lower fee levels."

These days, to charge only a performance fee, and not a management fee, is thought by some to be dangerously eccentric. One UK manager has done exactly this: Bedlam Asset Management, self-avowedly quixotic. This firm has an admirably commonsensical and old-fashioned approach to investing. Its founder, Jonathan Compton, has described rival firms as "lazy, sharp and misleading" with fee structures "ethically very close to simple fraud." The firm, named after a London lunatic asylum, does not collect fees from clients until the rate of return is above +1.25% in any quarter. This is not too hard a hurdle. Originally, when the firm was launched, their performance hurdle before charging any fees was more demanding. But too brave a business model may have the counter-productive effect that the firm's senior people have to spend much of their time discussing whether they can cope with it.

The pecking order in fees

For a long time it was regarded as not really acceptable that a long-only fund should charge as much in management and performance fees as a hedge fund. Hedge fund managers and those who made a speciality out of investing in hedge funds tended to be sniffy about such long-only managers. There was something rather clubbish about hedge funds. This clubbishness has faded as more and more hedge funds have appeared. Moreover, the poor performance of many hedge funds compared with equity markets during the last few years has led to a new generation of long-only funds, managed by hedge fund managers, and charging the full hedge fund standard fee.

The market in fees is therefore all over the place. At one extreme in the pecking order is the very low fee charged by index tracker funds, those who simply try to replicate the performance of the indices.

Next are the low fees of big institutional firms with emphasis on active risk, and aiming to do just a little better than the indices.

Next come the boutique fund management firms with generally long-only portfolios who tend to charge around 1.5% without a performance fee, or about 1% in management fees plus a performance fee.

Frontier Asset Management, drawing on the findings of Peter Bernstein in *The Intelligent Asset Allocator*, analyses the costs of a typical index fund, in three categories: first, the cheapest, funds investing in US large companies; next, those in US small companies and also international funds; and third, emerging markets funds. They then compare the total cost of investing through an index fund in each of these categories with the total cost of investing through a typical fund run by a manager who is trying to beat the index – an active fund. The results are as follows:

	Large companies	Small companies & international	Emerging
Index funds			
Fees (mainly investment)	0.18%	0.20%	0.57%
Dealing commissions	0.01%	0.10%	0.10%
Dealing impact on markets	0.04%	0.30%	0.80%
Total indexing costs	0.23%	0.60%	1.47%
Active funds			
Total active costs	2.20%	4.10%	9.00%

The cost advantage of the indexing approach is nearly 2% for the most straightforward type of fund, and over 7.5% for an emerging market fund. It is not surprising that indexing has its adherents.

Next up in the pecking order are the hedge funds with their standard 1.5 % and 20%, or 2% and 20%. Then there are long-only funds managed by hedge fund managers, also charging these hedge fund type fees.

In private equity, the fee burden is higher still. Typical fees are 2% of commitments and 20% of profits. But the commitment fee is paid irrespective of how much money has been drawn down by the private equity manager to invest. Since it is normal for a manager to take several years to draw down the full commitment the investor has made, a 2% commitment fee can equate to a fee of around 4% or more on investments actually made. A survey by *Private Equity Intelligence* in 2006 found that investors in over 700 funds paid an average of 12.8% in commitment or management fees, as a proportion of the amounts actually invested, over the life of the various funds. This is before performance fees. The effect is huge. *Private Equity Intelligence* said that, to give an internal rate of return to the investor of 25%, the average fund would have to triple the value of its investments. If they were to increase the value of investments by 1.5 times, the return to investors would be only 7.6%.

Summary

It may be worth paying high fees. But the investor has to be strongly aware just what a slice fees can take of the overall return, and how much more difficult it is for the manager charging high fees to produce good net, after-fee, performance for the owners of the money.

Investors should care. Even the most sophisticated and experienced do not. I went to a hedge fund conference in 2002 when a speaker asked whether the audience thought hedge fund managers' fees were too high. I was the only person, out of 30, who stuck up his hand.

Investors therefore need to think about fees and to be sure that the fee differential between one manager and another is worth it. Equally, they have to be sure, in investing in an asset class like private equity with especially high fees, that the managers are doing something likely to provide the necessary extra performance to justify the fees.

FIVE

Indices and Index-hugging

THE investment management industry is in some ways puzzlingly unsatisfactory. The industry as a whole does nothing useful. This is not its fault. It is an inevitability. The average fund manager managing an equity portfolio is bound to produce an investment performance in line with (or, because of costs, a little lower than) the stock market. The only exceptions to this are in markets which are so undeveloped that fund management professionals are not the dominant influence on market activity. There are not now many of these left.

In any developed market it is axiomatic that in the long run half the managers will outperform the market index and half will underperform. This is because they are the main participants in the market, and together they therefore compose the average, which is the index. Over short periods of a few years, more than half may outperform (to the disadvantage of other participants, which means principally individuals looking after their own affairs) but these periods will be offset by others in which more than half underperform (to the advantage of the others).

Indeed, the position is worse than this: the average manager underperforms the indices, rather than performs in line, because there are costs to deduct from performance – investment management fees

94

and the commissions which have to be paid to brokers who carry out every transaction.

This makes the industry unusual. Postmen are doing a good job if they deliver letters to the right place, say, 99.9% of the time. Builders are doing a good job if none of their buildings fall down; magicians if no one rumbles their tricks, and they manage to avoid actually sawing anyone in half. Accountants expect all their figures to add up. Proof-readers expect to get rid of all typos. But investment managers are conditioned to an extraordinary rate of failure. They are doing a good job if they manage to outperform the market index 55% of the time, or cumulatively by a small margin. Compounded over the years, that small margin may still make an immense difference to the investor.

That is the difficulty of investment management. It may be simple, but it is not easy. Owners of money often have an unduly inflated idea of what a good investment manager can do for them. Experienced managers know just how difficult it is to outperform by a decent margin and with some consistency.

In fact, confident though managers may be, rightly or wrongly, in their ability to outperform over the next seven or ten years, they know with virtual certainty that there will be periods of underperformance. Wholly consistent outperformance is a myth. The periods of underperformance may be as short as a few months or as long as a few years. There will almost certainly be, in a seven-year record, a duff year or two.

Indexing

During the 1960s academic work argued that the securities markets, or at least the main ones, were efficient. An efficient market sounds quite a good thing, but an efficient market is as grim an idea as the efficient Baxter in P.G. Wodehouse's books about Blandings Castle. Efficient markets make investment life no fun at all. Inefficiencies in markets are what enable active managers – those who try to outperform indices – to be effective. In a totally efficient market active managers are totally ineffective.

One of the tests of the efficient market hypothesis is that all public information is discounted instantly in markets. It is fairly obvious these days that genuinely public information must indeed be reflected in share prices immediately. It was not always so obvious, because the speed of dissemination of information was slower. The British victory at Waterloo was in theory a piece of public information, but it was the fact that the Rothschilds got hold of it earlier than others that enabled them to invest ahead of the crowd.

The idea that, even now, public information is discounted not only immediately but efficiently is different. There is plenty of evidence that in practice markets do not adjust correctly to every piece of information. If it were otherwise, how could one explain, for example, the fall in share prices of 25% in a day in October 1987, in response to almost no information at all, except the news that share prices were falling?

On the contrary, in a world in which vast amounts of information are instantly disseminated by the internet and financial news services like those of CNN, Bloomberg and Reuters, it looks as though the discounting mechanism frequently gets itself into overdrive by mistake, and that price movements in response to news are exaggerated, providing an opportunity to those who do not base too much on what has happened in the last hour or twenty-four hours, or what may happen in the next week, month or even quarter.

Another test of the efficient market hypothesis is that on average 'active' managers do not in fact outperform those indices. But this is no more than a truism, proving nothing, since professional managers are overwhelmingly the major active players in markets. This was not always so. In 1963 more than 60% of shares in the UK market were owned directly by individuals. Only 6% were owned by pension funds. Now more than 80% of shares are owned either by institutional investors such as pension funds or by some kind of professional firm on behalf of individuals. Individuals themselves, making their own decisions, account for less than 20%.

Of course, if the market is in effect composed of active managers, only half (or strictly speaking half the assets managed by active managers) can do better than the average which is represented by the index, and half will do worse. This does not mean that it is impossible to choose managers who are more likely than not to be among the outperformers in the future (and may have been in the past) and that is the subject of another chapter.

Before the last 30 or 40 years, it was assumed simplistically that professional managers could be expected generally to outperform. The discovery of the opposite rather depressing truism led many investors, especially institutional investors, to give up completely trying to beat the market by hiring active managers. Instead they invested in index funds, whose components were more or less exactly the components of the index, and which could therefore be relied upon to perform roughly in line with the index.

The desperation of indexing

Index funds have one great advantage, and that is that they do not cost very much, as discussed in the last chapter. There are no highly paid professional investment managers making decisions; just machines imitating the index.

The movement into equity index funds is the product of a doctrine of despair – if the chances of choosing managers who will outperform are slim, then it is thought by many clients better not to try to choose, and instead simply to accept what the market average provides, which should over the long term be a satisfactory real return.

That does not appear a completely unreasonable policy. Choosing managers who stand a decent chance of doing better than the average is not excessively complicated but it does require some time, effort, and knowledge of what the various managers do, and even if all these are applied still the results may be bad. That is the risk. So to avoid this risk altogether, and just to accept the return of the equity market which should be well above the rate of inflation over the medium term, is understandable. It is a little like deciding that the risk of a rotten dinner, and the possibility of a really good one, are such that, if a restaurant opened offering the 'average' dinner obtainable anywhere in London and at a knockdown price, one should jump at it. It might not be very exciting, but at least cheap and filling.

A study by Frontier Capital Management concludes that, over a variety of five-year periods, the percentage of actively managed funds underperforming the index is as much as 76% in the case of European funds and 73% in the case of the US. Over ten-year periods, the figures are higher. If the chances of an expensive and disgusting dinner are that high, it is not surprising that many investors are happy to accept the cheap though cheerless alternative provided by the index approach.

However, there are some peculiarities about an index fund approach of which the investor should at least be aware before embarking on this course.

Most indices are based on market capitalisation. The composition of the FTSE 100 Index in the UK, for example, is decided upon by an index committee of City luminaries. They use some discretion, but what they are after in principle is the 100 largest companies by market capitalisation (share price times number of shares). They are not putting their seal of approval on the investment merits of a company when they include it in their index. They are just saying that it is big enough to deserve to be part of the index, whose purpose is to reflect, in a clearly measurable way, the state of the market.

Similarly, the distribution of the MSCI World Index between different countries is determined by market capitalisation. If the current market value of the Japanese market is 10% of the market value of all developed markets, then the weighting of Japan in the MSCI World Index is 10%. The MSCI Index compilers are, again, making no judgement about whether Japan is a good or bad place to invest right now. They are merely putting together an index whose movements are supposed to give a measurable idea of how world markets in aggregate are doing.

The fact that most indices are based on market capitalisation has perverse consequences for anybody who decides to invest in an index fund. In the UK context by way of example, someone who invests in a FTSE All Share index fund has more and more of the portfolio in a particular company if that company's share price goes up. The more expensive the share price, the greater proportion of the portfolio. There is no mechanism, within an index fund, to take a profit on a share which has gone up too much.

Similarly in a global context investors have more and more of their portfolio in any country which does particularly well. If, say, the Dutch market doubles, and nothing else moves, then the proportion which index investors have in Dutch shares doubles.

Most indices are not static. Their composition changes quite frequently. Devised to give an indication of the overall performance of a market, indices are ill designed to be mimicked exactly by investors when they change their composition.

Index funds and the tech bubble

The peak of the tech boom in 2000 shows the strange consequences for the investor of adopting an index fund approach.

In March 2000 the index committee of the FTSE indices, responsible for shifting companies in and out of its indices, took nine companies out of the FTSE 100 Index and put nine in to replace them. The additions and removals are shown in the table below.

Company	Price-earnings ratio
Deletions	
Associated British Foods	12
Allied Domecq	12
Hanson	11
Whitbread	9
Scottish & Newcastle	8
PowerGen	7
Thames Water	7
Imperial Tobacco	9
Wolseley	8
Additions	
Cable & Wireless	104
Freeserve	★
Thus	★
Baltimore Technologies	★
Psion	★
Nycomed Amersham	32
Celltech Group	★
Capita Group	155
EMAP	37

★ no price-earnings ratio because the company was loss-making

Of the additions, six were either telecom or technology companies. The index committee was just doing its job. The indices were supposed to reflect the markets, and the guiding principle was that the FTSE 100 contained, broadly, the largest 100 companies by market capitalisation. The market capitalisation of each of the companies added had gone up because their share prices had shot up. Anything with the faintest whiff of high tech had roared to unimagined heights while many first class companies were languishing, neglected by investors because they were too boring. The market capitalisation of each of the companies thrown out of the index had gone down, so they no longer, based on the committee's criteria, deserved their place.

Index funds followed. They chucked out stocks which had, as the table above shows, very moderate price-earnings ratios, and added stocks which were exorbitantly expensive. The old stocks were Old Economy, regarded as dinosaurs facing extinction. The new stocks were New Era.

There were many signs, not only in valuations, that the bubble had got too big and must burst. I was at the time a director of a UK small companies investment trust whose managers told the board, in February 2000, that they were slightly nervous of what was going on in tech and telecom and therefore had what they described as a moderate position, only 36% of the portfolio. They went on to explain that their competitors had an average of 52% in these two sectors.

At Morgan Stanley conferences devoted to the technology sector, rubber balls and yo-yos were handed out. It was an indication that work had become play, a dangerous stage for markets to have arrived at. Around this time the chief executive of a Swedish internet consulting company, who had become on paper the sixth richest man in Sweden, came into our offices wearing shorts, another ominous work-is-play indicator.

The bubble burst in March 2000. In the UK, the peak was marked by the initial public offering of the shares of LastMinute.com, last minute in more ways than one. This is an internet travel agency which at the time was spending £100 on marketing for every £10 it generated in revenue. It had sales of £1.4m. Its market capitalisation at the time of the offering was £570m. It peaked two weeks later with a market capitalisation of £800m and a share price of £5.32. Two years later, at its low before it started to recover, the share price was 18p.

At the height of the excitement, one leading fund manager, Gilbert de Botton, founder of the phenomenally successful Global Asset Management, recited a palindrome: "Are we not drawn onward, drawn onward to new era?"

He did not give the answer, but the use of a palindrome was ironically apt. A palindrome is circular. Full circle is exactly what the markets turned. In the three months after the FTSE index changes, the performance of the old and the new FTSE stocks was as follows:

Old economy and out	Change in price %
Associated British Foods	+24
Allied Domecq	+29
Hanson	+14
Whitbread	+23
Scottish & Newcastle	+41
PowerGen	+55
Thames Water	+36
Imperial Tobacco	+30
Wolseley	+1
New era and in	
Cable & Wireless	-10
Freeserve	-26
Thus	-55
Baltimore Technologies	-57
Psion	-44
Nycomed Amersham	+4
Celltech Group	-14
Capita Group	+4
EMAP	-26

The index committee of the FTSE reacted predictably to these price changes. Obedient to their guidelines that size matters, they responded to the fall in market capitalisation of the stocks they had added in March by now removing some of them from the index, and putting back in some of those they had ejected in March. Index funds naturally did the same.

Although the technology bull market was over, there was one last twitch. In the next three months, Baltimore Technologies rose by 58% while Scottish & Newcastle and AB Foods both fell by 26%. In September 2000 the FTSE committee announced that Baltimore Technologies was back in the FTSE 100 and Scottish & Newcastle and AB Foods were out. The committee commented, perhaps slightly sheep-faced, that "changes simply reflect movement in the market." Baltimore Technologies then resumed its steep decline, and in due course left the FTSE 100 once more, never since then to return.

It is obviously better to invest in an indexed equity fund than in actively managed funds which underperform. But index funds have the serious disadvantage that they behave as lunatics.

Index-clinging

During the 1980s the difficulty of consistent outperformance led much of the UK investment management industry, indeed the majority of it, to cease to try to outperform by much. Active managers, supposedly trying to beat the market, became less and less ambitious about this goal. They remained in name active managers, and charged fees accordingly. But in practice the contents of their portfolios looked much like the contents of the indices.

Active managers who cling to indices are clinging to the coat-tails of a lunatic. This was perfectly illustrated in 2000, when the indices reflected the technology boom and bust, and index-clingers imitated in real portfolios the tergiversations of the FTSE index committee.

In the UK a few large firms had become predominant, especially in the management of portfolios for institutions – largely pension funds. A large firm begins to have goals which are different from those of a small firm. In a large firm, a high proportion of fee revenues drop to the bottom line of profit, because, after a certain threshold, there is little extra cost in the management of extra assets.

A large firm thus begins to worry more about conserving its cash flow from existing fees than about getting new business. To conserve cash flow it must not be sacked by existing clients. In order not to be sacked it must not disappoint them too much. And if it manages portfolios in such a way that it is sure not to disappoint too much, it is also sure not to provide performance which is especially pleasing.

There were other reasons around the turn of the century for large firms to shift the focus from really good performance to the avoidance of really bad performance. One factor was the Unilever case in 2001, when the trustees of the Unilever pension fund sued their manager, Mercury Asset Management, for negligence.

Mercury had achieved returns much lower than those of the benchmark set by the Unilever trustees. The trustees had set risk limits which were supposed to limit the extent of the underperformance, and they alleged that Mercury paid no attention to them. After an embarrassing time in court, Mercury ended up settling to pay an amount widely estimated to be around £75m.

The Unilever case accelerated a trend among UK managers. The trend had been towards index-clinging. After a few years of generally poor performance, the big managers had already been running for cover. The emphasis had moved from investment risk – the risk of losing money – to business risk, which is the risk of losing clients. In order not to lose clients, and not to be sued, managers felt that they must, above all, not underperform the index benchmarks which they were set by more than a smidgen.

Another reason for large firms to focus on avoidance of bad, rather than achievement of good, performance is size itself. A large firm is constitutionally at a disadvantage. A large firm is obliged either to present itself as a collection of individuals who all do their own thing, or as a collegiate entity with a corporate image and a corporate product which will be much the same for every client.

Presenting as a collection of individuals is commercially difficult: clients worry that they have got the wrong individual looking after them; and when they hear that x has done much better for their friends or competitors than y has for them they may feel aggrieved. One of the most damaging disclosures in the Unilever/Mercury case was that the person supposed to be in charge had actually handed over personal responsibility for managing the Unilever portfolio to a colleague, without initially telling Unilever about it. Ironically, the hand-over would have been with the very best of intentions: with the conviction that the successor was an excellent manager and might quite likely do better than the previous manager with other responsibilities. Unfortunately (though he probably was and is, in the long term, an outstanding fund manager), he did very badly indeed in the years concerned.

Commercially, it is easier for large firms to take the collegiate line that the individual is irrelevant and that clients have the benefit of the whole firm's collective brilliance. But, if put into practice, this means consensus, and consensus means compromise, and compromise means the introduction of lowest common denominators in decision-making.

Moreover the whole process of decision-making, when it has to involve a large number of bright people all of whom feel they have something to say, becomes turgid and slow. The easiest compromise is to copy the index.

I remember when these index-hugging tendencies started to prevail. In the US equity team at Mercury in the early 1990s we began to worry for the first time about the effect that not holding a particular stock had had on our performance during the last quarter – the effect, for example, of holding nothing in Coca-Cola, a large company with therefore a significant weighting in the US market index, the Standard & Poor's Composite Index. We began for the first time to talk about overweightings and underweightings – an underweighting being a position in a stock which was a lower percentage of the portfolio than that stock's weighting in the S&P. We started to hold underweight positions. Previously, if we had thought a share unattractive we did not hold it. Now, even if we were negative about their prospects, we sometimes held at least something in companies which formed a large part of the index because of the danger that we might be wrong and that having nothing in them would hurt performance. We began, in common with most of the other leading UK institutional investment management firms, to lose the courage to have convictions.

Active risk

The push in the direction of index-clinging was helped by improvements in the technical capabilities for performance measurement and monitoring of the characteristics of portfolios. "Improvement means deterioration" was the aphorism of the famous *Sunday Telegraph* City editor Patrick Hutber. It applied here.

For many years there has existed a measurement known as tracking error. This term is used in relation to index or tracker funds and it is apposite. Tracking error measures the extent to which an index fund fails to achieve the return of the index, which, that being its objective, is indeed an error.

In the late 1980s this measurement began to be used for a different purpose, and under a different name: active risk. The emphasis on active risk did more harm to the investment management industry, at least in the UK, than anything else in the last 30 years.

Active risk – measuring the extent to which the performance of a portfolio is likely to diverge from the performance of the index with which it is being compared – is based on analysis of the composition of a portfolio, and the way in which each equity within a portfolio behaves: how volatile it is, and to what extent its movement correlates with that of other holdings in the portfolio.

There are several problems with this. The first is that the measurement depends on past correlations and past volatilities, which will not necessarily hold good in the future. In reality there have been several occasions, always moments of crisis, when correlations and volatilities were not what they had been, so that the active risk figure gives a false picture of what might actually happen.

Second, active risk is a limited concept anyway. An active risk of, say, 4% means that there is theoretically a two-thirds probability that performance in each year will be within 4%, plus or minus, of the market return – so if the market return is +10%, a portfolio active risk of 4% means that the portfolio return will probably be between +6%

and +14%. Two-thirds probability leaves a lot to be surprised by. One year in three the portfolio return is likely to be outside this range.

To improve the odds, the range of possible returns has to be widened. A 4% active risk means that there is, again in theory, a 95% probability that performance will be within 8%, plus or minus, of the market return. Even this leaves room for a shock.

Reliance on past patterns which may not be the same in the future, and the fact that the outcome anyway may be outside even a wide range of possible returns, are both technical handicaps.

The other problems with active risk are much more fundamental. Active risk is a misnomer. It does not really describe the risk to the client of an investment. A client's real risk is to lose money permanently, rather than to diverge from a market return. A portfolio consisting entirely of cash has a high active risk vis-à-vis an equity index; but it cannot truly be said to represent much risk to the client. After all, the value of a cash portfolio cannot go down (though it may not do as well as inflation).

The risk in active risk is really that of the investment management firm, not that of the client. The large firms who majored on active risk wanted to control the likelihood of giving a shock to their clients.

Use of active risk as a measurement has encouraged index-clinging: determined not to shock, managers, supposedly active, produce portfolios which differ only minutely in composition from that of the index. The extent of divergence from the index is policed mercilessly by risk control and portfolio construction departments. These departments, with improved technical capabilities and quantitative methods, look over the shoulders of the investment managers and provide a critique intended to be helpful but in effect often putting managers off their stride, distracting them, and making them more sensitive to short-term aberrations in performance from that of the index.

The Vodafone debacle

The story of Vodafone is another illustration of the bizarre effect of index-clinging.

Vodafone is a newish company. The mobile telephone operations of the defence company Racal were spun off in this separate company in 1985. By 1999, with the help of the acquisition of Airtouch, it had become the largest company in the UK by market capitalisation. In February 2000, at the height of the bubble, Vodafone bought Mannesmann, issuing new shares to pay for it. The consequence was that Vodafone moved instantly from representing around 8% of the FTSE 100 index to representing around 14%.

Many pension funds had maximum limits on the proportion of their portfolios which could be invested in a single company, often 5%. This was a problem to the index-clinging brigade, because if they stuck to these limits they would be hugely underweight and so exposed to the risk that if the Vodafone share price went up a lot more than the market as a whole their portfolios would underperform.

Some investment consultants, whose specialist business is to advise institutional clients, mainly pension funds, on asset allocation and on which managers they should choose, encouraged pension fund trustees to change the rules to allow investment managers to buy more Vodafone.

At one pension fund of which I was a trustee, the manager wanted the investment committee to remove the 5% limit. His argument had nothing to do with the merits of Vodafone. In fact, he said, their firm was rather negative about Vodafone and so wished to remain underweight, but would want to buy more so that their position was 12% of the portfolio they managed compared with the 14% index position. The consultant agreed. Only two trustees – Leonard Licht vociferously and I supporting him – demurred.

Leonard Licht was the man who, many would say, was responsible more than any other for the Mercury Asset Management approach to investment in its glory days. This approach put a strong emphasis on convictions, on courage, on instinctual and quick but well-informed judgements. Licht believed in investing in assets and cash flow. He would appear at one's desk and flick through a tray piled high with research notes until he alighted on one which made him pause for a moment. The next day one would see that he had bought shares in the company concerned, and within a week or two he might have amassed a stake of 2% of the company. Impatient of committees and bureaucracy, he did not stay on this trustee board for long.

The trustee meeting about Vodafone was a classic in chairmanship. The chairman of the investment committee was a former Cabinet minister. Faced with this unexpected disagreement with the consultant and fund manager, he looked at his watch. He noted that the full trustee meeting was due to begin shortly and that the investment committee needed to get a move on. He summed up. The limit should be removed. He looked around the room over the heads of all present, two such heads, those of Licht and me, rather open-mouthed.

"Are we agreed? Good, next item." The manager duly went out and bought lots more Vodafone shares.

"Are we agreed?" How to chair a committee

To his great credit Leonard Licht returned to the fray at the next meeting. Vodafone's share price had already fallen, but it had much further to go over the next few years. He asked for the decision to be reversed and the 5% position limit to be reinstated, and it was. He saved this pension fund from an enormous loss.

The systematic tendency to underperform

It might be thought that the worst thing that could be said about index-clinging, supposedly active, managers is that they charge fees for producing performance roughly in line with the index – a little lower because of the fees. It is a bit worse than this. Index-clinging has a systematic tendency, cumulatively serious even if in each year mild, to produce a performance poorer than that of the stock market index (less fees), because it leads to a wholly reactive process.

A manager might have a portfolio which resembles the market very closely. The top ten holdings in a UK equity portfolio, for example, might be the top ten holdings in the FTSE 100, and in roughly the same proportions. The top ten holdings in the index have accounted, in recent years, for around half of the total FTSE 100, so this alone would help ensure that the portfolio would do much the same as the index.

In one or two stocks, the manager may have a position significantly different from the index. The reactive problem is that if a stock in which the manager is overweight goes down, there can be great pressures, self-generated and from the portfolio construction teams who monitor this kind of thing, to reduce the portfolio weighting to neutral – in line with the weighting of the index.

Conversely, if an important stock in which the manager is underweight goes up, the pressure is on to bring up the portfolio weighting to the neutral level. In this way such managers are always chasing their tail, buying something which has just gone up and selling something which has just gone down, a formula sure to result in underperformance.

For years up until 2000, despite providing something which was not very satisfactory for their clients, the large managers could at least take comfort from the fact that they were not disappointing their clients too much and were therefore conserving their firms' cash flows. But once returns became negative because markets were falling, clients became more sensitive to the flaws in the whole business of index-clinging. Nonetheless this remains the paramount method of fund management in London.

A factor in the increased awareness of indices in the last few decades has been increased short-termism. One of the reasons for it is that, as it became technologically easier to report on market values quickly, performance figures increasingly were calculated more frequently and provided promptly to clients. Dwelling on performance over periods as short as three months, a month, a week, or even a day resulted in nervousness about underperformance compared with indices over these short periods.

Other indices

The Dow Jones Industrial Average and the Financial Times 30 Share Index are indicators of market behaviour not devised in a particularly sophisticated way. Most more recently invented stock market indices are based on market capitalisation, so that if two shares start with an equal weighting in the index and one share outperforms the other, the weighting of the outperformer rises and the weighting of the underperformer falls. This means that index funds, and index-clinging managers, tend to have more invested in shares which, having done well, may be expensive, and less in shares which, having done badly, may be cheap. To get round this problem other indices have been invented.

The main index for international equity markets is the Morgan Stanley Capital International World Index. Countries in this index are weighted by their market capitalisations. MSCI have for many years had an alternative to this, weighted by size of economy (gross domestic product) rather than by market capitalisation.

In the late 1980s the Japanese market boomed. Its weighting in the standard MSCI World Index went from under 20% in 1985 to 39% at the peak of the market in 1990. A global index fund, based on this index, held 39% in Japan. Between 1985 and 1990 Japan's GDP as a proportion of the GDP of all developed economies moved only from 15% to 18%. A global index fund, based on the GDP weighted MSCI World Index, therefore held 18% rather than 39% in 1990 – and just as well, because the Japanese stock market fell by 75% over the next ten years.

To committed indexers, determined that they cannot find active managers who will outperform indices, these GDP weighted indices provide a respectable improvement on market capitalisation weighted indices. They still suffer the shortcoming that, within each country in the world index, the weighting of every company is determined by market capitalisation. There remains, therefore, the tendency to hold more in shares of a particular company whose share price has already done well.

Another lot of indices deals with this. Devised by Robert Arnott of Research Affiliates LLC, 'fundamental' indices are ones in which the weighting of each company is not based on market capitalisation and therefore on the vagaries of share price movements but on the company's revenues, profits, or dividends.

If investors feel they have to index, they could look in the direction of these GDP weighted international indices and fundamentally weighted country indices, rather than on traditional indices which are based on market capitalisation.

The reaction to index-clinging

In the late 1990s, despite the excitement of the rise in markets, the fund management industry became an enervating place. The old axiom was still true – that the industry as a whole provided no benefit. But also many clever and highly paid people became demotivated because they were now required not even to try: they were expected to imitate, more or less, the performance of the market index rather than attempt to outperform it significantly.

Many disenchanted managers turned their backs on these practices and left. One of my present colleagues finally threw in the towel at the large firm for which he then worked after a team meeting at which a certain stock, Total, was discussed. He had 1.2% of his portfolios in this company; other members of the team had 1.1%. The conclusion of the meeting was that he should reduce to 1.1%. It all seemed rather pointless.

Out of this bouillabaisse of increasing mediocrity, in some respects inevitable and in others self-imposed, emerged two dissident overlapping forces. Most of the departing disenchanted set up or joined hedge funds, the particular attractions of hedge funds being first the generous standard fee structure and second more investment (and other) freedom.

The minority set up or joined boutiques – small investment management businesses, with an approach recently designated by investment consultants as Long-Term Long-Only or LTLO.

LTLO is really a throwback to an earlier era. Long-only managers, the old-fashioned sort who do no short-selling, just have long positions in stocks they have bought. In the early 80s and before, investment managers had concentrated portfolios – portfolios with not very many holdings – and they owned only what they liked. The index was there to measure performance. Its country, sector, and stock weightings were not slavishly imitated. When I joined Warburgs in the late 1970s, the international investment team led by Manfred Adami held a large amount, more than 25% in some portfolios, in gold mining shares in Australia and South Africa. These two markets constituted less than 2% of the international market index and gold shares less than that.

The new LTLO managers regard index-clinging as anathema. They have no underweightings. If they do not think much of the prospects for a stock, however large a part of the index it is, they do not hold it.

They generally run much more concentrated portfolios – with

fewer holdings – than they were required to have, in order to meet active risk requirements, in the places they have come from. They tend, though this is not necessarily the case, to hold shares in a particular company for quite a long time – longer than the average of ten months. As for particular style, for example emphasis on growth or emphasis on value, these managers may follow either or any.

One thing such managers can be pretty sure of is that their portfolios' performance tends to diverge a good deal from that of the index – for better or for worse. The consultants' soubriquet – Long-Term Long-Only – includes Long-Term, not so much because that is what the managers are, but because their clients need to be long-term: in any quarter, indeed any year or series of years, performance is likely to be very different from that of indices and that can mean worse rather than better.

The special designation, LTLO, seems to imply that this method of fund management is somehow rather recondite and specialised. It is actually the most ordinary type of fund management, with commonsense principles, but, from being wholly the conventional approach in the early 1980s and before, it has become unconventional and even oddball.

I was asked in 2006 by one consultant to speak about LTLO to a group of pension fund trustees and to explain why what we did differed from what 'normal' equity managers did. Consultants still regard this type of activity, as opposed to index-centric and potentially index-clinging management, as that of some sort of monkey, but they are now prepared to visit the zoo.

In their asset allocation advice, consultants do not include LTLO among normal equity managers. It forms part of the alternative space, in a sub-set labelled equity risk premium, where it sits alongside long-short equity hedge funds.

Managing portfolios in this way, rather than index-clinging, naturally gives no assurance of good performance. To abandon index-clinging ensures performance which is different from that of the index but not necessarily better. Index-clinging afficianados may doubt that the different approach does anything to improve the likelihood of good performance.

This understates the drawbacks of index-clinging, in particular, the tendency to be reactive: to reduce an overweight position in a share whose price has just fallen, and to increase an underweight position in a share whose price has just risen. That tendency seems likely to guarantee a performance which, over the long term, is worse than the index by the extent of fees, plus costs of transactions, plus a little bit more. It is also an approach not calculated to maintain the enthusiasm of the most interested and able investment managers.

Studies, by Hewitt Associates and others, do show a tendency to outperformance on average by those who have concentrated portfolios consisting of their best bets, rather than portfolios with 50 or 60, or more, holdings.

Most of the investment management industry remains index-clinging and short-termist. From the point of view of those who are not, this is excellent. It is the existence of short-termism and index-clinging which creates the major opportunities in markets from which others can benefit. Long live short-termism.

SIX

Benchmarks

BENCHMARKS, like fees, are boring. Benchmarks are likewise
important. They have attracted a bad name in the last ten years or
so because they are seen, quite correctly, to have led managers to index-
cling in the way described in the last chapter. They have been used as
the drunk uses a lamppost, for support rather than illumination, and
during a period in which markets went down provided little of either.

This index-clinging is voluntary. The index does not have to
be slavishly imitated. There is, anyway, an important distinction
between a benchmark which is a composite of various indices, and
a benchmark which is just one index on its own. As discussed, most
stock market indices (though now not all) are composed of shares
which earn their place in the index, and their weightings, by market
capitalisation. If two shares start with the same weighting, and one
does much better than the other, the index-clinger ends up with a
higher percentage in the share which has done best, which may not
be the best recipe for future performance.

Benchmarks composed of a combination of various indices are
different, because the weightings of these indices in the benchmark
can be decided deliberately, and do not automatically change if one
index happens to do better than another.

In any event, index-clinging behaviour is an abuse of the point of a benchmark. The purpose of a single benchmark, composed of a number of indices, is twofold: first, it represents, with its different weightings, the mixture of asset classes which, in the extremely long term, the investor would be happy with; second, it provides a single measure of performance so that the investor can see whether the overall portfolio of investments is producing the goods or not.

If the investor is investing in a fund, the fund should have a benchmark set by the manager so that the manager is held to account, and it is clear what the manager is trying to do.

If investors are investing in a number of funds, or appointing a number of managers, they should construct their own benchmark which reflects their objectives and against which they can measure the performance of the combined portfolio. Such a benchmark brings everything together.

Jan Leschly, former head of SmithKline Beecham, in an earlier incarnation was a world-class tennis player, ranked 16th in the world. He has said that "if you don't keep the score, you are just practising." Without a benchmark, it is impossible for investors to tell whether they are doing well or badly. They are just practising.

Objectives

A benchmark is not quite the same thing, necessarily, as an objective, though it can be.

Investors who want to be sure that they never get a return less than the return on cash deposits have that as their objective. It makes sense for their benchmark too to be the cash deposit rate of interest.

Investors whose objective is to maximise the rate of return over the long term need a more specifically defined benchmark to get them to that destination. If the index is down 5% a year for three years it makes no sense to say that the investors' objective is fulfilled by beating the MSCI World Index for equities by a couple of per cent. No one in their right mind has the ambition of achieving a rate of return of −3% per annum. Nonetheless the MSCI World Index may still be the appropriate benchmark to provide the investor with the best chance of maximising the rate of return over the long term. Managing against that benchmark may achieve the right long-term result even if it means that the odd period of minus returns has to be tolerated because the alternative, to switch into and out of equities and other asset classes at the right time, is improbably Utopian.

Types of benchmarks

There are different kinds of benchmark, and they all have pros and cons.

1. Precise but unenlightening

A benchmark can be a particular target return. Many hedge funds and some other managers state their objective as an absolute return, for instance 10%, or as a return over the rate of inflation, say 5%, without any distinction between objective and benchmark.

The trouble with this is that the benchmark does not really allow the investor to judge whether the manager is doing a good job. If equity markets are exceptionally strong, say up 25%, bond markets also strong, say up 15%, and cash gives a return of 4%, should the investor be pleased if the manager produces a return of 15% compared with an absolute return benchmark of 10%?

That depends partly on how managers go about achieving the performance. Invested mainly in equities, a portfolio giving 15% compared with an equity index giving 25% is not very satisfactory. The managers may be doing something more subtle to try to do better than 10% consistently. If they truly are, and if that is what the investor wants them to do, fine. But the mere setting of an absolute return benchmark can give an illusory comfort. In fact, to achieve this level of return, the manager may have to take on the normal volatility of equity investment – in which case an equity index is a more appropriate benchmark.

2. Well-meaning but vague

One chief investment officer of a family office told a conference that his objective was "long-term growth with minor losses in declining markets". This sounds like a good idea but is vague.

3. Bold but unrealistic

The growth target for this same family office was then more precisely defined as 8% real return after taxes. This makes no sense at all as a target or as a benchmark. An 8% after-inflation return is very demanding – it is more than equities or any other class of assets have achieved except over short periods. To combine this with the expectation of minimal losses in declining markets makes it unrealistic. The only way to aim plausibly at an 8% real return would be by taking a lot of risk, with the likelihood that from year to year returns would be highly volatile, and sometimes negative.

4. Interesting but odd

Other professional investors, such as family offices, say that their benchmark is their peer group. That is fine if their peer group's performance is measured, and if it really is a peer group. But nobody puts together performance figures which represent the average achieved by all European family offices, and even if they did, it would be a rather dubious set of figures, because such family offices are utterly different, one from another, in their objectives and hence investment strategy.

One family may be keen on no account to lose money. Another may be prepared to take a great deal of risk.

One family may have a great chunk of its assets in a single quoted company of which it is the major shareholder. Another may be highly diversified.

One family may have a handful of unquoted investments, difficult to value, and perhaps generally kept in the books at the cost of investment until sold. Another may have no unquoted investments.

So any attempt to put together a peer group of like-minded families with large fortunes to be managed and measured could result in an odd assortment, whose average performance would not be much good for the purposes of comparison.

US college endowment funds are probably the most highly regarded group of investors, with excellent results often from unconventional asset allocation as well as good manager selection. In that world, and in the world of pension funds, the standard benchmark for performance is a peer group. This makes more sense because, although college endowment funds may have different pressures and objectives, they are a more homogeneous group than rich families. Moreover, with a culture of openness US investors are quite ready to provide independent performance-measuring firms with the figures which allow averages to be calculated.

Institutional investors are usually happy also to allow their own asset allocation to be fed into surveys so that they and their peers can see how the average such fund is invested in different assets. The figures are even broken down to deeper levels of distinctiveness, so that, for example, there is a peer group not only for US college endowment funds, but also for college endowment funds with more than $1bn each in assets.

But for the ordinary private investor none of these alternatives quite does the trick. Despite the problems in deciding on an appropriate benchmark, it is worth persevering because without a benchmark managers are all at sea. They must just try to do their best. Investors are all at sea too. All they can have is an impressionistic and unsatisfactory opinion, influenced more by the confidence with which managers express what they are doing than by the results.

One of my colleagues used to have a sign on his desk saying "don't confuse brains with a bull market." Not to have benchmarks is to take the road to this sort of confusion.

Constructing a composite benchmark
– clear and simple

Some investors may feel that, with the chunk of capital at issue, they have no immediate requirement for the money, and a limited need for income. There may be sources of income elsewhere, but with this particular chunk – which might be a large proportion of total assets or not so large – they can put up with a good deal of volatility in the value from year to year in order to accumulate a lot in the long-term. In that case they may decide that their objective with this capital is to maximise the rate of return over the long term.

It is to this type of investor that this book is biased. As Sir John Templeton said, "for all investors, there is only one objective: maximum total real returns after taxes."

A suitable benchmark for a Templeton investor could be a mixture of indices, the overwhelming majority of them equity indices but with something to cater for catastrophe. For example:

50% of the total return of the Morgan Stanley Capital International World Index (for developed markets)

+15% of the total return of the Morgan Stanley Capital International Emerging Markets Index

+10% of the total return of the Datastream World Property Index

+15% of the total return of the JP Morgan Global Government Bond Index

+ 5% Gold bullion

+ 5% of the 3 month US dollar deposit rate (3 month LIBID)

There are all sorts of difficulty in putting together benchmarks to represent the mixture of asset classes in which the investor might be interested, with appropriate weightings for each.

Private equity is particularly difficult. The nature of unquoted investments is that it takes years to get a result. Only when the investment is listed on a stock exchange, or sold, is it clear what it has been worth. Funds which invest in unquoted investments, private equity funds, are therefore hard to value, and it is even harder to get reliable figures on what the average such fund is achieving.

An investor may want private equity included in the portfolio. Rather than over-complicating the benchmark problem by trying to devise some kind of index for the performance of the private equity component of the overall benchmark, it may be better to keep it simple. Using an ordinary quoted equity index as a proxy for private equity is a short cut to avoid the delays, the ambiguities and the inadequacies of special private equity indices.

The same goes, to a slightly lesser extent, for hedge funds. There are many peer group indices for the different types of hedge funds, and they are increasingly reliable. Investors ought to decide exactly what they are looking for in any hedge fund component of their strategy, and choose the right hedge fund index accordingly.

Benchmarks in asset allocation

Apart from comparing themselves with peer groups, US college endowment funds think carefully about what they call their long-term policy portfolio. This represents the mix of assets which they believe would achieve the best results (in risk-adjusted returns: the most return for a given degree of volatility). This is therefore a more immediate benchmark than the peer group.

The long-term policy portfolio is what it says: long-term in intention, it is typically reviewed every year and sometimes tinkered with, sometimes not. At Yale University an investment committee, mainly non-executive, decides on the long-term policy portfolio, with recommendations (pretty influential) from the investment office, the executive team. The investment office then implements. In 13 of the last 20 years (to 2005) the Yale investment committee has changed their long-term policy portfolio. The changes in each year are small but over several years the cumulative change has been significant. In the six years 2000–05 the total of the percentage changes out of some asset types and into other asset types varied between 9% in the most active year (2000) and 3% in the least active, 2004. The total of all the changes in these six years comes to 42%. The amount added to, for example, commodities in three years, 2000–02, was 7%.

The long-term policy portfolio of Yale in June 2005, compared with the average for similar educational institutions in the US, had weightings in the various asset classes as follows:

Asset class	Yale target	US Educ. Average
US equity	14%	32.0%
Non-US equity	14	17.4
Private equity	17	6.1
Fixed income	5	16.3
Absolute return	25	17.6
Real assets	25	7.5
Cash	0	3.2
Total	100	100

In their actual portfolio Yale sticks closely to the long-term policy weightings. They have a strict rebalancing rule. If one asset class has outperformed another, its weighting will automatically have risen in the real portfolio. The rebalancing rule is that Yale must reduce investment in the area that has done well and increase in the area that has done less well.

The magic of this rule is that it takes emotion out of the decision. The natural instinct is to become more enthusiastic about assets which have done well and discouraged by assets which have done badly. The rule makes sure that Yale buys low, sells high.

Benchmarks as road maps

A slight variation on this use of the benchmark is that it serves as a sort of road map. The investor does not expect managers to stick to the route marked on the map at all times, but they should always know what it is.

People driving to Scotland do not always go straight up the M1 and M6 without stopping or deviating. They may decide to stay the night somewhere on the way. They may hear that a stretch of the motorway is in a complete jam because of roadworks, and take a detour. With a cup of tea here, a nap there, a petrol fill-up and a detour later on, there are all sorts of little stratagems which will produce for the motorist the optimal journey. It is not necessarily the quickest. The quickest would bear the big risk that they fall asleep at the wheel, a risk better avoided. But if they chuck away the road map altogether, and head in whatever direction the mood takes them, they are unlikely to get to Scotland at all.

A benchmark, and its composition, can serve a similar purpose for an investor. A benchmark need not be an inflexible recipe for a portfolio concoction which must always have exactly the prescribed proportions. This is benchmark-hugging.

The growth of benchmark-hugging is why there are so many enemies of benchmarks. The existence of a benchmark does not mean that it has to dictate portfolio activity precisely.

At the asset allocation level it may be a guide to the Rip van Winkle investor. It should represent, in its mix of assets, the assortment of investments with which an investor would be happy if he or she were to decide, once and for all, on an investment strategy, and then depart to the moon for the next 50 years, heedless of short-term hiccups, however severe.

The argument for tactical tweaking

If investors do not want to play Rip van Winkle, they can tweak – or tell their managers to tweak – this mix of assets to try to improve on the result which the unaltered mix would give.

Investors should not try to move wholly from one asset type to another in the hope of always being in the right one at the right time. To do this successfully is exceedingly difficult – and to do it successfully consistently is impossible.

Some people get lucky. In 1929 Carl Loeb, having made a fortune in his family's commodities business, had a row with his partners and sold out for $8m. For the next two years he went on a world cruise while his money was in US Treasury bills, the equivalent of cash. So the row and the cruise kept him out of the market fortuitously. This was the foundation of the Loeb fortune, Loeb remaining a name to conjure with on Wall Street for the rest of the century. Carl Loeb's son was, incidentally, a legendary investor who had a number of aphorisms:

When in doubt sell half.

Extreme situations do not last forever, no matter what the apparent justification.

Borrow in bad times; pay back in good times.

Never chase a money manager – there's always another one coming round the corner.

Carl Loeb was the sort of general Napoleon liked to have around, a lucky one. Sir James Goldsmith was another lucky general. At the age of 16 he won several thousand pounds on a three-horse accumulator at Lewes races. In his twenties, jointly with his brother in charge of a heavily indebted French pharmaceutical company, he stayed in bed one Monday when the banks were due to foreclose, getting up and shambling along in mid-morning to buy a paper in which he found that the banks were on strike. They stayed on strike for a few weeks, long enough for the company to sort out its cash flow and survive. Before the crash in 1987 Goldsmith famously sold all his equities.

Normally a policy involving large scale movements between different asset classes does not work out well. Wholesale abandonment of an asset class is unlikely to work repeatedly. The chances of getting out and getting back in again at the right time are only one in four. When the mood is sufficiently strong for this kind of wholesale move it is all too likely that the market has been overwhelmed by exaggerated gloom or exaggerated enthusiasm, and that it is too late.

Sir Isaac Newton was canny enough to sell all his shares at a late stage in the South Sea Bubble, but as the bubble went on getting bigger he could not resist the temptation to hurry back in. When the bubble burst he lost £20,000 and bitterly concluded (more critical of the actions of his fellow-men than of his own), "I can calculate the movement of the stars, but not the madness of men."

Investors need to decide what sorts of assets they are happy to invest in, and what sort of mixture of these assets they would be happy with for the very long term, given the impossibility of jumping wholesale from one to another – market timing.

Then smallish deviations from time to time, which could cumulatively add up to something significant, are likely to make for a better journey than large ones. Gradual moves in one direction or another objectively stand the same chance of success as a wholesale move, but in practice those with any skill in the area of asset allocation may be able to add something worthwhile to performance by being bold rather than as heroic as Goldsmith, Loeb, or Newton.

Why tweak at all? If the benchmark represents the mix of assets with which the investor should be happy in the very long term, the critic might ask why the investor should allow the manager to engage in deviations from this strategy – sometimes known as tactical asset allocation. After all, tweaking risks subverting the long-term policy.

A long-term policy is based on certain assumptions about future likely returns and risks. The assumptions are themselves forecasts by another more palatable name. The forecasts are either that the future will be roughly the same as the past or in specific ways different. The most unreliable type of forecast is that an exceptional trend is likely to continue. The reason that it is unreliable is that returns tend to revert to the mean.

In real life, investors have to steer between the Scylla of assuming no change and the Charybdis of expecting change. A sensible compromise position is to assume that the future will be something like the long-term past, but not so good when it has just been very good in the short term, and not so bad when it has just been very bad. Basing actual allocation on the long-term weightings, but aiming off, in particular by adding an assumption that returns revert to the mean and searching for value, is less dangerous than sticking inflexibly, instead, to long-term policy weightings derived from extrapolation of sometimes abnormal movements.

Such tactical asset allocation around a central long-term policy does involve the risk that the tactical allocation will do worse than the unmodified long-term policy. But a long-term policy, reflected in the benchmark weightings in different asset classes, should not be regarded as some scientifically produced piece of perfection, and anything different as subversive. Both the long-term policy and any tactical asset allocation are imperfect in different ways. While it is not necessarily right to do two imperfect things rather than one, nor is it right to put all eggs in one imperfect basket.

Allowing tactical asset allocation leaves room for opportunism. Many of the best investment decisions are not based on a pre-existing strategy but are thoroughly opportunistic. Markets move quickly and create windows of opportunity which do not stay open for long. Whole asset classes may suddenly have attractions which a year earlier they did not seem to have – securities in 'distressed' companies after the 2002–3 Enron debacle, for example. Investors who feel they have to turn away opportunities because they do not fit may be allowing themselves to be tied up in the red tape of their own strategic framework, to the detriment of performance.

A benchmark reflecting assumptions, with deviation from that policy to take account of excesses, may be the least bad approach just as democracy is the least bad form of government.

The asset allocation framework

With a benchmark and its weightings in different asset classes, the investor has a framework for making decisions, managing expectations, and monitoring performance. The tables below are an example of this sort of framework.

Table 1: Background – historic and expected returns per annum

Asset class	Historic return %	Long-term asset class expected return %	Current asset class expected return %	Current manager expected return %
MSCI World	10%	8%	7%	9%
MSCI EM	12%	10%	9%	11%
JP Morgan GGB	5%	5%	5%	5%
Cash	4%	5%	5%	5%

All the figures in these examples are in US dollars.

The developed and emerging markets are represented by the Morgan Stanley Capital International World and Emerging Markets indices respectively, bonds by the JP Morgan Global Government Bond index, and cash by the present rate of interest on three-month US dollar deposits.

The historic returns are the approximate figures for each of these asset classes over the long-term past. The long-term expected returns are not the same, because it seems reasonable to expect for equities a slightly lower result than in the past since the starting point today is a higher valuation than at most previous starting points; and for bonds and cash the actual present interest rates.

The current asset class expected return is for a shorter period: it shows what the manager, or investor, thinks reasonable, subjectively, over the next two to three years.

The final column reflects another piece of hopeful supposition, or enlightened aspiration: investors will be hoping to appoint managers who outperform in at least some of the asset classes. In the cash category they will probably not do any better than the ordinary large depositor; and in the bond category they will be lucky to outperform the average by more than a smidgen. But in equities they may think, rightly or wrongly, that they can choose managers who will do better than the index. The manager expected return reflects some outperformance, compared with the asset class expected return. The latter is what the asset class in general is assumed to do. The former is what the particular managers chosen are assumed to do.

The table below then applies the weightings, first of the benchmark and then of the actual portfolio, to the assumed returns shown in Table 1.

Table 2: Portfolio expected returns

Asset class	Benchmark weighting %	Contribution to overall long-term benchmark return %	Contribution to overall current benchmark return %	Portfolio weighting %	Contribution to portfolio %	Allowed weighting range %
MSCI World	60%	4.8%	4.2%	66%	5.9%	40–75%
MSCI EM	15%	1.5%	1.35%	20%	2.2%	5–25%
JPM GGB	20%	1.0%	1.0%	6%	0.3%	0–20%
Cash	5%	0.25%	0.25%	10%	0.5%	0–20%
Total	100%	7.55%	6.8%	100%	8.9%	100%

The outcome is that, in this example, the benchmark is assumed to give a long-term return of 7.5% and a return over the next two to three years of 6.8%, while with actual portfolio weightings and assumptions about outperformance by the chosen managers the overall portfolio is assumed to give a return of 8.9%.

Needless to say, the usefulness of this model rests on the assumptions. Garbage in, garbage out. One of my first bosses, an American, used to write out the word ASSUME in capital letters, draw a line between the second S and the U and between the U and the M, and declaim: "the word ASSUME makes an ASS out of U and an ASS out of ME." Disasters in every field are usually because people have assumed something that they should not have assumed. Investment is no exception in this.

It helps if the assumptions are vaguely realistic. A recent advertisement in *Investors Chronicle* has a fine example of ambitious assumption.

38% return p.a.
I have been using this unique investment system for 22 years. My average return is 38% a year. Any investor could employ the system for himself and get the same results as I do. Send for the Users Manual.

Thirty-eight percent a year for 22 years means that the lucky advertiser would have managed, starting with £10,000, to accumulate £11,949,230. If the advertiser kept at this for another 22 years, the portfolio would turn into £14,278,409,000. The Users Manual was very reasonably priced, at $10.

The Nobel prize winner Kenneth Arrow had to make predictions when he was employed by the meteorological department of the US Air Force during the Second World War. He was asked to make medium- and long-term weather forecasts. He quickly concluded that his results were no better than randomly right and asked to be relieved of this responsibility. The reply came back: "The Commanding General is well aware that the forecasts are no good. However, he needs them for planning purposes."

This sums up pretty well the status of assumptions, a vague enough word, or expectations, a bolder one, about future returns: unlikely to be right but essential for planning – like the Cavaliers in *1066 and All That*, "wrong but wromantic."

Summary

'Benchmark' should be regarded as shorthand for 'long-term policy portfolio'. In this sense, long term means at least 25 years.

A benchmark also helps the investor judge the success or failure of the chosen investment strategy.

A composite of various market indices is the clearest and simplest benchmark.

Benchmarks should be reviewed at intervals, but with a long-term perspective and not too often.

Asset allocation in practice may differ from the benchmark weightings in asset classes. Asset allocation should be carried out with a medium-term view of say two to three years, and not based solely on the extremely long-term assumptions which lie behind the benchmark.

For the investor who, with a particular parcel of assets, has no need for income, is not concerned about liquidity of investments, and has temperamentally, a truly long-term view and a high tolerance for volatility, it makes sense for the long-term policy (the benchmark) to be overwhelmingly equity.

The long-term policy should take account of possible catastrophes, deflation or hyper-inflation. This could argue for a fixed income component or a hard asset component – gold or real estate, for instance.

Once a benchmark is established, it is not only a yardstick for performance measurement but a neutral position for the investor. Investors may want to limit the extent to which they can succumb to over-enthusiasm or over-gloom by having some ranges, with a minimum and maximum for each type of asset around the neutral weightings.

SEVEN

What to Look for in a Manager

HAVING sorted out objectives and a benchmark, investors will normally want someone to manage their money. If they have enough money to justify meeting managers they are thinking about appointing – more than a few hundred thousand pounds – they should make sure they do. The choice of the right manager can make, over the long term, an enormous difference to returns. Investment management, being a highly individualistic business, requires knowledge of the individuals. Reading about them, or reading what they say, is second best, but better than nothing.

The Counter-Presentational Principle

The good managers are not necessarily the ones who make the best presentation. An erstwhile colleague, overweight and unkempt, used to appear for meetings with potential clients with traces of gravy on his tie and his tummy protruding where a shirt button or two was missing. He would drop all his papers on the floor, rummage around in them, and declare despairingly from time to time "I know it's in here somewhere." The prospective clients often saw that, since he was no good at presenting to prospective clients, he could not have been hired for his presentational skills and they suspected he must be a very good investment manager. He was.

The brilliant investor Leon Levy, partner of Oppenheimer and later of Odyssey Partners, was about as far from the stereotype of the smooth-talking and smart-dressing banker as one could imagine. When I first met him in 1982 he was trying to give up smoking and constantly fiddled with a realistic plastic cigarette. He caused consternation when he left it on the fine mahogany Warburgs meeting-room table.

Levy was wonderfully absent-minded. Once, allegedly, he and a lady colleague hailed a taxi in Manhattan. Faultlessly good-mannered, he opened the door for his colleague, closed the door behind her, walked round the back of the taxi and opened the opposite door, looked in, said "Oh, I'm so sorry, I didn't realise this taxi was occupied," and shut the door.

The Counter-Presentational Principle states that the ability of investment managers may be in inverse relationship to their ability to present well at meetings. Some of the best and most interesting managers are rotten presenters.

One of the best managers I have come across was so unaccustomed to presenting (because for years he had not needed to present) that he opened with the words, "I'm going to make a terrible hash of this," and did. Another excellent manager was dragged in by a colleague to give a presentation to my firm. He arrived trailing unhappily some yards behind his enthusiastic colleague. Everyone sat down. We waited for him to produce some papers, 'presentation material' as it is unattractively known in the trade. He produced nothing and looked uncomfortable. We asked him some questions. Haltingly he replied. Gradually he warmed to his theme, sufficiently in due course to exclaim, "I hate this. I find this very disagreeable. I never do it. I never make presentations. This is very unusual for me." It was this manager who described investment as something to do rather than to talk about.

On another occasion, I went to visit him in his office. His room contained his own chair, a desk with a computer monitor on it, lots of paper, and a large and immovably heavy armchair. I sat down in the armchair. This, the manager's chair, and the computer screen were positioned so that the computer screen produced a total eclipse of the manager. He was thus fully protected from any intrusive sightings by his interlocutor.

Such bashfulness is in refreshing contrast with the slick investment bankerese to which many big investors are accustomed. Beautifully dressed and beautifully mannered bankers arrive with well-honed pitches and well-laminated presentation documents. They express astonishment at the excellence of their hosts' offices. They laugh gratifyingly at their hosts' jokes. They marvel at the acuity of their hosts' investment strategy. They brush invisible specks of dust from their immaculate trousers. They have the manner of Lord Curzon.

"My name is George Nathaniel Curzon.
I am a most superior person.
My cheek is pink, my hair is sleek,
I dine at Blenheim once a week."

For Blenheim one might substitute Davos, and add a verse:

The job is first to find the loot.
My presentation style is cute.
I tell them they have nought to fear
And when they've signed just disappear.

Many of those presenting about investment management are not investment managers themselves but are minders, gatekeepers, or client relationship people whose forte, not surprisingly, is client relationships. Their main job is to get the money in for others to manage.

A good friend, Mr X, was one of my colleagues on this side of things. He was famous for his cheerfulness. One German client said of him: "Ah yes, Mr X. He comes, he smiles, he takes the money," a contemporary veni, vidi, vici. The smile got him into trouble when he and I met the right-hand man of a noted Australian corporate thug. X smiled. "What are you laughing at," the henchman snarled, and X stopped smiling.

Many presentations have elaborate organograms showing the different companies in the fund management group. I only realised how appallingly tedious this is when on the other side of the table as a prospective client. For years I had been explaining what proportion the parent company owned of its subsidiaries, how Warburg Asset Management related to Warburg Investment Management International, and in what year the latter was first registered with the Securities and Exchange Commission in the US. Nobody wants to know this kind of thing except as a late step in what is called the due diligence process. Due diligence is what you have to do to show you have been diligent. Not all of it is useful, or ever referred to.

The first rule of choosing a manager is to look beyond the presentation.

Venables ratings

The investor learns something about an investment management firm by meeting client relationship people, but it is hard to make a proper judgement without meeting the investment managers themselves.

For the last ten years, with colleagues, I have applied to managers the Venables ratings, named after the England football team manager who had his own ratings system. He marked each player out of ten on a number of different criteria: technical, tactical, personality, and pace. We adapted this, marking out of ten under four headings: people, approach, practice, and environment, summarised in the acronym PAPE and the mnemonic Polite Africans Protect Elephants. I would add, for smaller clients especially, another criterion: reporting.

A virtue of this rating system is that if two or more see a particular manager, they can have a sensible conversation afterwards. They do not come away in the taxi muttering simply, "Well, he was all right, wasn't he?" They can refer to these different headings.

It helps to have more than one person looking at a manager so that it is possible to debate the manager's pros and cons. While too much consensus in looking at investments is counter-productive, because of the peculiar nature of markets, a consensus about a manager is not a bad thing at all. Generally there is such a consensus. It is quite rare for one interviewer to think a manager is good and another interviewer to think the opposite, and if two interviewers think a manager is good there is a decent chance they are right.

1. People

Investors need to be looking for a number of qualities in the people to whom they entrust their money. Here is my check-list.

Convictions and the courage of convictions

The first quality is the ability to have convictions, of the non-criminal sort. Investment managers must be truly interested in what they are doing, in markets, in companies and businesses. If they are interested, they are bound to have convictions.

A manager ought not be expected to have convictions about everything. People often demand opinions of investment managers on all sorts of subjects – economic prospects, prospects for a company, bird flu, global warming. But it is as unrealistic to expect an investment manager to know about everything as it is to expect a politician to have an opinion on every issue. Investment managers who profess to know and to have a view about everything should be regarded with circumspection. For much of the time managers may have nothing to say about interest rates or economies or most companies. But they will tend to have strong convictions about a few things, including some companies.

Managers need also the courage of their convictions. The world is full of people whose judgements always seem to have been right, but the rightness is somehow not reflected in results. Managers must act on their convictions. Whether they do so will be evident in the composition of their portfolios and in the record of transactions.

Commonsense: diversification and concentration

Commonsense matters much more than brilliance. "Investing is not a game where the guy with the 160 IQ beats the guy with the 130 IQ. Once you have ordinary intelligence, what you need is the temperament to control the urges that get other people into trouble in investing," said Warren Buffett.

Commonsense is an ordinary enough virtue in the ordinary world, but in the investment world, it often flies out of the window, propelled by all the pressures of an over-crowded profession, with the concomitant cacophony, the short-termism, and the pressure to do things all the time.

Part of the commonsense is that managers, though having convictions, must not be too convinced that those convictions are right. They need to be conscious of probabilities. (A leading manager of managers always asks investment managers whether they play poker or bridge.)

If managers are right 55% or 60% of the time they are doing fine. They must therefore be prepared to act on the strength of their convictions but also not to back them to the limit. This means balance. In *The Merchant of* Venice, Antonio explains his shipping policy:

> "My ventures are not in one bottom trusted,
>   Nor to one place; nor is my whole estate
>   Upon the fortune of this present year;
>   Therefore, my merchandise makes me not sad."

Diversification of risk, within an equity portfolio as well as in asset allocation, helps to keep one not sad. People who have a hugely convinced, and convincing, view of the world, which they allow to penetrate to every nook and cranny of their portfolios, are betting the farm. A portfolio needs to be more than a one-stop-shop where only one idea is bought: a view, for example, that deflation is the main threat, or that Iran is about to develop a nuclear weapon. Even those who turn out to have been the cleverest and best will still have had a 40% chance of being wrong, and if wrong with such a world-view, reflected in every stock, they will be wrong in spades, and their performance awful.

Often those who propound such world-views most convincingly, and indeed are frequently right, are in practice unsuccessful investment managers. They are extremely useful people for an investment manager to listen to, because they are stimulating and interesting and they provoke ideas and debate; but they are not necessarily the people to run the money themselves.

Diversification is known sometimes as diworsification. This pejorative description applies to the continual reduction in exposure to any particular company or any particular risk so that in the end you have a portfolio which stands for nothing. This has been the pattern of index-clinging over the last two decades.

Not all diversification is diworsification. There may be little point in a portfolio of a hundred holdings in companies all of which are large and liquid. But it is possible to achieve plenty of diversification with a much more concentrated portfolio, in which the risk of any one wrong decision swamping everything else is low while the portfolio does still stand for something. The academics show that, if managers aim at diversification, they can get almost all the diversification there is to get with a portfolio of as few as 15 stocks. After that, every additional holding does very little in terms of risk reduction.

A portfolio with no more than, say, 25 stocks is generally regarded as pretty concentrated. The effort at concentration of the portfolio concentrates the mind. A portfolio with a hundred stocks tends to be the product of a manager with too few convictions; often the product of a management team whose members have been obliged to compromise with one another.

In practice, once the number of stocks has proliferated, it becomes all too easy to tolerate passengers who are not pulling their weight.

Typically, the manager starts to sell a position, finds the share price moving down, and then ceases to sell. There is then, lingering in the portfolio for possibly years, a small remnant position, uncherished and unloved. A concentrated portfolio does not allow for this kind of excessive tolerance.

But there are other views about this. There are many good managers who own many more than 20 or 30 stocks. Sir William Stuttaford was a legendary fund manager, specialising in smallish companies. He told me once that he thoroughly disliked selling even very small positions, because he never knew when one of them would begin to twitch into life. He therefore let the number of holdings increase.

Some wonderful managers profess not to believe in diversification. Warren Buffett, the greatest of them all, has said that he does not believe in the maxim 'don't put all your eggs in one basket'. Instead, he likes to put all his eggs in one basket and then to watch that basket extremely closely. Nonetheless, although there are fewer than 20 major companies within Berkshire Hathaway, Buffett's holding company, the portfolio is spread among quite a variety of companies, in different industries. They have some financial attributes in common – high free cash flow especially – but they are exposed to different economic trends, and thus give diversification.

Others are clearly less diversified. A manager regarded by one of my colleagues as the most brilliant stock picker he has ever come across is tremendously dogmatic about no more than two or three sectors at a time: coal miners and home-builders, for example, two narrow sectors, have been where he concentrated nearly all the assets at his command in recent years, with mainly fabulous though inevitably volatile results.

Investors may be happy with this extreme concentration, but they are relying on the manager being outstanding, and on their own tolerance, as investors, for some especially scary moments. The investor could well put a few but not all eggs in that particular manager's basket.

A concentrated portfolio is a plus. Every decision should have a significant impact. On the other hand, the exposure to any one country, sector, idea, or company, should not be so great that if the decision is wholly wrong its performance would dominate the performance of the rest of the portfolio – assuming the portfolio is the investor's only one.

Entrepreneurs may own a single company. Being a portfolio manager is different from being an entrepreneur. An owner can choose to stake everything on one activity. A portfolio should not, and investors should not expect it of their portfolio managers.

2. Approach

"I 'ad that Bertrand Russell in the back of the cab," recalled a London taxi driver, "so I said to 'im, 'what's it all about, then, Guv.' And do you know, 'e didn't 'ave the answer."

Investment managers ought to have the answer in the sense of having an investment approach, sometimes known rather fancily as a philosophy, which they can explain succinctly and convincingly. They should be able to express in a few sentences what their fundamental beliefs about investment are, and what they are looking for in making investment decisions.

Portfolios ought to stand for something. If they stand for nothing, nothing will come of nothing.

Managers should also have a clear idea of what they are good at. No one is good at everything. They need to stick within their circle of competence.

There are various things a manager might be good at.

(i) Some are good at activist investing – getting involved closely in trying to redirect companies, by influencing the managements, and even by seeking to change managements.

This has become a faddish field, but it is not for all. One of the disadvantages of activist investment is that it is too easy for a manager to get embroiled in a particular situation which needs a lot of attention, and to be distracted from all other investments. More fundamentally, management of a portfolio of shares and company management are quite different things, and there are few people who can carry off successfully a parcelling together of the two functions. A lot of activist investors should not be activist.

(ii) Some are good buyers and less good sellers. This is often the case with value managers. Managers buy full of conviction because the shares look outstandingly cheap. They may be right or wrong, but they are confident. Selling is much more difficult. The shares might by then look fully valued, but could become much more so. Often the manager will feel forced to find something, rather regretfully, to sell, because of better opportunities to buy.

(iii) Some are good at spotting good value in the long term, rather than a quick turn. Some excel in spotting major changes in an industry, or the potential of a new product to produce strong earnings growth. Managers may, in other words, put more or less emphasis on value, and more or less emphasis on growth. They may put more or less emphasis on the cash which a business generates, rather than the potential for growth long into the future which justifies, for some years to come, reinvestment by the company of all its earnings to maximise that future growth.

The strengths and weaknesses need to be evident from managers' own accounts of what they do. Managers have to believe in themselves. They may be shy with people and dislike presenting, but they must give an impression of knowing and liking what they are doing.

Of course, some are good bluffers, and it may be hard to tell. One successful manager of managers employs a psychologist who sits in all meetings, silent but constantly scribbling notes. Glass tables are revealing in meetings: as with a duck paddling, people often give away their uncertainties with their restless twitching of legs and wringing of hands below table. People are used to making sure that above the surface of the table all is serene.

3. Practice

"Fine words butter no parsnips."

Making a judgement about people, and about their approach, from one or two meetings is tough. A client ought to try to get a grip on what a manager actually does.

The eloquence of transaction records

Transaction records provide the most eloquent evidence as to what sort of manager someone is, and yet they are not much looked at. The staple package presented by managers to prospective clients consists of lots of charts about their firms, some statements about philosophy and approach, details of the current portfolio, some statistical characteristics, maybe a few well-chosen and usually flattering examples of decisions made; but almost nothing otherwise in the way of a transaction record. The latter answers several questions:

Does the manager...

- do a lot of buying and selling?
- trade in and out of stocks, and, if so, does the trading in and out generally, more often than not, seem worthwhile?
- move in decisive chunks and occasionally, or dabble in the market nearly every day, adding a little to this position, taking a little away from that position?
- arbitrage between different companies in the same industrial sector, moving, say, from one pharmaceutical to another, or is the style more eclectic?

There is no right or wrong answer to any of these questions, but clients ought to know what they are getting and to be sure that they want it. When performance turns sour, which at some stage it is bound to, clients could be self-damagingly impatient unless they have found out at the outset what kind of investment style they are settling for. When performance is good nothing else seems to matter very much.

Turnover

High turnover in a portfolio is not invariably a bad thing but it needs to be looked at sceptically. It costs more than low turnover.

As a result, on average, the busiest managers perform less well than the least busy. Turnover has escalated in recent decades. Much more information and better trading systems have made it easier to trade. That does not mean that it has got easier to make a success of it.

In the first investment offices I worked in, there might be one or two share price screens shared between five or six people. There was no question of there being a monitor or computer on every desk. There was of course no email. The fax was a new-fangled invention. The main source of information about share prices was the *Financial Times*. To get early information on the level of the main stock market indices for international markets, the Capital International indices, it was necessary to telephone the office that calculated them. One of my early tasks was to ring up the lady in Geneva in charge of these indices and ask her, a few days after the end of the month, at what levels they stood. This lady is now one of the leading investment managers at the Capital Group.

The pervasiveness of Reuters and Bloomberg share price screens covering every market and every type of security, and later of hand-held devices so that the obsessive can look at share prices when they are halfway up a mountain on a ski-lift, has allowed managers to be much more short-term.

They have taken full advantage of the technology. In recent years, there has even been an acceleration in trading activity. In 1995, the value of shares traded, divided by total market capitalisation, in the New York, Tokyo and London markets combined was 35% – so the average share was held by the same investor for roughly three years. In 2005, the comparable figure was 109%. The average share now stayed in the same hands for 11 months. For NASDAQ, the US exchange on which are listed a disproportionate number of technology companies, the figure in 2005 was five months.

Those figures cover all investors, of every shape and size – from the most placid individual to the most hyperactive proprietary desk of an investment bank. Professional investment managers have always tended to trade more than the average private investor. When I started managing portfolios in the early 1980s, the average turnover rate (the lower of total purchases or total sales during a year, divided by the average portfolio value) in professional investment managers' portfolios managed for institutions was around 30%. It is now said to be around 120% – and these are supposedly long-term investment institutions such as pension funds and insurance companies; hedge funds, usually though not always much more active, and the proprietary desks of the investment banks, more active still, are not included. This means that in the early 1980s a fund manager for one of these institutions held shares in a particular company for more than three years on average. By 2005, such a fund manager held shares on average for less than ten months.

In his book, *More than you know: finding financial wisdom in unconventional places*, Michael Mauboussin, of the eminent fund management firm Legg Mason, says that the rate of turnover of US mutual funds has increased from 20% per annum in the 1950s to more than 100% today. He also finds that over the one-, three-, and five-year periods to the end of 2004, the best performances were achieved by funds with turnover in the 20–50% range. The same was true of earlier periods which he examined.

The generally damaging effect of short-termism on performance was demonstrated in a study by Messrs Odean and Barber, quoted in *The Motley Fool*. This study was based on the returns of 78,000 individual investors' accounts at a large discount brokerage firm in the US from 1991 to 1996. The average annual turnover was 80% – slightly lower than the average annual turnover of equity mutual funds during this period of 84%. The least active 15,000 accounts had average annual turnover of only 1% and an average annual return of 17.5%, higher than the Standard & Poor's Index (16.9%). The most active 15,000 accounts had average annual turnover of more than 100% and returns of 10%. The authors of the study concluded that "trading is hazardous to your wealth…Trigger-happy investors are prone to shooting themselves in the foot."

Not every busy manager will underperform, but the odds are against energetic activity because of the extra costs. Investment managers are tempted to react to information. Every trade has a cost, in terms not only of commission to the broker, but the market impact of selling a chunk of shares.

In aggregate the extra transaction costs are money down the drain. Constructive indolence is an underrated virtue. Doing nothing is often a much wiser policy than doing something. One of my former bosses used frequently to advise, "Do nothing." It was good advice. At moments of emergency especially, but also more generally, the best sell discipline is often a walk round the block until the feeling subsides. Think busy, act idle.

Investment management in a bear market

In the great bear market of 1973–4, two excellent investment managers at what later became Mercury Asset Management used to pass the time by adopting a raindrop each and betting on which raindrop would reach the bottom of the window first. This was a more sensible way to spend their working hours than gratuitous buying and selling. They also played a great deal of ping-pong during working hours.

These days, in a bear market, the eyes of investment managers are fixed upon the share price monitors rather than on rain-swept windows.

Chasing the crowd

There is a school of investment, momentum investing, which recommends buying stocks which have been going up and selling those which have been going down.

The momentum approach has its moments, and the moments can be long ones. But what it comes down to is chasing the crowd. Those who try to keep up with the Jones's rarely overtake them. If it were always, or even generally, right to buy shares because their prices have risen (or 'are rising', as the defenders of this approach would put it), then there would be a virtuous circle as a result of which trees grew to the sky, and trees do not grow to the sky. This is the stuff of which bubbles are made.

Momentum eventually comes to an end. The bigger the momentum on the upside, the bigger it is on the downside. A momentum investor relies on being clever enough to get out immediately the momentum turns and back in again if momentum turns positive again, and few are clever enough to do this successfully.

The brilliant investor Sir John Templeton, founder of a highly successful eponymous firm, said once that the most dangerous four words in investment were "this time it's different" (five, actually). Perhaps as dangerous are the four words 'go with the flow'.

Another contender is the wounding phrase, 'you just don't get it' – the sentiment of those who are participating in a bubble about those who are not. The wounded manager has already to cope with the pressure of underperforming. There is the awful possibility that the wounder might well be right, which is what the market is screaming.

A senior investment manager did say "you just don't get it" to a colleague just before the apogee of the technology boom in 2000. Within months, the wounded had retired prematurely – his retirement coinciding with the turn in the market, so that his style of investing, focussing on valuations, did superbly over the next several years. Two years after his retirement, when the bubble had burst, the wounder also retired prematurely and with a damaged reputation.

Buffetings

The transaction record may betray a fundamental weakness. Some managers may be buffeted around by markets, scared into selling shares when their prices go down, lured back into buying them later just because their prices have gone up.

Transaction records reveal these buffetings. One management firm I have monitored sold lots of shares (at losses) in blue chip companies, such as Nestlé, on 14 September 2001, three days after 9/11. Two weeks later, they bought back many of the same shares at much higher prices. Their nerve had failed after 9/11, not surprisingly. As confidence returned to markets, so they recovered their poise, thus moving harmoniously with the herd at each stage. They had locked in losses, missed out on 15% or so of gains, and handed two sets of commissions to the brokers.

In a way, this particular firm at least implicitly acknowledged its error, by buying back exactly the same shares earlier sold. Often managers try to draw a veil over their foolishness – perhaps even denying it to themselves – by buying back shares in companies similar to but not quite the same as those they have sold at lower prices.

This kind of failure of nerve can be forgiven once, maybe twice, but if the transaction record reveals many such instances in which managers are motivated by short-term momentum and the mood of the moment, then their services should be avoided.

The Bernstein paradox

This pattern of transactions – in, out, and back in again – reflects a lack of conviction.

Buying more of a stock whose price has gone down, on the other hand, reflects plenty of conviction – which is not to say that it is necessarily the right thing to do, and frequently it is not. But generally, being prejudiced to regard as more attractive a share whose price has fallen, and conversely to regard as less attractive a share whose price has risen, is beneficial.

This principle is enshrined in more academic terms by Peter Bernstein in his book about risk, *Against the Gods*, in a formulation which has become known as the Bernstein paradox: when the price of an asset falls its expected return rises.

The objection to this principle is that shares do not fall without a reason. A share which is cheaper than it was yesterday is cheaper for cause. I will try to deal more with this in the chapter on investment styles.

The transaction record, in any event, is helpful in sorting out those who have convictions about the shares which they buy, which result in them buying more of the same if initially the price goes down.

Convictions are a prerequisite to long-term good results. There are plenty of managers with strong convictions and rotten results; but there are few managers with good results who do not have strong convictions.

Changes in habits

Transaction records also tell one something more general: if the level or pattern of turnover changes significantly, this too is something to watch out for.

If for years a manager has turned over the portfolio at a rate of around 30% (in other words, holding every share for an average of three years), and suddenly turnover increases to 100%, it needs investigating. Something has changed. Maybe there is actually a different manager running the portfolio, or new colleagues, and especially new bosses, have changed the manager's style; or maybe the manager is reacting in a different way to market circumstances in the belief that they have changed.

A move to untypical inertia deserves as much investigation as a move to untypical hyperactivity. I remember being told of some portfolios being managed by a firm in Hong Kong. For several months, there were, untypically, no transactions at all. It turned out that the individual manager had been suspended because the regulatory authorities were investigating alleged insider trading. The firm concerned had not thought it necessary to tell its clients.

4. Environment

The qualities discussed above under 'people' – convictions, courage of convictions, commonsense – are intrinsic to a manager. The manager is what matters. But the firm for which the individual works is not irrelevant. The firm needs to provide the right sort of background to the individual. The right background means the right ethos and environment.

Alignment of interests

It is a plus to see investment managers who invest a large proportion of their own assets in the funds which they manage. One manager explained to me that he did not invest in his own funds because he was already quite enough at risk through what he did professionally and wanted to spread his risk by investing personally elsewhere. This was not reassuring.

Another well-known hedge fund manager told me after a disastrous year that at least at the end of the previous year, in which he had earned a performance fee of more than £10m, he had not invested it in his own fund.

Investment managers should be prepared to take their own medicine. If the manager is investing in all sorts of things which are not in the clients' portfolios, it is disquieting.

The right place

The cultures of investment management firms vary enormously. Some put a strong emphasis on asset-gathering, marketing what they do intensely; others eschew marketing on the view that if performance is good assets will follow. Some are quiet places; others are noisy. In some, investment managers and researchers each sit in their own little room; in others, they sit in an open plan office and there is more cross-desk chat.

A good manager can be ruined by being in the wrong place. To generalise about culture and environment, the atmosphere most conducive to good decisions in investment is a relatively tranquil one, with as little external disturbance as possible to what the investment management team do. A rush of adrenalin from time to time in investment is inevitable but it is not altogether a good thing because the chances of moving with the crowd, emotionally rather than dispassionately, are greater once the adrenalin is whirring round. A frenetic atmosphere, with much noise and activity, is potentially harmful.

The lonelier the investment manager, the more likely to be able to resist the siren song of the consensus. The larger the team and the company, the less likely to resist. Every day thousands of people converge, in the big firms, on their desks in the City of London, Canary Wharf, and Wall Street and mid-town Manhattan. They are surrounded by cacophony, and subjected to enormous pressures, mostly self-generated, to do things. With an intense focus on what happened yesterday to share prices, the overwhelming pressure is to do something in the direction in which the market was moving yesterday, to go with the flow, to move with the consensus.

The investment business does not need to have a schoolish atmosphere. It can be a relatively easy-going place. Of course I am talking my own book. My firm's offices have a garden at the back, and in the summer we have investment meetings on benches in the sun. Our decisions in summer are naturally much better than our decisions in winter.

Investment strategist at work in Australia

When I was a non-executive director of an Australian subsidiary, the energetic chief executive worried that the head of strategy used to wander in at about a quarter to ten. I thought this did not matter at all. If he did his best thinking in a rather leisurely bath, that was fine. A respected Japanese fund manager does almost all her research at home.

One of the oddities of the investment world is that it is, along with politics, perhaps the only profession where at most times of the waking day those engaged in it are thinking about some aspect of their professional life. When investment managers go to Sainsbury's they look around to see how busy it is. When they fly they note how many seats are occupied. Ringing Vodafone to cancel the monthly fee for a daughter's mobile which she has just announced she lost six months ago, the manager wonders about the fact that the call is immediately put through to a department called Customer Save, where the benefits of maintaining the subscription are extolled.

When calling their bank, managers count how many times a recorded message, including the phrase 'your call is important to us', is played and they are asked to choose from four numbers to press on their keyboard before they can speak to a real person.

Investment management is not a nine to five job. The business of investment goes on, in a manager's mind, most of the time, though often in the background rather than the foreground. It does not matter whether at a desk, in an aeroplane, or on a factory floor: whatever the manager finds most conducive to good decision-making is what is best.

Too much of a good thing

One further point about investment firms, rather than investment people, is that the firm must be structured and staffed in such a way that it can cope with the business it has. Since small is beautiful in decision-making, there may be limits to the amount of money and the number of portfolios which a firm can optimally manage.

Not surprisingly, studies show that small firms tend to do better than big firms. Rosemont Investment Partners looked at the top 10–40 managers in various categories between 1998 and 2002, and found that 19 out of the top 20 US large cap growth and value equity managers had assets under management of less than $2bn; and all of the top ten US small cap growth and value equity managers had assets under management of less than $10bn.

Similarly, a Northern Trust study found that 40% of firms with less than $2bn under management were in the top quartile of performance. Management firms of this size – less than $2bn – have less than 1% of all assets which are managed by investment management firms.

It is a great advantage to a firm, and to its clients, if it is able to run all portfolios of the same type identically. Many clients shy away from pooled funds. They do not like the idea that they will simply own units in a large fund with lots of other participants, and they feel that they will be losing the advantages of a personal service from their fund manager.

This is a mistaken view of what a personal service can achieve. A large pooled fund is a convenient way for an investment management firm to lump together what would otherwise be lots of portfolios of the same type, and clients can be sure that a large pooled fund, probably with a public performance record, gets the full attention of the firm and its particular manager.

Pension funds and charities are tax-exempt. Separate portfolios for these institutions can be run identically. There is some small incremental administrative burden in the acceptance of each new portfolio, and the client must therefore watch out that the administrative burden is not getting too great for the firm, or for the individual portfolio manager, to handle.

But the problem is greater with firms looking after a multitude of private client portfolios. Such firms may need particularly careful scrutiny. Each portfolio arrives with a different capital gains tax position, and the manager, or the client, may be reluctant to realise large capital gains and land up with a hefty tax bill. Every private client portfolio therefore tends to be a little different from every other.

This means that managing private client portfolios is fundamentally different from handling tax-exempt institutional funds, or pooled funds. Managers cannot make a decision and then apply it proportionately across all funds, because they have to check each portfolio to see what its peculiar tax position is.

Moreover, because private client portfolios are on average much smaller than institutional or pooled funds, each manager usually manages a large number of portfolios. Clients would be horrified if they knew quite how many portfolios some managers look after – and how many clients they have to report to, in person, each year. The number is sometimes well into three figures.

One private banking department of a major bank, a household name, has 38,000 clients with separate portfolios. When the bank wants to sell a stock, every portfolio has to be looked at one by one. The orders to deal are not all bundled together in a single package so that everyone gets the same price, at the same time. The sale is made for each portfolio, one after the other, through the bank's in-house broker. By the time the last few thousand clients are being looked after, it is more than likely that the selling will have moved the price. To prevent people whose names begin with a W or a Z suffering unduly, the order in which the clients are attended to is varied.

There are exceptional private client managers, who cope with the burden of these numbers and the differences between each portfolio, but the odds are against them. On the whole, it is better for clients with a portfolio of, say, up to $20m to make use of pooled funds rather than to hope that they will find an exceptional manager among the firms which specialise in private client portfolios.

5. Reporting

Finally, among the things to look for in a manager is good guff-free reporting. Large clients are able to dictate to managers what they want to see in reports. Even so, a lot of guff in the standard reporting package is a warning sign. Smaller clients are not able to decide the type of reporting they get, so it is especially important for them that they see upfront the standard reporting and are happy about it.

Sometimes there is a mass of largely irrelevant information, quantity substituting for quality. This is really disinformation. Managers often provide pages of economic commentary but do not explain what connection it has with what has been going on in the investment portfolio. They give no overall picture of the effect of what they have been doing. Most of these reports can be chucked in the dustbin. The useful part could generally be covered in a couple of pages rather than 12.

Many investment management firms managing money for private clients report to their clients in such a way that it is quite impossible to tell whether they are doing well or badly. Not only do they provide no benchmark with which to compare performance; they frequently provide no information at all on the movement of stock or bond market indices generally. The investor is given vague statements about the market background, and details of capital gains and losses, and income. But whether the capital gains and income, taken together, are more or less than should be expected, in the circumstances, is a mystery.

A typical hopeless report covers the following subjects, in 18 pages:

- Portfolio profile
- Financial overview
- Sector summary
- Valuation of investments
- Dealing
- Earnings
- Acquisitions
- Disposals .
- Schedule of other changes
- Cash movements
- Comments and notes

The word performance is not mentioned. Neither the total return of the portfolio nor of that of the market indices is shown.

At the very least a client needs to be able to compare the total return of each part of the portfolio – for example, equities – with the relevant market indices. Even this can be more confusing than enlightening. If the manager shows portfolio returns and relevant index returns for six or seven separate parts of the portfolio, the client can be overwhelmed with information. There is still no idea how the client has done overall. If no information is ever given about performance, it is quite likely that the manager is not truly motivated to produce good performance.

A good report is not long and not necessarily frequent. Another report, 32 pages, from one of the major private wealth managers tells the client almost nothing. There are detailed analyses, but they are either incomprehensible or misleading. An analysis of the portfolio by currency regards a UK unit trust invested wholly in Japan as providing sterling exposure. The analysis by country treats this unit trust as a UK equity. This sort of misleading and low-quality reporting is unhappily frequent among major as well as minor private banks and asset management firms.

These 32 pages could be reduced sensibly to one page. What the client needs to know is:

- What the portfolio has in it and its real geographical and currency exposure;
- What the performance has been, compared with a benchmark, over the year to date, last year, each of the last three years, and since inception;
- What the main successes and failures have been;
- And what transactions there have been.

Where performance is covered, a favourite trick, practised on supposedly sophisticated institutional clients as well as on less sophisticated private clients, is to report almost exclusively on the last quarter only, a period so short as to be irrelevant.

Good reports have almost no economic commentary – or at least limit economic commentary to what is truly an unconventional view. There is no point at all in reading that your manager is expecting GDP growth in Germany to be 2.5% while the consensus among commentators is 2.25%.

The worst reports are like the most turgid Christmas round robins in which no detail is spared as to Alice's academic achievements and James's success on the football field.

EIGHT

What Not to Look for in a Manager

THE traditional approach to choosing managers puts overwhelming emphasis on two things above all: performance and process. One adviser recommends a version of Venables ratings with 40% of the rating depending on process and 20% on performance, the rest on organisation, people, and fees.

The previous chapter made little of either performance or process as criteria for choosing managers, even though, looking back, performance has to be the yardstick of success. It is no good saying, "we had brilliant managers though they performed very badly."

Clients need lucky managers as armies need lucky generals. But looking forward, focussing on past performance too heavily is at best useless and at worst harmful.

Past performance really is no guide to the future

All that a client really cares about is performance: that the portfolio should outperform, as much as possible, whatever the chosen benchmark happens to be, and secure the long-term objective, with just a few provisos.

The main proviso is that most clients prefer that their managers stay within the law and are not therefore expecting or hoping that their managers are acting with the advantage of inside information.

A second proviso is that some clients may feel strongly that their managers should not do certain things – should not invest in tobacco stocks, for example – and others that their managers should not take certain risks – investing in Iceland or small companies in Indonesia, say.

The first proviso is encompassed in laws and the second in guidelines which the client sets. But these things aside, it is performance that the client is after.

We are all familiar with the rubric at the bottom of every unit trust advertisement: "past performance is no guide to future performance." But familiar though we are, most investors regard this as a tiresome piece of regulatory necessity, and as basically untrue. It is not. It is true.

The investment consultants Cambridge Associates have produced analysis which compares the performance of a large sample of quoted equities portfolio managers over successive five-year periods. Those managers who are in the top quartile (i.e. the top 25% of all managers in the survey) over the first five-year period are pretty evenly distributed between the four performance quartiles over the next five-year period. Equally, those in the bottom quartile in the first period are pretty evenly distributed over the performance quartiles in the next period.

Another consultant, Mercer Investment Consulting, has found the same thing. They looked at 12,500 performance records from 2,300 managers. Analysis of rolling three-year periods showed that under half of those who had just outperformed were able to do so in the ensuing period. Only 22% of those who were in the top 25% of all large cap managers repeated the trick in the next period; among small/midcap managers 23% of the top quartile did it again.

"Play it again, Sam," the hopeful client implores the satisfied manager; but Sam often does not.

There is not even an inverse relationship. It would be nice if it were possible to conclude that a star over one period was likely to be a duffer over the next period, and vice versa; but there is (usually) no correlation at all.

This unpredictability does not apply just to the stars (first quartile) and the duffers (fourth quartile): those closer to the middle in the first period, the second quartile who are just above average and the third quartile who are just below, are likewise evenly distributed in the second period.

This is disheartening. From many similar surveys comes the same conclusion. This conclusion, incidentally, applies to investment managers of quoted equity portfolios. The results for private equity managers – managers of investments in unquoted companies – are more confused. A McKinsey survey concludes that there is, with private equity, some degree of repeatability: the top quartile in one period are, mostly, successful in the next period. Conversely, of those in the bottom (fourth) quartile in a first fund, only 28% were in the first or second quartiles in their next fund. This suggests that those who do well go on doing well and those who do badly go on doing badly, and this seems to be true especially in venture capital.

The data for private equity is contradicted by other data, however – for example, that after successful first funds, 41 out of a sample of 49 follow-on funds of private equity managers underperformed. If there is any 'sustainability' pattern among private equity managers in aggregate, there may be special reasons why it is so. In private equity, it may be that the companies in which investments are made have a preference for those managers who have a successful record, and so the bad deals gravitate to the unsuccessful managers. In quoted equity markets there is a saying that you must not fall in love with a stock:

the stock does not know you own it. In private equity this is not so. The company does know it is owned by the private equity manager, and there is a different relationship.

But in quoted equity, past performance is emphatically no guide to the future. This does not mean that the quest for a manager who will outperform in the future is hopeless. Some of the managers hidden among the first and second quartiles of managers over past periods are managers who will outperform in the future. Choosing some of them is not necessarily a matter wholly of luck.

Likewise, there are managers in the first and second quartiles who will underperform in the future. Avoiding some of them may, again, not be wholly down to luck. But the point is that the mere fact of past good performance should be regarded as irrelevant. This is one of the reasons that investing is, though simple, more difficult than it looks.

Hirings and firings based on past performance do not work

It follows that when an investor is choosing a manager the thing to care least about is past good performance. But experience shows that past performance is the main factor in making people hire and fire managers – with disastrous results.

A Cambridge Associates study compared the results of managers whom their clients had fired with managers whom their clients had hired. The managers hired had outperformed the managers fired by an average of 11% over the year just before the hiring and firing – not surprising, but certainly demonstrating a prejudice in favour of good immediately past performance. What is alarming is that the newly hired managers then underperformed the newly fired managers by 4.1% over the year immediately after the hiring and firing.

Even more disturbing is a study by John Bogle, head of the US fund management group Vanguard, in the *Financial Analysts Journal*.

This showed that, over the 21 years 1983–2003, the Standard & Poor's Composite Index of the top 500 US shares gave an average annual return of 13%. The average equity mutual fund gave a return of 10%.

That alone is bad news, and testimony to the fact that the average fund manager performs, after all fees and costs, worse than the index.

But the really disturbing extra information in Bogle's study was that the average equity mutual fund investor made only 6% a year.

The difference between the 10% and the 6% is accounted for by the fact that habitually investors switch funds at the wrong time: out of the fund which has performed badly and into the fund which has performed well. They chase their tails on a monumental scale. They constantly buy high and sell low, the antithesis of the rule of successful investment.

The investment consultants Watson Wyatt came to the same conclusion in a study in 2006 based on work by Messrs Goyal and Wahal in 2005, 'The selection and termination of investment management firms by plan sponsors'. This was based on a study of around 4,000 hiring and firing decisions by US pension funds between 1993 and 2003.

"The stronger the pre-hiring relative returns, the weaker the post-hiring returns…In the cases where the pre-firing returns were negative, post-firing returns were positive. In other words, the fiduciaries would have been better off retaining the managers. Institutional investors tend to destroy value when changing managers."

The managers hired had an average outperformance of 14% in the three years before hiring, while those fired, having underperformed by around 6% in the three years before dismissal, outperformed by nearly 5% – for other clients – after dismissal.

The Watson Wyatt study concluded that 32% of manager terminations were performance-related. I do not believe this. I suspect that much, much more than 32% of firings were performance-related, but respondents would have been reluctant to admit this because all know very well that past performance is a lousy reason to fire a manager. All it does is to punish the manager. It does no good for the investor.

So investors seize upon other pretexts to explain away firings, when in fact, lurking consciously or possibly sub-consciously in their minds is the real reason, the knowledge that performance has been bad.

These were long-only managers. The same points appear true of hedge fund managers, according to a study by Morgan Stanley. Those hedge fund managers in the top quartile of all similar hedge funds in the three-year period to October 1999 had an average return of 27% per annum. Their average return in the next three years was 5.5%.

Global Asset Management, one of the leading investors in hedge funds over many years, has also found little evidence of persistence of returns, either within particular strategies or within individual hedge funds.

"We compared year-on-year periods, month-on-month periods and just about everything else," David Smith, investment director of GAM's $20bn manager-of-managers programme, told the firm's annual conference. "The evidence is that returns are little better than random."

There are all sorts of facets of the past performance record which are relevant and interesting, but the fact of outperformance itself is not one of them. It is worth banging on at length about this because it is so hard to get rid of the prejudice which the past performance record creates.

Anyone meeting a Nobel Prize winner is likely to think that the Nobel Prize winner is highly intelligent, and is likely to be right. Anyone meeting an investment manager with an excellent performance record is likely to think that the manager must be good. Not necessarily. It may just have been luck. And even if it was not luck, it may have been the climate of the times, which could be about to change.

Good managers sometimes perform badly

Good managers have bad patches. One of the most successful managers in recent years is Bill Miller, the manager of the Legg Mason Value Trust which did better than the Standard & Poor's Index for 15 years in a row, to 2005. In mid-August 2006 this fund had fallen by more than 10% while the S&P was up 3%. Miller described his fund's performance as dreadful. *Barron's*, under the sub-heading 'Has the fabled manager lost his touch?', rather cruelly noted that Miller had recently bought a 190-foot-long yacht and asked the infamous Wall Street yacht question, "Where are his customer's yachts?" They wondered whether time and pressure were taking their toll.

Jonathan Davis in the *Financial Times* pointed out more level-headedly that the 15 consecutive years of outperformance were a statistical quirk and that in some ways Miller was lucky to have that particular monkey off his back. "Periods of excruciating short-term underperformance are a burden that all genuine value investors have to endure."

Warren Buffett made a speech entitled 'The Superinvestors of Graham-and-Doddsville' in 1984, printed in Columbia University's magazine, *HERMES*. This was about seven investment managers with exceptional long-term track records, all of them devotees of the value-oriented approach described by the legendary Graham and Dodd in their seminal series of books on investment, *Security Analysis*.

None of the seven outperformed the relevant index (the Standard & Poor's Composite) every year. Stretches of consecutive annual underperformance ranged from one to six years. In a later issue of *HERMES*, Eugene Shahan commented: "unfortunately, there is no way to distinguish between a poor three-year stretch for a manager who will do well over 15 years, from a poor three-year stretch for a manager who will continue to do poorly."

Warren Buffett himself, like Homer, is occasionally found nodding. In 42 years, Berkshire Hathaway's asset value has underperformed the Standard & Poor's Index for US equities six times. But over the whole

42 years, the annual rate of return has been 21.4% compared with 10.4% for the index – so the cumulative gain has been 361,156% for Berkshire Hathaway, 6,479% for the index. Asset value has increased from $19 per share in 1965, to $70,281 at the end of 2006.

From worst to best

There may be special circumstances which make it sensible sometimes to focus attention on those whose performance record has just been thoroughly bad. The two best manager appointments I have ever made have been of managers whose immediately past performance record was poor.

Both appointments were in 2000, *annus mirabilis* or *annus horribilis*, depending on your point of view. This was the last of three extraordinary years in which the tech bubble had got bigger and bigger. Finally, it burst. But during this bubble it was not simply that technology and telecom stocks became absurdly expensive. Other companies, with essentially strong businesses and good balance sheets, were neglected in the rush to the exotic, and became severely undervalued.

Both the managers appointed in 2000 were 'value' managers who had altogether missed out on the tech boom, not understanding at all the valuations of such companies, and instead focussed on the latter sort of company.

One was an international equity management firm based in Tennessee. They had just had three years of seriously dud performance. The other was a UK equity manager. I went to see the individual concerned, on his own. I said that we were inclined to add money to the portfolio he was already managing, which had done badly; but that, since he was getting on and had had some 13 years of excellent performance (for others) before these two years of dud performance, we wanted to check that he would still be around in six months' time.

There was rather a long pause. "I suppose I had better tell you something," the manager said. He then told me that in fact he was in the midst of negotiating his exit from his current employers. We went on to appoint him to manage a portfolio in his new guise. Both he, and the Tennessee firm, had a dazzling five years ahead, because the nature of the market changed completely. The tech bubble burst and 'value', after years in the wilderness, flourished.

Many old-fashioned value managers who did not take part in the tech boom performed so badly in the last couple of years of the 1990s that they gave up altogether. Tony Dye, the head of Phillips & Drew's fund management operation, was one of the most notorious of these diehards, and a casualty. He had long been sceptical both of the level of stock markets generally and more particularly of the tech stocks. Eventually, in March 2000 – absolutely the peak of the tech boom – he threw in the towel at Phillips & Drew. In 2000, 75 of Phillips & Drew's UK pension fund clients fired the firm – nearly 30% of their accounts. In the year to 31 March 2001, the main Phillips & Drew fund outperformed by 24% the leading growth manager – which had done well throughout the bubble period.

The year 2000 was truly exceptional. It was a serious policy to look among those who had not done well in the previous few years – then selecting not on the basis of worst possible performance but for the usual, more positive, attributes covered in the last chapter. On the whole, though, it would be a nerve-racking business to concentrate wholly on those who had done badly. We all tend to look, because of the prejudice that is impossible to eradicate, at managers who have done at least reasonably, or better. Given that that is likely to be the starting point, it is important to try to minimise the influence that past performance has on the decision about whom to hire.

Gilding the lily

Another reason to be sceptical about performance records is that they are remarkably easy to embellish. As with all industries the investment management industry has been subject to increasing regulation, either externally imposed or self-imposed, and this has affected the measurement of performance.

Over the years, various bodies have introduced standards which are supposed to be observed and which are intended to make more credible and comparable the performance records of the different managers.

In the early 1990s, a new lot of performance standards was introduced in the measurement of international portfolios for US clients. Every fund management firm was supposed to overhaul its published records, making sure that its methods of measuring, and the portfolios which were included in certain averages for each peer group, complied with the new rules. Every firm duly set about the overhauling.

The interesting result, a few months later when all the careful number-recrunching was complete, was that in every case of around half a dozen different sets of performance groups, the peer group average return in the overhauled sample was higher than that in the pre-overhauled sample.

Investment management firms had seized the wonderful, officially provided opportunity to weed out from their figures one or two portfolios which lowered their batting average, wherever they could find a pretext for doing so. There was always some quite plausible pretext.

This was a classic case of perverse consequences. The intention was to provide figures which really stood up to objective scrutiny, were put together in the same way for every firm, and which could therefore be compared properly as a true reflection of what a firm had achieved. The result was that many firms looked for loopholes which would let them improve on the performance they had been reporting.

The bureaucratisation of performance figures has not led to purer figures, just to pages of explanation. One chief executive of a fund management firm told me that their latest publication giving full details of their international equity portfolios' performance ran to 132 pages and he did not understand half of it. A footnote to another firm's figures states (referring to GIPS which is a globally agreed standard for performance measurement):

"This data is GIPS compliant if presented as supplemental to the GIPS compliant presentations contained in the GIPS Performance Presentations booklet."

Pretty baffling, but leaving the impression that the investor should probably ask to see the GIPS Performance Presentations booklet, which no doubt would turn out to have 132 largely incomprehensible pages.

There are all sorts of tricks. The most blatant is simulation, when the performance record you are shown is not a record actually achieved, but the record the manager claims would have been achieved if the proposed method had been followed. "All above figures are pro forma calculations based on application of the fund's strategy."

In this, of course, there is wonderful hindsight. The manager is not likely, when looking back, to follow a method which would have resulted in poor notional performance. Yet managers do frequently come along to prospective clients and present some black box, computer-driven, approach, on which they say they have done a simulation which has been proven to provide outperformance.

This is tautology. Managers tinker around with different algorithms, in different permutations and weightings. Once the best possible results for the past have appeared, they stop tinkering, and present this method to clients. There is in real life no assurance whatever that the conditions which would have created this outperformance in the past will be obtained in the future. Actual past performance is no guide to future performance, and imaginary past performance is no guide either.

Another trick is to rummage around in the cupboard for the right set of numbers. Choosing the right start date is half the trick. It often pays to enquire as to what happened immediately before the set of performance figures with which the potential client is confronted. There may be good reasons that the performance series starts when it does, but then again there may not.

Large investment managers have a huge range of types of portfolio, many very similar, but managed by different people with different approaches. A large firm may have, for example,

- global equity portfolios;
- global equity portfolios with an income objective;
- global equity portfolios with ethical constraints;
- global equity portfolios managed by the charity team;
- global equity portfolios managed by the private client team;
- global equity portfolios managed by three different teams in the institutional division with three similar but different approaches;
- global equity portfolios managed by a UK unit trust manager;
- and global equity portfolios managed by an offshore fund manager.

These may differ, slightly or radically. Whatever is best of these may be the record which is presented to the hapless potential client. The presentation may be entirely truthful. The client may be told, quite rightly, that this is the performance of Wondermanagement Global Equity Fund over the last five years, that it has always been run by the same manager, and that it is a big fund with £500m. What may not be revealed is that the reason for showing figures for this fund, rather than those for Wondermanagement Global Trust or the averages for Wondermanagement's pension fund global equity portfolios, is simply that Wondermanagement Global Equity Fund has done much better than the others.

Another area to probe is whether there has been any change in the management of the portfolios for which figures are being provided. At large institutional firms, especially, there frequently is change. Managers leave. "She was a good cook, as cooks go," wrote Saki, "and as cooks go, she went." The same is true of investment managers. Good managers especially leave the large firms. The performance record presented may be the record of three different managers in five years.

Although the specialist investment management firms in the US tend to be staffed by people who have worked together for years, that is not so much the case in the investment departments of investment banks. One US investment bank in my experience never really saw the difference between the investment management arm of the bank and other more transaction-related divisions where the particular deal was the thing. They used to move their people around regularly, and that included into and out of the investment management division.

A team in Singapore ran Asian portfolios. It had nine members. They did well. A year after I first met them, only three of that nine-man team were still there. They had not been sacked or retired hurt. On the contrary, the head of the team had been promoted to an investment banking team, and his colleagues too had been shifted around, often flatteringly because of their success. But it meant that the performance record signified nothing: it was the product of a different lot of people.

Patterns in performance

So performance figures need to be treated with a large dose of scepticism. Nonetheless, they are useful. It is not the fact, or the amount, of outperformance, which is useful, but the patterns which can be seen in them. These patterns, like the patterns which can be seen in a transaction record, tell one something about the style of management, and may tell one about changes. The client therefore needs to see at least quarterly figures, preferably monthly, going back several years, and to be able to compare these with relevant benchmark returns.

A pattern which often occurs is that performance has been startlingly good at the beginning of a period – much better than the benchmark – and perhaps quite volatile, with less outperformance in the more recent past. This can be something to be wary of, because what it can indicate is a shift in the motivation of managers. The initial period may be one in which they are concerned wholly with managing portfolios and with performance. If they do very well they may then become more concerned with the business aspects of what they are doing rather than the performance. They may become more restrained, less bold, in order to present to potential clients a picture of steadiness and consistency, to help to attract business. In that case they are not quite the same managers that they were.

This pattern occurs especially often when there has been some serious accident. Managers steam ahead for years, investing with conviction, wildly different from the index, on balance outperforming by a wide margin. Then they go through a period when it goes drastically wrong: some individual months (and they may well be managing funds where clients focus on individual months) where they chalk up big minuses, and big underperformance compared with the index. Thereafter they can become a milder version of their old selves: convictions more restrained, more consciousness of the index. Again, they are not the managers they used to be.

Another situation in which this pattern occurs is when a firm gets big. A firm which started with little money to manage and a determination to do it well for clients so as to get more of them can become, once large and successful, more focussed on not disappointing the clients it already has, and therefore more inclined to cling to the index in order not to do much worse than it.

Excess of process

So much for performance. The other big area of emphasis is normally process. "Is the process robust?" is a standard question consultants ask themselves about investment managers. Quantity and quality are easy to get muddled up. Managers produce masses of evidence of lots of process to persuade clients that this means the process must be a good one. But process, in investment management, should be treated almost as warily as performance.

Investment management relies on people, and on the individuality of those people. Individuality frequently becomes squashed by process.

As a firm grows it becomes inevitable that individuals are organised. The individuals are allotted, by themselves or their bosses, different areas of speciality. That is the first step. The second is that with further growth there is more than one person in each area of speciality, so in each area a team has to be organised. Each team has to have some sort of code of conduct. The relationship between the teams has to be codified too. This is process.

Where there is a big team there may be a temptation to try to balance the views of all of its members for the sake of teamwork. Once there is a whole series of teams, the way in which they relate with one another can slow down decision-making. A phrase like 'global leverage into our global research platform', advertised as a virtue, should fill the investor with foreboding.

The nonsensus of consensus

Consensus is not a good way to manage investment portfolios. Consensus in other walks of life may have its pros and cons. But in investment management it is fatally flawed because of the plain fact that, when all are positive about something, they are already invested in it and that, when all are negative, they are already underinvested.

This characteristic is not true of other disciplines such as economic or weather forecasting. We can all forecast that it will rain tomorrow and all be right. We can all forecast that John McCain will be the next president of the US and all be right. But if we all, without exception, forecast that Japan will be the best performing market next year, we are almost bound to be wrong. It is axiomatic in markets that the consensus, if truly universal, is overwhelmingly likely to be wrong.

No consensus is ever entirely universal, but it may come close. There comes a time when just about everyone thinks that the price of oil is bound to go up; or that the new era means that a new breed of technology companies have to be valued in a completely new way, or that the rarity of a particular type of tulip bulb justifies an enormous price. In retrospect it always appears rather ridiculous that nearly everyone should have succumbed to what turns out to be a delusion. But when their friends and competitors are making money from oil or tech or tulips, even the sceptics get lured in. Once in, we can have the zeal of the converted. This is human nature.

In the mid-19th century, Charles Mackay wrote about these human failings in *Extraordinary Popular Delusions and the Madness of Crowds*: "Whole communities suddenly fix their minds upon one object, and go mad in its pursuit ... millions of people become simultaneously impressed with one delusion, and run after it, until their attention is caught by some new folly more captivating than the first ... Men, it has been well said, think in herds; it will be seen that they go mad in herds, while they only recover their senses slowly, and one by one."

A herd of six with the same view is not as dangerous as a herd of 60,000. A committee of six might well be right. All the same, a strong consensus about markets and shares among just six people is more likely to be wrong than right. A manager may well want to listen carefully to the views of a wise adviser. If 12 wise people have the same view, the manager should be sceptical.

This is demonstrated particularly vividly in various so-called sentiment indicators. I have followed for 25 years something called the Investors Intelligence Survey of Advisory Sentiment, compiled by a firm in upstate New York. This firm looks each week at 150 or so advisory newsletters published by commentators on the US stock market, and then rates their conclusions about the overall direction of the market either bullish, or bearish, or looking for a correction.

For much of the time the figures are in a no man's land, where they tell nothing in particular. But when they are at an extreme − when there are many more bulls than bears, or when there are more bears than bulls (which is rare because on the whole such market commentators do not like to be bearish) − this indicator has been almost infallible about the near term direction of the market. If opinion is generally very bullish, the market is about to go down; if opinion is generally bearish, it is about to go up. It is as simple as that.

This indicator cannot be perfect because there cannot be, in markets, any such thing as a perfect indicator − since if there were, its perfection would be speedily recognised and, by making use of it, people would quickly arbitrage out its usefulness and make it useless. But I know that every time I have ignored what this indicator was telling me I have regretted it. I have too often ignored it, because the whole tide of human emotion is to share the convictions of the crowd. The crowd is not dim. The crowd has its strong feelings for sound reasons; it is just that the mere fact that the crowd has these feelings in itself moves market prices to the extent that it nullifies the likelihood of it being right.

Such inverse indicators may seem somewhat cynical bits of witch-doctory but they usually work.

In a large firm, with large teams and a process organised to ensure that decisions are the product of teamwork, consensus is almost inevitable. A share which is deeply unpopular in the market as a whole is likely to be fairly unpopular within a large firm, because the members of that firm represent more and more closely a cross-section of the market as a whole.

All investment managers recognise the importance of not merely being conventional. But it is extremely difficult to avoid the human inclination to be part of the crowd. At parties, one end of the room, however large, is full, and the other has a few scattered eccentrics who have strayed. They do not look cool. They look as though they do not belong, and we all like to belong.

John Maynard Keynes, who had an excellent record as an investor both for his Cambridge college, King's, and for his old school, Eton, famously said that it is easier to fail conventionally than succeed unconventionally.

"My central principle," Keynes wrote in 1944 to a fellow money manager for Eton, "is to go contrary to general opinion, on the ground that, if everyone is agreed about its merits, the investment is inevitably too dear and therefore unattractive."

A touch of autocracy in portfolio management is positively desirable. The responsibility for decision-making is absolutely clear. The decision-maker cannot hide behind a veil of collegiality – "but we all thought…" Nor can a manager, subconsciously or consciously, take the line about a mistake that it is not his or her problem, but the problem of the person mainly responsible for putting the mistake stock in the portfolio in the first place – "but you thought…"

Most of the truly successful firms have started life dependent on a very few decision-makers. As they get bigger, they naturally tend to take on more people, and thus to change, often for the worse. When a firm has gone through this process, though still bearing the strong stamp of its founders, the question for the founders could be this:

"You started this yourselves. It is your distinctive philosophy, and your distinctive investment policy. As you have grown, successfully, you have recruited lots of clever people around you. Which should we fear more: that, having recruited all these people, you ignore their views; or that having recruited them, you pay attention to them?"

Looking big, thinking small

A firm, however large, is expected to provide much the same outcome for its clients to whom it is giving a supposedly identical service. One of the largest investment management companies in the world, the Capital Group, recognised at an early stage that there was a conflict between what was necessary for it as a firm with a corporate image and what was desirable for its clients.

Capital Group organise themselves so that for each of their funds there are six or seven managers. But the managers do not have to agree on anything; and nor do they manage specialised, non-overlapping, sub-portfolios. Each is responsible for a sub-portfolio, which may have positions which are the same as that of other sub-portfolio managers, or positions which are quite contrary. It is possible for one manager to be selling something at the same time as another is buying it. When this happens, Capital has an internal clearing system so that the deal does not actually have to be carried out, with the attendant costs, in the market; it is simply transferred from one sub-portfolio to another.

The beauty of this arrangement is that the individuality of the investment management process is preserved. Each manager feels wholly responsible, and can take decisions quickly. But the client sees a portfolio which cobbles together these sub-portfolios to provide a corporate product, the same for all clients who want that particular service.

Other firms have copied this set-up. This is much better than imposing consensus decision-making. But when managers are finding life difficult, they may tend to seek the comfort of doing the same thing as others within the same firm. Sub-portfolios may, from time to time, gravitate towards one another, so that in the end, as a result of a cultural inclination to togetherness, they look very much the same. There may, therefore, be a disguised tendency to consensus.

Committeeitis

An elaborate process can depend too much on consensus. It can also result in decisions taking too long.

Experienced prospective clients, who have seen masses of presentations, are all too familiar with Powerpoint, the main Microsoft software programme for presentations. Powerpoint is good at drawing boxes and connecting them with arrows. Too many boxes and arrows indicate that an investment decision is staged, and stages take time. Too many stages take too much time. Decisions which start in a research team and then go through several layers of ratification by committees are unlikely to be good ones. Even if they would have been good if implemented on day one, they are not likely to be good by the time they are finally polished up to be ready for implementation by the umpteenth committee.

Sometimes the process is so elaborate that research about a stock seems to turn into a holding of that stock by some sort of osmosis, without it being apparent, in the miasma of collegiality, who firmly pushes the button, and who truly cares if it goes wrong.

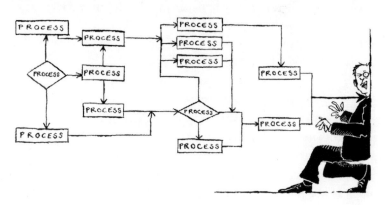

How to kill good investing

One of the best possible processes is close to none at all: where an individual or a small team is clearly accountable for all decisions. It is not necessary then to draw a diagram showing different parts of the brain in boxes linked by arrows, and there are no research teams whose different parts in the operation have to be explained. Decision-making may be disciplined but idiosyncratic and in part serendipitous.

Overspecialisation

A single decision-maker could theoretically be supported by any number of people doing research. In practice, there is a limit to how many researchers can really be optimally employed. If there are lots, they will tend either to have overlapping areas of responsibility, in which case the same problem of consensus and compromise arises in the research team in putting together its recommendations as arises if there are lots of people in the decision-making team; or they will have separate, non-overlapping but therefore highly specialised responsibilities, in which case a different sort of problem can arise: that of overspecialisation.

Along with its increase in short-termism the investment world has become steadily more specialised as more and more people have joined it. The range of interest of the average fund manager, or of the average researcher, is usually quite narrow. Their job is, for example, to manage Continental European portfolios, or to research Asian telecom companies. The shortcoming of this is the loss of the big picture and of the big decision.

In early 2004, to take an example, the price of oil was $32 per barrel. All the economic forecasters, with a few honourable outlying exceptions, were predicting a price of $24. The oil company analysts, again with some honourable exceptions but not many, simply adopted this $24 forecast. It was not their job to forecast the oil price; that privilege belonged to someone else in their large firms. The analysts imputed the forecast into their models and projections for individual companies. With their narrow range of speciality, they focussed on which companies looked most attractive with a future price of $24 per barrel. They weighed carefully the merits of Anadarko Petroleum and Devon Energy and Apache Petroleum.

The forecast as it happened was completely wrong. Over the next 18 months, the price of oil doubled. The only thing the investor had to do was to be doubtful about the forecast – and it is rare that a forecast is so far below the current level of whatever it is for which the forecast is being made, whether gold or copper or earnings or a currency. It was the big picture, viewed with the dispassion that distance brings, which mattered more than the intricacies of one company's exploration activities compared with those of another.

Specialist, in-depth knowledge is not to be sneezed at. Knowledge is better than ignorance. But knowledge of the trees can obscure judgement about the wood. In looking at the virtues of an investment management firm which has a bevy of knowledgeable highly specialised researchers, the question for the investor is whether the manager has sacrificed anything, or too much, in terms of a quick and incisive decision-making process.

NINE

How to be a Successful Client

THE worst client I have ever had was a charming businessman. He was a friend of the chairman of the merchant bank, Warburgs, and also of the chairman of Mercury Asset Management, for which I worked, and which was, at the time, majority owned by Warburgs.

Rodney used to ring me every day to talk about the state of the market and find out what I had done in his portfolio. Invariably he homed in with flawless instinct on the bits of the portfolio about which I felt most defensive because something had gone wrong. On one occasion he rang, reversing the charges, from South Africa.

"Did I hear you say, my boy, that you bought me some IBM yesterday?" He had observed that the price of IBM had gone down $4 overnight, as in those days it frequently did.

Mostly Rodney was charm itself. He was especially charming when he visited our office and one of the two chairmen, David Scholey or Peter Stormonth Darling, would look in to say hello. Then he would put his arm round my shoulders and make flattering references to "my boy". At other times, when they were absent, his friendship with them was a constant veiled threat. "I am playing golf with David on Saturday," he would say. He wanted to leave me in no doubt that I had better perform or else. Although of a certain age, he had great vigour and forcefulness. He once overturned his car on a motorway but was on a golf course within hours.

Hire, support and fire

It may seem arrogant for an investment manager to be choosy about clients, and to make the distinction between a good client and a bad client. But good clients help themselves; bad clients harm themselves. Managers do not give their best for a client if they fear that the client is going to be on the telephone at the merest whiff of a mistake. A manager in those circumstances is tempted to try to avoid trouble, and to take little risk, buying the most stable and uninteresting investments. Determination never to lose money, in a portfolio invested in shares, results in the impossibility of making money, because there is no such thing – no such legal thing, anyway – as a sure-fire winner.

Sure-fire winners are deeply suspect. A colleague of mine described to me a Coca-Cola bottling company in an emerging economy as a no-brainer, a licence to print money. Six years later, the company went into liquidation.

Rodney was a client at one extreme. At the other extreme were the clients whose affairs I advised on for eight years as head of a family investment office. The head of the family had been a hugely successful businessman and entrepreneur. The years in which I looked after them included some very good years, but also some of the worst in the history of the stock market. There were several occasions when stock markets slumped, notably the Russian crisis and the collapse of the hedge fund Long-Term Capital Management in 1998 and the attack on the World Trade Centre in September 2001. My clients never flinched. The head of the family used occasionally, at such awkward moments, to ring up and ask, "Is there anything left?" This was cheering because there was of course always something left. I could always answer yes.

The most interested member of the family was by inclination a deep discount value manager, managing herself a substantial portfolio for her charity and achieving embarrassingly excellent results through brave contrarianism. This meant that she was immensely supportive at the times when support is most useful, which is when things are going wrong. Nobody needs support when things are going well.

Good clients decide the course and stick to it. They choose the managers who they think stand the best chance of following that course and doing better than the average. Then they say to the manager, "Do your best", and encourage them to get on with it.

Good clients think about their objectives and the risk they are prepared to take. They preferably do this explicitly, by putting in place a benchmark by which to measure performance, and which also serves as a reminder of the long-term strategy which they have chosen. Alternatively, they set the course implicitly, in their choice of managers who have, or a fund which has, the same long-term strategy. They should expect the managers to report on how they are doing in relation to the benchmark.

The one thing clients mindful of their own interests might hesitate to do is to shake the confidence of their managers. Homing in on mistakes is a natural temptation. The mistakes are always much more interesting than the successes. But managers are just as aware as a client, more so in fact, if something is going badly. If they are to be dispassionate about it, it does not help to have the owner of the money reminding them of their stupidity. What is past is past. Managers need to look at the investment afresh, at what may be a new improved price. As far as possible they have to dispense with the baggage created by the knowledge that so far it has been wrong. It is difficult to get rid of the baggage if a client is taking pains to remind you of it.

The best clients therefore hire, support, and fire. They do not give any hint of dissatisfaction until the moment they pull the trigger. There is no point in doing so unless the portfolio shows obvious signs of neglect. A manager clearly concentrating on things other than a client's portfolio may benefit from a shot across the bows. If clients find they have hired the sort of firm which allows a manager to focus on some portfolios rather than others, they have hired the wrong firm and should change.

Otherwise, managers are probably doing their best. If they are doing badly they know it. Being put under some sort of notice will not make them take better decisions. To take good decisions requires confidence, and enlightened self-serving clients boost the confidence of their manager by expressing confidence themselves. If their own confidence in the manager vanishes, they pull the rug.

An unhappy story in recent years is that of an investment trust set up by a leading investment management firm. After a short period of good performance, the fund started to do badly, and never stopped. Investment trusts are funny animals because they often bear the name of the investment firm doing the investment management, as this one did. They have, like all quoted companies, boards of directors of whom a fair proportion are independent, but changing the investment manager is a big decision for the board if the company was set up in the first place by the investment management firm and bears its name.

The board lost confidence in the managers but was reluctant to bite the bullet. At the worst point to do so, they changed the mandate of the managers so that their benchmark was no longer to beat an equity index but to beat short-term deposits through investment in equities and cash. This coincided with the bottoming of the world equity markets after the 2000–02 bear market. A year on, after further misery, they moved two-thirds of the fund into the hands of third parties.

Finally, after yet more misery, they ditched the original managers altogether. The whole affair was extremely expensive in terms of fees to advisers, and much more so in terms of lost performance. The managers concerned felt throughout that they were being retained for bad reasons – public relations – rather than because the board had any confidence in them. The managers were permanently nervous. They really had little hope of getting back on the right track, and never did. They were doomed.

The long-term view

Self-interested clients should be careful not to focus on too short a period of performance. They must not be in too much of a hurry. The wise commercial banker Lord Overstone said, "no warning can save a people determined to grow suddenly rich." Our firm's funds are called Overstone, not because of his banking wisdom (he also described the market cycle: quiescence, improvement, confidence, prosperity, excitement, convulsion, pressure, stagnation, distress... and back to quiescence), but because he gave his name to a road in Hammersmith in which I bought a house in 1976 for £13,250. This house has good value associations for me.

Good self-interested clients have realistic expectations. Not so good clients tend to be disappointed by talk of an expected rate of return from equities over the long run of 9% or 10%, but that is what, in the long term, the return has been.

A very short-term focus, as well as high expectations, can have ruinous effects, as they do for many hedge funds. One potential client of ours wanted to have weekly performance figures. (We value the funds we manage monthly.) I told the client that he could not have them, because I did not have them. The head of operations at our firm knows performance from week to week, and even more frequently; but I have an eccentric rule that I am allowed to ask the performance of our funds intra-month only once each month. To know more frequently would not be useful and could be harmful: a distraction, but also a cause of complacency if performance is good and of neurosis if bad, and in any event unnecessary clutter. It was not acceptable for the client to know more than I did about performance, and I did not want to know more, so we agreed that we would not provide the weekly figures, and the potential client went away, which is probably just as well.

Types of client

Some managers are particularly critical of a certain type of client, the fund of funds. A fund of funds is what it says it is. It invests in a variety of funds, so that the client is saved the problem of choosing individual managers. On the other hand, the client suffers double-charging: management, and sometimes performance fees, both on the underlying funds and on the fund of funds.

There must be many excellent funds of funds, but the funds of funds sector is much criticised by other professionals. Miles Morland, the admirable investment manager who founded Blakeney Management, which specialises in investment in Africa, wrote on his retirement in his wonderful valedictory newsletter:

> "We are blessed with the clients we have. The bulk are educational endowments, foundations, and family offices. These are the highest quality clients anyone could wish for. There is not a shit among them. They, unlike the sleazy flotsam that makes up the fund of funds industry, take a genuinely long-term view of investing. Their cycle is fifteen years long. This allows them to ignore short-term blips, to be buyers when the walls are crumbling and to be sellers when the moon is full and the dogs barking in the streets." (He made an exception for Blakeney's sole fund of funds client.)

The excellent, and thoroughly unconventional, fund manager Jonathan Ruffer has a story about a client whose family was one of the long-term owners of a chunk of London real estate. The client said that they would certainly monitor quarterly performance. "And if, after the first 25 years…"

There are exceptions to everything, but a general rule is that those who are owners or who think most like owners are the best clients. Family offices are staffed by people whose only interest is to act for the owners.

Pension fund trustees, on the other hand, have two disadvantages. First, their membership of the trustee board is often a sideshow to their real occupation, since most trustees are in some way connected, as employees or directors, with the company whose pension fund it is, and are asked to take on the trustee position, without having much experience of investment matters. Second, they are tied up in regulatory red tape. They are battered by the demands of actuaries who often force them to do things which they would not dream of doing as individuals.

Such trustees are sometimes completely at the mercy of bureaucratic requirements. I once headed a team managing a portfolio for the pension fund of the employees of a US city administration. At short notice I was asked to appear in that city. I happened to be on holiday, but this looked a rather menacing request, and we thought I had better get there myself. I interrupted the holiday, flew to the place, and met the trustees. It was puzzling because they did not seem much bothered by anything. They asked no questions. The meeting was over in half an hour. A few weeks later I discovered that there was some bye-law in their terms of reference which obliged them to meet every manager at least once a year, and they had forgotten until late in the day to do anything about us.

TEN

When to Fire a Manager

T HE fact of investment life is that investors nearly always change horses after their first horse has performed poorly. Poor performance alone is a very bad reason to change. Investment consultants often set performance targets which cover a five-year period, and recommend sacking the manager if after five years the manager has not beaten the target. This is not in the client's interests.

Bad performance is a bad reason

Even those who know perfectly well that past performance is no guide to future performance find it difficult to pay much attention to this sobering truth. They cannot suppress knowledge of the performance they have suffered or missed out on when they are deciding whether to hire or fire a manager.

People sometimes ask over what period a manager should be judged. This is the wrong question. There is no proper answer. Of course, if an investor chooses a manager who does very well over ten years, at the end of that ten years that is good, and if the manager does badly over ten years disappointing. But no particular action flows from the result. It may be tempting to fire a manager who has performed poorly over three years, but it is not necessarily the right thing. Sometimes it may be the worst thing to do, giving up just when market conditions are about to turn in the manager's favour.

The US is much better than the UK at dealing with poor performance. It is said that institutions are very short-term in their performance requirements, but I do not think it is so in the US.

Moreover, the ethos of the typical US investment partnership is much stronger than that of the large UK institutional firms. There are several reasons for this. One is that the US long ago accepted that different managers have different investment styles: some are temperamentally value managers, some temperamentally growth managers. Different firms, or teams within firms, have different style specialities. A value manager makes sure that new recruits have a similar investment philosophy. Colleagues understand each other. Clients accept that a value manager is unlikely to do well during a period in which growth investing is the mood of the market, and vice versa. This means that there is much greater tolerance of periods of poor performance.

A second reason is that investment managers in the US tend to be older than investment managers in the UK. Experience is worth something. At times when the going is rough, there is a much greater sense of partnership in the typical US firm than in England. In the US, they deal phlegmatically with such periods.

In some firms in the UK the mood more easily degenerates into that found in Dad's Army when at moments of crisis Corporal Jones shouts "Don't panic!" in an increasingly agitated manner until silenced by the world-weary Captain Mainwaring.

Change in people

If bad past performance is not a reason to fire, what is? Investment being overwhelmingly an individualistic business, the loss of the key individuals is an obvious reason to worry. Investment management firms make every effort to smooth over departures, but blithe assurances of continuity should be treated with scepticism. People are different, and a new investment manager is unlikely to be a clone of a departing one. When performance has been all right, clients tend to inertia: it is tempting to accept reassurances rather than face the tiresome business of finding a new manager. The investor should therefore start with a prejudice to fire if the manager changes. The new one needs to be assessed afresh.

Turnover among fund managers has risen alarmingly in recent years. According to the *Financial Times*, the average tenure of a fund manager in 2006 was about three years. A research group, Investment Solutions, claimed even more remarkably that turnover among fund managers was 51% in 2006 – every other manager changed firm. This is hard to believe.

Sometimes it is not quite clear that there has been a change in manager. Investment firms are well aware that a change in people frightens clients, and they try to disguise the change.

I once went to see a manager in New York. He had been doing wonderfully for a couple of years. I was disconcerted to find that the room in which the manager sat, which used to contain just him, now had three or four others packed into it. It was not at all evident to me what they did. He had been doing marvellously without this extra help. I did not think it necessarily good news that he now had these assistants, no doubt bright, complicating the decision-making process.

It only became clear at the end of the meeting what was going on. "There is just one other thing," the manager told me, "that I should say, and that is that my physical circumstances have changed. I am now living in Aspen, Colorado." In a flash all was clear. The manager was skiing in the winter and doing whatever it is that people who live in Aspen, Colorado do in the summer. All the assistants were doing his job. This explained also the large increase in transactions in the portfolio: more people responsible generally means more activity, because people who are employed on large salaries generally feel unhappy unless they are visibly doing something to justify them. Benign neglect is not usually regarded as sufficiently meritorious. The specific mandate which they had been given by the man from Aspen was to increase or reduce to 1% of the portfolio every holding, more or less every day. There was thus ceaseless fringe activity, pointlessly.

It was both a reason to fire that this 'change in physical circumstances' had happened and that the manager had not thought it necessary to tell his clients when it happened. Clients have to be able to trust their managers, in the most basic sense.

Change in investment approach

A change in investment approach is a serious matter. Managers should be hired because their investment approach rings true and because the investor thinks they are the right people to carry it through. If the investment approach changes, the reason that they were hired in the first place has gone.

The most frequent reason for a change in approach is performance. Managers may worry that their approach is not working. This often happens shortly before it would have worked if stuck to.

It is a cause for concern if a manager starts to do something which is not apparently a core strength. One management firm told us one day that they were planning to use short-term instruments to try to enhance performance – which had not been good. They might write (sell) call options and buy put options. Three years before, they had emphasised the long-term nature of their portfolios and that aberrations in markets had to be disregarded. They explained this change: they had now "learned to walk" and felt they could be less rigid. But their investors, three years earlier, had not appointed them because of their walking abilities.

Another manager, of European portfolios, had been very far from an index-clinger. They did not know their active risk, which I always take to be a plus. They did not know how large a proportion of the index Nestlé was, even though it was actually a big component, around 9%. But over a period of months their portfolio came to look more and more like the index, with the same weightings. We were unhappy with this and were considering sacking them when we got a letter announcing that the whole of the team had jumped ship. We saw what they had been doing. They had been preparing for their departure, and they had been tidying up, abandoning all the positions which had represented their own convictions.

Miles Morland reflected with typical modesty and realism on Blakeney's departure from their own straight and narrow. "Initially we did very well and, by the late nineties, drunk with our own brilliance, we decided that being a passive investor was fine but how much better to be an active one." They started to take large stakes, sometimes a controlling interest, and to get involved in the strategy and management of these companies. "So brilliant were we that in 2000 and 2001 we lost 100% of our clients' investment in African Lakes and African Plantations and about 80% in Lonrho Africa." Encouraged by David Swensen of Yale to find out what they were good at, Blakeney concluded that they were "the world's worst strategic investors" but good at their basic business of identifying and buying wrongly priced stocks traded on inefficiently priced stock markets. They got back to basics.

Bad reporting

Then there is bad reporting in person. Really bad reporting, in a meeting to review the portfolio, may be a reason to be concerned, but only if it is really bad reporting by the manager. If it is really bad reporting by someone other than the manager – a relationship person, for example – it may be irritating but, just as a tremendously slick presentation by someone other than the manager should not persuade one to hire, so bad reporting by someone other than the manager should not persuade one to fire. It is not truly significant.

It is questionable anyway how often a client should want to see the manager. The job of the manager is to get on with managing. Some clients feel an obligation to see their manager from time to time and the manager can easily overrate the importance of reporting meetings. At a meeting with a group of clients I noticed that one of them was scrawling notes on the written report, and showing them to her husband. At the end of the meeting several people, she among them, left behind their papers for me to dispose of. In her papers I was enthralled to find some words written backwards in the style of Leonardo da Vinci. Anxiously I hurried to a mirror. "Adam can write backwards," I read.

Institutional clients are sometimes just going through the motions, too. As a trustee I have participated in boring sessions in which the manager pontificates, a couple of cursory questions are asked, and while the manager is shoving papers in a briefcase and getting out of the room, the meeting moves on to another subject without any discussion about the manager. This is just bureaucratic agenda-filling and is worthless.

Others really do want to see their managers. A paradox of client relations is that clients may want their manager to meet to report on progress, but not to waste time seeing any other clients. They want the manager to be concentrating on fund management, not on client relations except relations with themselves. Fund management firms struggle to resolve this paradox by providing relationship managers who do the reporting, sometimes misleadingly disguised as portfolio managers and appearing to have some part in the decision-making process, when in fact their role in any decision-making meetings is simply to be informed. There is no substitute, if you are trying to understand what goes on in the mind of a manager, for meeting the manager.

Meetings with managers – whether actually the portfolio managers or their representatives – are often full of padding. Investment managers are prone to drone on about the likely rate of growth in the economy and the rate of inflation. We seem to think this is expected of us.

These predictive liturgies are worthless and turgid, both because prediction is a hopeless task (in that very few predictors are right more than 60% of the time, and one may listen especially carefully in one of the 40% moments), and because the broad sweep of the canvas may have little to do with what actually happens in portfolios. What matters is what portfolio managers do, not what they say.

The Counter-Presentational Principle is important. A bad presenter may be a brilliant manager. A good presenter may be a hopeless manager. Alternatively, good managers may speak with the tongues of angels, but what they say may be different from what they do, which may also be good. I can think of two notably class acts, both delightful to listen to – unconventional, eloquent, provocative – and excellent managers, but what they say, tremendously persuasively, about the state of the world is only loosely connected with what they do.

It is a well-known rule of thumb that it takes longer to report bad performance than it does to report good performance. Constant late reporting may simply be the effect of poor performance – perhaps stemming from latent psychological urges to suppress or at least delay.

Total absence of reporting can be positively beneficial. In early

1975, a portfolio manager at what became one of the largest London investment management firms, later himself to be chief executive of that firm, looked at a December 1974 valuation which he was about to send out to a client who had been allowed to borrow against her portfolio and saw to his horror that the figure at the bottom was a minus number. As a result of the collapse of the UK market, down 55% in 1974, the borrowings were bigger than the much-dwindled value of the investments. Appalled, he asked a colleague what he should do.

"Tear it up," advised the colleague, later to become co-chief executive. He did.

The client never saw her valuation and never missed it. Three months later, the UK market had risen 77%. The portfolio was back in positive territory. The client got her valuation. In later generations many hedge fund managers, who similarly borrow against the assets they invest in, must have wished that such relaxed standards of reporting still prevailed.

Admin in disorder

With the 1974 client and the minus valuation, tearing up the valuation was the last resort, deliberately chosen. Bad reporting in itself signifies not much. But if reporting is full of errors and omissions it can be one of a number of indicators of more deep-rooted administrative problems which cumulatively add up to enough to be truly alarming.

There are other symptoms, such as frequent mistakes in trading, so that details of transactions have to be corrected. If the administrative malaise is bad enough to be observable on the outside, then administrative systems are probably in a state of disorder. If that is the case, it is likely to be affecting the ability of the manager to manage, and hence probably performance.

One of the most frequent causes of administrative malaise is overload. A fund management firm may take on too many portfolios of different types. If an individual manager is managing too many types at the same time, some of those types are likely to suffer. In an article in *Financial Analysts Journal*, John Bogle of Vanguard Group, looking at returns of managers in 1994–2003, found that six of the seven best performers managed 15 or fewer portfolios. The five worst performers managed an average of 39 each.

Sometimes the administrative shortfalls may be almost deliberate. I went once to see a manager in a rather inaccessible corner of Ohio – a manager with all sorts of attributes such as courage, firm convictions, a vision of the world, and a commitment to the long term which had led us to hire him. Remote Ohio, far from the madding crowd, was one of those attributes, but the fact that it is a nuisance to get there meant that I had not done so before the hiring.

Having spent some time with him, I passed the time of day with his assistant. I then discovered something about the practicalities of the way in which he managed portfolios which, if I had done my job properly, I should have found out earlier. Every day the assistant carried in to the manager a pile of portfolio valuations. Every day he went through some of those nearest the top of the pile and put on orders for transactions in those portfolios only. The assistant varied the order of the valuations in the pile, so that everyone got a look-in, but all the same this struck me as too whimsically antediluvian a process to be what consultants love to call 'robust', a much over-used jargon term. Sadly, we sacked the manager. He had done very well.

Change in ownership

Another reason to think about sacking is if the fund management firm is taken over. Firms in this position produce sophisticated explanations as to why it is in the best interests of the client to be looked after by a bigger firm. It never is. The best that can be hoped for is that it is neutral. In his newsletter on departure from Blakeney Management, Miles Morland wrote:

"Boutiques are notorious for failing to survive the departure of their founder. Most sell out just before that happens and pocket the cash, leaving the clients at the mercy of whatever behemothal asset-gatherer has just bought the firm. We have at times discussed selling the firm to one of the several people who have offered to buy us. None of the partners had the slightest interest. We are not in it for the money; we are refugees from the uniformed world, here for the game, to do something we enjoy that we believe in. It also keeps us off the streets on wet afternoons."

David Swensen, in charge of the phenomenally successful Yale University endowment fund, has a rule that if a firm which manages money for Yale is taken over it should (almost) invariably be sacked. There are exceptions when the firm continues to perform well, but much more often it does not. In his experience, the odds favour the harshest judgement.

The same rule might be applied to companies which are not taken over by another firm but instead go public, floating their shares on a stock exchange. This may be too harsh. If it is understandable that managers of money are interested in money themselves, it may be preferable for the investor that managers make a lot of money by selling some shares in their companies in a flotation rather than by extracting enormous fees directly from the investor.

Unfortunately, managers sometimes are doing both. Huge fee levels lead to huge valuations of fund management companies. In early 2007 a private equity and hedge fund management company floated its shares. A few days after the flotation the market capitalisation of the company was half the total value of its assets under management.

Almost always those selling will claim a sound business reason to sell. The business reason most frequently trotted out is that the sold firm's activities can be marketed more vigorously by the buying company than the selling company could do itself. That is understandable, but existing clients will get no benefit from this, and they may suffer. What often happens is that the investment managers who have sold become swamped with the demands on their time to make presentations to new prospective clients, and spend less time on investment.

They also have the extra administrative burdens that come with managing more money. These may be marginal, but even the mildest of unnecessary frictions may upset the delicate balance which produces good performance.

Finally, the increase in the amount of money under management may affect the manager's investment approach. This is the most serious disadvantage of acquisitions. If a manager likes to hold, typically, say 20 stocks in the portfolio, and if the average market capitalisation of each of these is say $30bn, the average percentage of each company owned will be 1% when the firm has $6bn under management. But if through vigorous marketing the funds grow to $12bn the average percentage rises to 2%, and it becomes that much more difficult to buy or sell a holding without significantly pushing the price up or down. So the manager and clients either suffer the consequences of this reduced marketability or the manager changes investment approach by buying bigger companies.

At least a principal, and sometimes the only, motivation for sale is money, not a business motivation at all. The sellers quite naturally want to release some value from the firm which they have built up. It is strange how reluctant they are to confess to this. After all, the business of investment is to increase the wealth of their clients. It should not be inadmissible to do the same for themselves. Investment managers do not have to be as heroically self-denying as the Blakeney partners. But when sales take place this motive is usually covered up. Press releases include fancy language about the synergies between the two firms, the taker-over and the taken-over, and the usefulness of the additional shared resources. Promises are made, and rarely kept, that nothing at all will change at the acquired firm.

Money itself sometimes changes things. Investment managers have investment management in their blood. They do not usually want to give it up, or find it easy to do so. But sometimes the temptations of the yacht, the golf course, or the tented safari are overwhelming, or it is just tremendously attractive not to have to continue the struggle to outperform. So managers, once they have sold, may get lazy. They may no longer have the same zest to invest that they had before.

This is often cited as a reason for deterioration in performance after managers have become rich, either through taking a big share of big fees or through selling part or all of their stake in their firm. The manager is no longer thought to be 'hungry'. No doubt this happens, but in general I suspect it does not. I can think of several managers who, despite their success, remain as committed as ever and just as anxious about performance as in the past. Such managers are concerned to do a good job for their clients, and to be seen to do a good job. They do not want to be spoken of as people who have done well for themselves but not for their clients.

Alternatively, sellers may be diverted by a sense of responsibility to the new owners. Anxious not to disappoint, they may fall into the same index-clinging trap that large firms, driven above all to conserve cash flow, fall into. Not prepared to take the risk of doing very badly, they forego the chance to do very well.

Another problem with takeovers is the effect on procedures. Investment management is no different from any other business in this. The taken-over firm may become entrenched in the more bureaucratic procedures of the large acquiring firm. If this bureaucracy encroaches into the investment management process, with committees, organisational charts and so on, it is damaging. Small is beautiful.

These factors result incidentally in takeovers being not much good for the acquiror, either. Acquirors often pay a much higher price than they should, because they over-estimate the ability of the firm they are acquiring, which presumably has done well (otherwise they would not be being acquired), to go on doing well in the new ownership. George Magan, an investment banker who was involved in many of the take-overs in the financial services sector in the UK in the 80s and 90s, told me that he had always thought investment management businesses were for selling, not for buying.

ELEVEN

Keep Your Distance

AMATEURS are nervous about their ignorance, and about their distance from the action. They tend to think distance is a disadvantage. On the contrary, while it would be overstating it to say that ignorance is bliss, too much knowledge can lead to over-confidence and information overload; and being too close to the action can lead to over-emotional decisions and hyper-activity. Distance is good. That is one reason that those amateurs interested in investing themselves, as well as choosing others to manage their portfolios, can do so.

Distance is not the same as ignorance or laziness. Professional investment managers have to spend a great deal of time thinking about investment, reading and learning. But they also want to keep some perspective and not become so enmeshed in the highly particular and the short term that they lose sight of the big picture and the long term.

In general, investment decisions should not be so fine-tuned that they require computerised modelling of the possible future, inch by inch. They should be capable of being summarised on a postcard.

This book is aimed at increasing the amateur's understanding of what the professional does. I do not want to get in a tangle by embarking on a DIY course for amateur investors who want to do some investing themselves. For full confidence to invest, more than this is needed: the guides to investing published piecemeal in *Investors Chronicle* are a good place to start.

Nonetheless the message of this chapter is that distance does not disqualify amateurs from themselves taking part, and doing well. The fact that interested amateurs are likely to be more distant from the market hurly-burly in some ways gives them an advantage to exploit.

According to Brian Tora, who writes and broadcasts on financial matters, only 18% of personal wealth in the UK is looked after, DIY, by its owners. Independent financial advisers (IFAs), banks and investment managers, accountants and solicitors do the rest. There is no reason why more should not manage their money and do respectably or better.

The visitee bias

In the old days people made money in stock markets by knowing more than others. The law, and technology, have changed this.

When my father was a stockbroker in the 1960s his firm had a winning streak when one of his partners, the former cricketer Gubby Allen, who was with the England cricket team in Australia, sent recommendations to buy shares in several Australian gold mining companies. On the spot, Allen had better information than investors in London. There was nothing suspect about what he was doing. Technology had not advanced far enough for all public information about a company to be available to all investors at the same time.

Insider trading is different: profiteering from clearly private, rather than public, information. For long frowned upon, it only became illegal in the UK in 1980.

Since then rules about what a company's management may tell some people but not others have got tighter and tighter. The result is that an investor is unlikely to find out anything which is not already widely known (even if not to that particular investor) by interviewing the chief executive or chairman or chief financial officer of a major company.

With small companies it is a bit different. In fact, I have often been amazed at hearing from what are called micro-cap managers – fund managers who specialise in investing in very small quoted companies – about their discussions with managements. Some of these discussions do seem to involve what looks at first sight like insider information, and thus information on the basis of which it is illegal to deal. But managements of large companies, under greater scrutiny and with tighter corporate governance, are unlikely to divulge anything new to one investor alone. When they want to divulge something new, they do it, in a carefully orchestrated way, to the investment world at large.

Meanwhile the ease with which information is disseminated means that there is an overload of information. With all but the smallest companies, the problem is too much information rather than too little.

When I was heading the US equity team at Mercury, I used to spend a lot of time visiting companies in America. But I came increasingly to wonder how useful these trips were. I saw Wal-Mart in Arkansas regularly. In those days – the mid to late 80s – it was reasonably easy for the representative of quite a large European fund management firm to get an appointment with the chief financial officer. I remember sitting in his office and admiring its frugality. It was a tiny room, with linoleum on the floor rather than carpet. The CFO pointed to his car in the car park, a seasoned old Ford of some sort. (I wondered if there was a Ferrari in his garage at home.)

All this was very reassuring. It testified to the admirably cost-conscious ethos of Sam Walton, the founder of Wal-Mart and an entrepreneur full of home-spun wisdom. I always returned home convinced that Wal-Mart was worth a price-earnings ratio at least two higher than the present one. But was it? I wonder.

Investors are vulnerable to what I call a visitee bias – the feeling that the company you have visited is worth more than the company you have not visited, simply by virtue of the fact of having done the visiting. This bias is made more likely by the fact that most people in top management positions are very compelling and persuasive. This is not surprising since it is one of the attributes which have got them to the top. The one thing, therefore, they nearly all have in common is the ability to spin a good line about their company.

There may be value in meeting managements and visiting companies just as there is in other sorts of research in the field. But the net benefit is open to question on two counts. First, the law and technology make it more unlikely than in previous eras that the investor can discover anything from these visits and meetings which is not already in the public domain, and if it is in the public domain it should be discounted in the share price. Second, charming chief executives can be dangerously persuasive.

These strictures apply as much to whole markets as to individual companies. It is quite possible to go to Russia and come away more cautious than before, but my own experience, having been lured by the romantic charm of the country, is to come back enthusiastic. But even in reverse the visiting can affect the judgement excessively. Twenty-four hours in Shanghai turns one into an instant expert. One jumps confidently to conclusions from which, at a safe distance, one might have shied away, and these conclusions are no more likely to be right than they would have been without the visit. Travel can narrow the mind.

Premature beatification of chief executives

Even in an era in which information was not so easily disseminated, Benjamin Graham, author of *The Intelligent Investor* which is the first gospel of value investing, felt it was prejudicial to meet managements or visit companies, and had a rule never to do so. He liked just to look at the figures.

Most investors will be reluctant to go quite so far as this. They may not want to run away from the opportunity to meet managements. Personal knowledge of individual company heads can sometimes be a helpful influence on decisions. Meetings with Lee Iacocca (chairman of Chrysler), Rupert Murdoch (News Corporation) and Hank Greenberg (AIG) made an impression on me.

With Iacocca and Greenberg, the atmosphere of deference amongst their immediate subordinates was overwhelming. I am sure none of them would like to have this atmosphere described as one of fear, but that was the impression. Even the most senior people referred to Iacocca as 'the chairman'. They did not call him by his first name. With Greenberg it was the same. When he swept into a conference room there was a palpable stiffening.

Incidentally, too much Mister This and Mister That is something to be wary of in looking at investment managers too. The presentation document for a fund launched by the veteran, extremely successful, US investor Carl Icahn refers to him reverentially throughout as Mr Icahn – Mr Icahn's team, Mr Icahn's philosophy. Investment managers should not be revered (except Mr Buffett). If they are revered, it is more than likely that they are riding for a fall.

Markets, representing the consensus of investors, are fickle. They cast aside quite readily old heroes and create new ones. One of the factors which prompted our firm to sell Renault shares in 2006 and to buy (more) Microsoft was the market's reverential attitude to Carlos Ghosn, the chairman of Renault, and its suspicion by contrast of anything which the Microsoft management dreamed up. Carlos Ghosn had worked miracles at Nissan in Japan before he returned to Paris to lead Renault (which owns 44% of Nissan). In the market's eyes he could do no wrong. Bill Gates and Steve Ballmer at Microsoft could do no right. Premature beatification of chief executives is a condition to be wary of.

Fear of a mighty chief executive is especially unhealthy. Autocratic decision-making is efficient and often desirable, but the autocrat needs to make an especial effort not to be feared. Otherwise, no one will dare to disagree. With Rupert Murdoch it was different. Everyone calls him Rupert. No one is afraid to disagree. Though he is indeed autocratic and comes to his own conclusions, the freedom to disagree makes it more likely that he will have a decent debate before he makes a decision.

Such vignettes can be instructive. But on the whole acquaintance with managements serves merely to confirm investors in views which the managements want them to have rather than to encourage objectivity.

Joel Greenblatt, author of *The Little Book That Beats The Market*, agrees:

"I used to meet CEOs and say to myself: 'This guy is smart.' Next day I met another CEO and said to myself: 'This guy is smart, too.' In the end, I feel meeting CEOs is not very important because I am not good at reading people."

Another wise commentator is Whitney Tilson, editor of *Value Investor Insight*. In the newsletter *The Motley Fool*, commenting on one successful manager, he wrote:

"The importance of having access to company managements and making site visits is way overblown. In fact, this too can work against an investor's interests. (There's an unfortunate amount of truth to the joke about how can you tell when a CEO is lying? His lips are moving.) Through the internet, Francesco can access all of the information he needs to make informed decisions, and his remote location [in the south of Italy] isolates him from the sound and fury (read: nonsense) of Wall Street. You can be sure that CNBC (Bubblevision) isn't blaring in his office, and since the US market doesn't open until 3.30 in the afternoon here, he has nearly the entire day to read and do analysis."

Short-termism hurts performance

There is another sense in which it is important for the investor to keep his distance, more so now than ever. Proximity encourages short-termism.

Short-termism tends to damage performance as some of the studies mentioned in Chapter 7 have revealed. At the very least those who buy and sell frequently have to stump up the extra costs in commissions of this trading. But, more fundamentally, a lot of trading is generally the habit of those who are buffeted around by the whims of the market. Only a small minority of investors are such able traders that they can do better than they would if they moved less often.

William Donaldson, former chairman of the Securities & Exchange Commission in the US, has remarked that "speaking out on the need for a longer-term approach to investment analysis is akin to speaking out in favour of baseball, hot dogs, and apple pie – it is something (almost) everyone supports in an abstract way." But in practice most professional investors act differently.

Short-termism among most provides the greatest opportunity for the rest. Those who are not short-termist may do better in the medium and long term; but they may even do better in the short term too, because they will not be a slave to momentum in the way that is almost unavoidable in a highly short-term environment.

Some 25 years ago the famous investor Sir John Templeton was quoted saying that it was a great advantage that his firm was located in the Bahamas, because the newspapers arrived a day late. This meant that he could not react to yesterday's news, because he did not know what it was. No doubt even when he said this it was a wild exaggeration. Someone told me that he had been spotted once sitting on a bench outside the chapel at Lyford Cay reading the *Wall Street Journal*. Perhaps it was an issue two days old. In any case, the principle is important.

Research in the Bahamas

Only the very first finger on the button stands any chance of benefiting from a piece of news once published. In these days of instant communication, any news which reaches the general public can be regarded as reaching enough of them immediately and simultaneously for it to be instantly reflected in share prices.

There is no point in trying to react instantly to published news. Yet that is what most of the investment world does. In the over-populated investment world of the City of London and Wall Street, the focus is on what has just happened – yesterday's earnings announcements, yesterday's and the last ten minutes' stock price movements. There is an overwhelming compulsion to do things, and generally speaking to do things in the direction in which the market has just moved.

The great battle in investment is to avoid becoming more enthusiastic about something which has just done well and to avoid becoming more gloomy about something which has just done badly. This is hard, because human beings like togetherness. To hold a view alone is uncomfortable. But in investment it is axiomatic that if all are enthusiastic they are wrong.

So it is important to treat a share price which has fallen as, *prima facie*, more interesting than it was before it fell. The expected return of an asset rises as its price falls. This is straightforward enough. But we naturally tend to become more enthusiastic when things have gone well and to become gloomier when things have gone badly. Trying to do the opposite is hard, and it is especially hard amidst the noisy peer pressures and short-termist obsessions of the City and Wall Street.

It is much easier to look at a fallen share price with equanimity in an environment far removed from these frenetic places. The Bahamas, for instance; or Omaha, Nebraska, home of Warren Buffett; or Henley-on-Thames where Martyn Arbib founded Perpetual Funds; or even Edinburgh.

In my early years of investing, while learning about it at a wonderful place to learn, I always imagined that the best place to run money would be in a garage in Battersea, happening as I did to own a garage in Battersea at the time. Only after I was 40 was I able to retreat to the equivalent, at least metaphorically, of a garage in Battersea.

Investors in places remote from the City frenzy are arguably at a huge advantage. They are more likely to be able to use commonsense. An investor may have all the inclinations to be anti-short-termist and commonsensical and dispassionate; but if in the wrong environment, an environment of ferocious activity and noise, the chances of being so are diminished.

Information minimalism

For the same reason those who get rid of the Bloomberg or Reuters machine, or any other machine which tells one stock prices, from their desks feel a sense of liberation. Those who have these machines stare at them for half the day, mesmerised. Many of us know how we behave when we stay in hotels and watch CNN, transfixed by the moving belt of share prices at the bottom of the screen, and even when the market concerned is closed watching the same stock symbols and same stock prices coming round again and again like an ever-optimistic victim of lost luggage watching the baggage carousel hopelessly long after everyone else's luggage has been and gone.

But worse than the idiotic distraction and waste of time, staring at the Bloomberg machine impels people to do all sorts of things which are better left undone. Indolence can be constructive. Distance is an underrated advantage.

A *Wall Street Journal* article in 2005 captured vividly the modus operandi of Warren Buffett. One summer day,

> "Warren Buffett … received a faxed letter about a company he had never heard of. Mr Buffett liked what he saw. The next day, Mr Buffett offered to buy Forest River. He sealed the deal in a 20 minute meeting one week later. He spends most of his time alone in an office with no computer. He makes swift investment decisions, steers clear of meetings and advisers, eschews set procedures. On a recent Wednesday, he received only 13 phone calls, including one wrong number."

Buffett himself wrote, in the 2006 Annual Report of Berkshire Hathaway, about his friend Walter Schloss, who managed a remarkably successful investment partnership between 1956 and 2002 (when he was 86). "His office contained one file cabinet in 1956; the number mushroomed to four by 2002. Walter worked without a secretary, clerk or bookkeeper, his only associate being his son, Edwin."

Doing without Bloomberg, or basing oneself in Omaha or its metaphorical equivalent, naturally does not ensure success. But it does provide a distinct, and easily achievable, advantage in encouraging the investor to focus on the things which matter – information minimalism.

TWELVE

The Folly of Forecasting

M ANAGING money does not involve tremendous prescience. It requires the commonsense to be doubtful about the flawed prescience of others.

Forecasting markets

One of the things which investment managers are expected to do is to make predictions. James and Alvilde Lees-Milne, writers and aesthetes, were once accosted by their neighbour and landlord the late Duke of Beaufort, furious after their dogs had caused some disturbance to his hunting. "What is the point of you Lees-Milnes? You don't shoot, you don't hunt. What is the blasted point of you?" Sensible investment managers who refused to predict might feel somewhat in the position, *mutatis mutandis*, of the Lees-Milnes. "You don't make predictions, you don't meet managements. What is the point of you?" If they timidly responded that they looked at valuations and thought about probabilities, the Duke would have regarded this as intolerably limp-wristed.

Christmas especially is a silly season for news in which the newspapers are full of quizzes about what happened and predictions about what will happen. But predicting happens to be something which human beings are not very good at doing, and no one has yet discovered the machine which will do it better. Someone said that the secret of making good predictions is to make them long-term, and make them often. Alternatively, if you give a date, give no numbers; and if you give numbers, give no date. The chances of being rumbled are thereby reduced.

In stock markets forecasts have a remarkably poor record, much worse than the medium-term weather forecasts which the Nobel laureate Kenneth Arrow was forced to make and found were no better than randomly right. Yet everyone still wants a forecast, and every pundit provides one. One of the worst recent years for punditry was 2002. As usual at the end of the previous year the *Sunday Times* asked ten leading firms to forecast the level of the FTSE 100 at the end of the year. Here are the results:

Pundit	Prediction for end 2002
Deutsche Bank	6200
NatWest Stockbrokers	5800
Credit Suisse	5900
Morgan Stanley	6000
Legal & General	6000
Barclays Stockbrokers	5800
UBS Warburg	5750
HSBC	5700
Gerrard	6350
Merrill Lynch	5500

The actual index level was 3940. Not one was within 25% of the outturn.

The usefulness of market forecasting surveys is as contrary indicators. If everyone is bullish, everyone is invested. If everyone is bearish, everyone is underinvested – hence the usefulness of something like the Investors Intelligence Survey of Advisory Sentiment as an inverse indicator, not much help except when there are extreme measurements, but at extremes extremely useful. When nobody can think of a kind word to say about markets, it is time to buy.

In practice, these measures are difficult to act on because at moments of severe bearishness all investors tend to have the same colly-wobbles. The investor needs to be disciplined enough to recognise that his or her own gloom is the same as everyone else's, and that therefore any surprise is likely to be a nice one.

Economic and earnings forecasts

While in aggregate unanimous forecasts about markets are bound, because of the nature of markets, to be completely wrong, this is not true of economic forecasting. Nonetheless, economic forecasting is notoriously unreliable, much more so than one might expect, perhaps because of what John Kay describes in the *Financial Times* as "naïve extrapolation." Roy Jenkins regarded the UK Treasury's forecasts as worthless, though they had become "almost a fetish among the mandarins."

Earnings forecasts by stock market analysts are, in aggregate, just as useless. Morgan Stanley compared the aggregate expectations for earnings growth in the US technology sector year by year with the actual outturn:

	Start-of-year growth expectations	**Actual growth**
1986	22.9%	-6.1%
1987	+21.7	+35.8
1988	+23.5	+13.2
1989	+12.8	-21.3
1990	+14.0	-15.7
1991	+10.8	-32.7
1992	+42.6	-1.3
1993	+23.2	+16.2
1994	+22.2	+66.6
1995	+23.5	+41.7
1996	+22.8	+6.1
1997	+24.4	+16.3
1998	+20.0	+12.7
1999	+29.3	+32.2
2000	+28.6	+27.6
2001	+1.2	-62.9
2002	+49.8	-3.3

In only six out of 25 years were the aggregate forecasts within 10% of the right number, and in seven out of 25 years the aggregate was more than 25% wild.

Although for each year there may be one or two outliers who predict something radically different from the average, most like to stick pretty close to the average. This is for two reasons. First, they cannot be too ridiculed if their forecast is not much worse than anyone else's. Second, in many cases they are merely parroting the 'guidance' about prospective earnings which major companies give. The companies themselves make forecasts which turn out to be wrong. It is easier to repeat the company's forecast, with a little tweak here and there, than risk the isolation, with less information than the company has, of a radically different figure.

Long-term forecasting about the most important big picture issues is just as suspect as quarterly or annual detailed earnings forecasts. Thomas Watson of IBM memorably opined in 1943 that, "I think there is a world market for maybe five computers." A Western Union internal note in 1876 concluded that "the 'telephone' has too many shortcomings to be seriously considered as a means of communication." Marshal Foch regarded airplanes "as interesting toys, but of no military value", in 1911. H.M. Warner of Warner Bros. asked in 1927, "Who the hell wants to hear actors talk?"

An alternative method

In August 1996, the *Wall Street Journal* published a letter from a student at Middlebury College.

"Your semi-annual survey of economists has come and gone (July 1) and I was not included again. This is a shame because I have developed a complex economic model for predicting the yield on the 30-year Treasury bond. Much of the process is proprietary, but I will share some of the details. I first gather all sorts of economic data … I then contact Eleanor Roosevelt to get her thoughts on the mood of the Federal Reserve. And finally, and this is most important, I reach into my left pocket, pull out a 1993 Canadian penny and flip it.

Astute readers will no doubt argue that my model gets the direction of long-term rates correct only about half the time. To these cynics I point out that there have been 29 surveys conducted since the *Wall Street Journal* began asking economists for their 30-year Treasury bond forecast. The consensus estimate of these highly paid economists for the 30-year bond has been in the wrong direction in 20 of these 29 surveys. Furthermore, 43 economists have participated in ten or more surveys. Only 13, or

30% have gotten the direction correct more than half the time, with only one economist breaking the 60% accuracy barrier.

Interest-rate forecasts are most important when the interest-rate movements are large, and this is where my model shines. The yield of the 30-year Treasury bond has ended up or down more than 100 basis points during the six-month prediction period on more than ten occasions. The economists' consensus forecast (and I use this term loosely) was in the right direction only twice. My model has predicted the right direction, believe it or not, in five of 10 periods."

Why bother? This kind of record shows that reality has very little to do with forecasting. The investor who acts on the basis of forecasts is unlikely to do spectacularly well. But the thirst for forecasts is so great, the same thirst which makes astrology so popular, that the game continues. The investor who stands aside from the forecasting maelstrom is likely to do better.

When I was at Mercury Asset Management I had a Japanese colleague (who has gone on to great success elsewhere). He was an excellent stock-picker. He was promoted to be head of his team, in part an admin role which did not suit him at all. He was required to come over to London every quarter to join our quarterly strategy meetings, an elaborate process of solemn prognostication. This was not at all his cup of tea. Asked to opine on some large issue of the moment, he often took some time to produce an answer. Then it would come. "Nobody know," he would declare.

This conclusion often reverberates in my mind. The most confidently produced forecasts may seem quite unchallengeable. But it is the nature of the unchallengeable that the view is universally shared. If it is universally shared, it is discounted in markets. And it may turn out to be wrong, so that markets can only be surprised by a forecast not coming true.

Forecasting the inevitable

There are some sorts of prediction which can be guaranteed to turn out right, eventually. A stopped clock tells the right time twice a day. Every year that an earthquake does not happen in Tokyo or San Francisco makes an earthquake more likely to happen, and more severely, the subsequent year, because there is an inevitability about the consequences of tectonic plate movements.

Many people have regarded the position of the US economy as earthquake-like. The growth in debt of US consumers was made possible by low interest rates and a housing bubble, which ultimately had to explode, and began to in 2006. In early 2007, the default rate on low quality loans rose alarmingly. There is certainly the possibility that, with these two pressures, consumer spending could fall sharply, damaging the stock market.

The problem with this sort of forecast, as with those for earthquakes, is the problem of timing. When will it happen? "Nobody know." Everyone regards the position as unsustainable. The Chinese and the Japanese central banks have been supporting the US dollar for years, which has allowed interest rates (especially of long-term bonds) to remain much lower than they should be (and the yen much weaker), which in turn has kept the housing bubble inflating and the economy growing, and consumers buying Chinese goods.

Investors react to this differently. The glass-half-empty type say that a position which is unsustainable will not be sustained; the Chinese and Japanese will drop their support for the dollar and the house of cards will collapse.

The glass-half-full type argue that since it is in everyone's interests for the show to continue, it will – even though that means that the severity of the ultimate earthquake could be worse. This view is abetted by the surreptitious suspicion that, although it is obvious that the end must be disastrous, some *deus ex machina* will intervene to change the ending. Things very frequently have a way of unexpectedly sorting themselves out.

Reversion to the mean

Another sort of prediction which can be guaranteed to be right is the sort which cheered up Daddy Warbucks in the musical Annie – "the sun will come out tomorrow," sang the eponymous heroine – and which propelled Chauncey Gardener to the confidences of the President of the United States in *Being There*.

Chauncey, an illiterate gardener, responded to questions about Keynesian economics with habitual conviction on a limited number of topics: "There will be growth in the Spring." Fed up with the verbose obfuscations of experts, the President greeted this as a profound truth.

Anyone who believes in the certainty of cycles, and in reversion to the mean, will see the point of Chauncey Gardener. The mathematician Francis Galton originated the notion of reversion to the mean; the idea that when, in a series of measurements, there is a movement far away from the average of that series, the next few numbers are likely to see a move back towards the average. In the investment world that means that when price-earnings ratios are well above average they are likely to come down towards the average; when market returns have been abnormally high, they are more likely to come down towards the long-term average than they are to continue going up.

Movements well away from trend can go on for longer than expected. But in due course, the further distant from the mean the movement has been, the greater the move in order to get back to the mean. The elastic can stretch surprisingly far, but in the end it snaps back.

These rules have been fundamental to market behaviour. Reversion to the mean has been described as the most important four words in investment, a counter-poise to the four words described by John Templeton as the most dangerous, "this time it's different."

By way of example, any investors of a Galtonian disposition would have pricked up their ears when they read Chris Dillow's article in

Investors Chronicle in April 2005. Dillow reported that a notional low-risk fund which he had created had outperformed all 276 managed UK equity unit trusts in the most recent quarter, all but five such funds over the past year, and all but four over the past five years. The sole basis on which he had constructed his portfolio was to achieve low volatility. The conclusion Dillow draws is that "fund managers are institutionally stupid": the industry is "staffed by morons" or so structured that it is "incapable of doing its job."

Be that as it may, as Miss Marple would say, the really interesting thing about the Dillow fund performance was what it suggested about the future. The Dillow fund was simply the set of large UK stocks, revised each quarter, which minimised the quarterly volatility of historic returns. The conclusion a Galtonian fund manager would draw was that, if in the past few years a very low volatility portfolio had outperformed almost every other, there was an overwhelming probability that in the next few years the opposite would be the case. If high volatility portfolios were to outperform, that in itself suggested a favourable outlook for the UK market as a whole.

In addition to reversion to the mean, a theory applied first to the height of humans from generation to generation, Galton also originated an unpleasant theory of eugenics, taken up among others by H.G.Wells and Lord Rosebery.

Galton was a cousin of Charles Darwin. In the investment world there is an aptness about this pairing of cousins since simplistically those who believe in reversion to the mean can be characterised as value managers, while growth managers are more inclined to the survival of the fittest, and to the view that the strong get stronger.

THIRTEEN

Valuation Matters

THERE are different ways of managing money, just as there are, purportedly, many ways of skinning a cat. My friend Charles Elliott had a formidable record as an analyst at Goldman Sachs. The word discovery is over-used in the investment world, but he can claim to have discovered, with a handful of other professionals, Nintendo, SAP and TomTom, all companies which produced dazzling growth in the years thereafter. At the party given for him when he left Goldman Sachs to set up a hedge fund in early 2007, one of his former colleagues pointed out that the price of Nintendo had risen 40 times since he first recommended it in the early 1980s. Charles quietly corrected him. "440 times, actually."

In his valedictory speech Charles Elliott told us:

"For me, the greatest fun has always been in identifying emerging growth companies, which might be tenbaggers or even hundredbaggers [i.e. companies whose share prices multiply ten or a hundred times]. Normally, companies like this do not have a really new, cutting edge product or service – they just have the first version which works, and can be commercialised. Typically, their valuations – relative to the earnings they will really generate – are quite low, partly because it is hard to see how high those earnings will be, partly because the first iteration which works is the fourth or fifth iteration of the product, and investors remember the previous failures and simultaneously worry about commoditisation. Rather than greed or fear, the strongest driver to investment is hope."

That is one way of doing it. No professional investor can be utterly dogmatic because so frequently what works in one period fails in another, and equally what one investor can make work brilliantly another will make a disastrous failure.

One of the sharpest thinkers in the investment business is Jeremy Grantham, founder of the fund management firm GMO. Fiercely intelligent about the theory but also rigorously empirical, he found in the 1990s that his approach, based on value and on the likelihood of reversion to the mean, was not working. It might well, eventually, have worked. But he was not sure that he or his clients could wait long enough.

He therefore incorporated in his quantitative models an element of momentum: most of the decision-making was still based on valuation, but a small proportion depended on momentum, in other words on whether the share price of the company under review had already started to move in the right direction. To the committed value investor – which he is – this is close to anathema, but he was pragmatic enough to acknowledge what his observations were telling him about what worked in practice. Momentum remains part of the GMO model.

Another successful manager, specialising in small US companies, has explained to me that his approach relies overwhelmingly on finding low valuations but that among the other factors he pays attention to are insider buying and momentum, in combination. Insider buying is (legal) buying by directors. Not surprisingly, insiders tend to know how their companies are doing. While the positive views of outsiders, in aggregate, are an inverse indicator, the positive views of insiders are a positive indicator.

But this manager has found that, perhaps especially in small companies, insiders have a tendency to be over-optimistic about the prospects for their companies and are inclined to buy their shares when the price falls, even if as it turns out business is going sour. He therefore looks also at momentum: if a director is prepared to buy shares which have already gone up a good deal, it tends to be a more reliable indicator.

So there are many ways of approaching investment, and different people are temperamentally suited to doing it in different ways. It is still fair to generalise that over the long term investors have an advantage if they keep their distance, are sceptical of predictions, and focus on a few simple measures of valuation and commonsense basic analysis of a business. It is perfectly possible for managers who are quite the opposite to do well, and many do. It is just harder.

This final chapter does not go into 'how to' detail, but does attempt to explain why the value approach works.

Distinguishing between value and growth managers

People who manage equity portfolios are frequently categorised, and the two most frequently applied categories are value and growth.

The simple distinction between value and growth is that a value manager is interested primarily in stocks with low price-earnings ratios, price-book ratios and price-sales ratios while growth managers are interested primarily in stocks which have high historic rates of growth in earnings. The latter tend to have relatively high price-earnings, price-book, and price-sales ratios, because the investor is prepared to pay up now for the prospect of high growth in the future.

Value managers are natural sceptics. They can be tiresomely argumentative and curmudgeonly. Growth managers are optimists, looking for the best in everything and everybody, and are much nicer to meet at a party.

The entrepreneur and journalist Luke Johnson made this same distinction in a slightly different context. In an article in the *Sunday*

Telegraph he divided capitalists into two types: those who believe in goodwill and those who trust only hard assets.

> "The former are more interested in growth, while the latter prefer income and security. Goodwill investors are perhaps more likely to be dreamers who have faith in a bright future, while asset investors tend to adopt a conservative outlook and regard positive projections with cynicism … Of the two richest men in the world, Gates is clearly a goodwill investor. Warren Buffett is a classic 'margin of safety' man …When both men are long gone … Gates, the entrepreneur, will be remembered, while Buffett, the financier, will soon be forgotten."

Johnson was speaking of businessmen, but the same distinctions apply to growth investors and value investors.

In the US the distinctions between growth and value investors are long established and generally accepted. Many managers do not mind too much being described as one or the other. Others are more wary, and place themselves in a middle of the road category, growth at the right price, acronym GARP.

In the UK there is much greater reluctance to accept this pigeon-holing. Managers frequently talk of the need to be flexible, according to market circumstances, and cavil at these simplistic categorisations.

Many managers are genuinely hard to pigeon-hole, but there are many others who are recognisably either value or growth. Some managers always think first about the valuation, and only second about likely rates of growth; and other managers think almost exclusively about prospects for growth, and just about ignore valuations.

No such thing as a value stock

While there is such a thing as a value manager, there is not necessarily such a thing as a value stock. At different times, companies trade in the stock market at different levels of valuation. In early 2005, I read

Pioneering Portfolio Management by David Swensen, in charge of the Yale University endowment fund for the last 22 hugely successful years. In it he suggested that, if you found a 'value' manager talking about Coca-Cola or Microsoft, you should run for the hills. This struck a sensitive chord as we owned Microsoft. But Swensen was writing in 1999. The price-earnings ratios of Coca-Cola and Microsoft at the end of 1999 were respectively 47 and 72. In early 2005, they were both around 20.

At about the same time I read that if you owned a portfolio of six US blue chip stocks, Coca-Cola, Microsoft, Pfizer, Colgate-Palmolive, IBM and Wal-Mart, your return since March 2003 would have been zero, while the return of the US market as a whole in that time (measured by the Standard & Poor's Index) was over 50%. The price-earnings ratio of these stocks, on average, at the end of 1999 was 50; in early 2005, the average was under 20.

So, valuations change. The table below shows the companies which were the top 10, in terms of market capitalisation, in the US in 1998, with their price-earnings ratios then and in 2006.

Company	PE 1998	PE 2006
Microsoft	77.9	18.9
General Electric	36.4	18.4
Intel	34.7	13.5
Wal–Mart	42.2	16.3
Exxon	28.3	11.5
Merck	34.3	17.7
IBM	28.1	15.1
Coca–Cola	47.9	21.3
Pfizer	63.1	17.9
Cisco	79.4	20.3

In 2000, many excellent companies with strong balance sheets, strong historic rates of growth, and consistent growth, were extremely cheap. This was because at the height of the tech bubble so many portfolio managers flocked to the exotic, leaving these other companies relatively neglected. Companies like Reckitt Benckiser, Federal Express, and Emerson Electric were all on price-earnings multiples in low double digits.

Later, after the tech bubble had burst, there were value opportunities even in the tech sector, which is normally regarded as the epitome of growth. Samsung Electronic, the Korean technology company, had a price-earnings ratio of only four. So, a value manager can often find attractive opportunities in sectors and companies which are normally seen as growth, but which for some reason have fallen out of favour as a result of the excesses of enthusiasm and gloom in the markets.

Value managers outperform

In the short term, anything can happen. Expensive stocks can get more expensive, and cheap stocks can get cheaper. But over the long term there is abundant evidence that valuation matters, as commonsense suggests it should. On average value managers have, over the long term, outperformed growth managers (which is not of course the same as saying that all value managers outperform or that all growth managers underperform).

A study by Morgan Stanley showed that, between August 1997 and May 2005, value stocks (those on low price-book ratios) outperformed growth stocks by 2.6% per annum in the UK and by 3.5% per annum globally. August 1997 was not a starting date chosen to make the results favour the value argument. It was then that Eugene Fama and Kenneth French published a paper in which they showed that value outperformed growth around the world in the years 1975–1995.

In 1992, the venerable value managers Tweedy, Browne Company published *What has worked in investing*, a summary of several dozen different studies, based on different countries' markets and over different time periods. These studies showed that buying companies which had low price-book value ratios, low price-earnings ratios, or low price-cash flow ratios, or whose share prices had gone down most, was nearly always, over any period of more than a few years, much more successful than doing the opposite. The only other successful strategy which they identified was buying shares in companies in which insiders – directors or executives of the companies themselves – are also buying. Tweedy, Browne's conservatively stated conclusion was:

> "Unlike science, where two parts hydrogen and one part oxygen always produce water, the partners do not believe there is an investment formula that *always* produces an exceptional return over every period of time. However, there have been recurring and often interrelated patterns of investment success *over very long periods of time*. Tweedy, Browne believes it is likely that many of the investments which will generate exceptional rates of return in the future, over long measurement periods, will possess one or several of the characteristics which have previously been associated with exceptional returns."

Why value goes on working

The cynic spots at once that anything which has been found to work in investment management should stop working. Nonetheless, Joel Greenblatt, author of *The Little Book That Beats the Market*, explains why value investing may continue to work.

> "It is hard for people to do, for two main reasons. First, the companies that show up on the screens can be scary and not doing so well, so people find them difficult to buy. Second, there can be one-, two-, or three-year periods when a strategy such as this doesn't work. Most people aren't capable of sticking it through that."

Seth Klarman of Baupost says the same thing:

"If the entire country became securities analysts, memorised Benjamin Graham's Intelligent Investor and regularly attended Warren Buffett's annual shareholder meetings, most people would, nevertheless, find themselves irresistibly drawn to hot initial public offerings, momentum strategies and investment fads. A country of security analysts would still overreact. In short, even the best-trained investors would make the same mistakes that investors have been making forever, and for the same immutable reason – that they cannot help it."

One reason for the vulnerability of growth investing, by contrast, is that in general investors tend to be too optimistic about the ability of companies to grow. The number of companies for which earnings growth is expected by the average analyst to be consistently more than 20% per annum is enormous, but the number of companies which actually achieve more than 20% growth is tiny. To score 20% every single year is virtually impossible. Bank of Ireland Asset Management found that over five years 10% of US companies clocked up 20% growth in each year; over ten years, 3% of companies; over 15 years, none.

Moreover, optimism about the future grows with success in the past. So, the expected five-year earnings growth rate in the US technology sector rose from 11% in 1992 to 21% in 2000 – when the bubble burst. In some companies the optimism was simply absurd, and the managements realised it and tried to dispel it, but could not. Scott McNealy, chairman of Sun Microsystems, tried in 2002 to placate shareholders:

"Two years ago we were selling at 10 times revenues when we were at $64 [share price]. At 10 times revenues, to give you a 10-year payback, I have to pay you 100% of revenues for 10 straight years in dividends. That assumes I have zero cost of goods sold, which is very hard for a computer company. That assumes zero expenses, which is really hard with 39,000 employees. That assumes I pay no taxes, which is very hard. And that assumes you pay no taxes on your dividends, which is kind of illegal. Now, having done that, would any of you like to buy my stock at $64? Do you realise how ridiculous those basic assumptions are? You don't need any transparency. You don't need any footnotes. What were you thinking?"

At the table in the investment casino marked Growth, the banker sweeps away a disproportionate amount of the money staked, because expectations are so frequently disappointed. At the table marked Value, the banker is more generous. He shovels, albeit erratically and unpredictably, money in the direction of the punters, because stocks which are genuinely cheap, in terms of the usual ratios, frequently provide to the investor a margin of safety.

This margin of safety will not stop things going wrong. Occasionally they go disastrously wrong, as what looks cheap turns out to be what is called a value trap, where the cheapness turns out to be for a very good reason, and the stock gets cheaper and cheaper. But more generally, companies with low valuations turn out to have had exaggeratedly gloomy expectations discounted in the share price.

At the least, the margin of safety is a help when the price, notwithstanding its cheapness, falls further. Investors remember why they invested in the first place, and that can be useful in preventing them doing something silly when the price has already gone down.

With a stock selling at a high valuation it is much more difficult to know what to do when things go wrong. To buy, for example, Google or eBay at say 70 or 80 times earnings requires a huge confidence that all will continue to go swimmingly. If these companies falter at all, it will be hard to understand why they should – even if they continue to grow reasonably strongly – sell at 70 rather than, say, 30 or 40 times earnings, still a valuation level which requires very strong future growth to be justified. But there is an enormous variation in share price if it is 30 or 40 which turns out to be justified, rather than 70 or 80.

This does not mean that it is always wrong to buy Google at 70 or 80 times earnings. One or two companies will turn out to be truly exceptional. But most, on extravagant valuations, will not. They only have these extravagant valuations because investors extrapolate the recent past.

The extrapolation flaw

Extrapolation is one of the fatal flaws of stock market behaviour. The word itself has been firmly in my mind as a thing to be wary of since I attended a company meeting with investors in the late 1970s. After some gung-ho presentation, an investment manager who had enjoyed his lunch became rather obstreperous. "But can you extrapolate?" he demanded of the chief executive, loudly and repeatedly. The chief executive was evidently greatly relieved when this manager seemed to be off, calling after him cheerily, "have a nice one", as the manager disappeared through a door. A few minutes later the manager reappeared. He had merely been to the gents. He resumed his rumbustious questioning about the extrapolation.

Investors (and managers) often extrapolate unreasonably. They assume that what has been will be. Often it will not. The English company Rentokil was a good example of this tendency. For years Clive Thompson assured the markets that the company could grow consistently at 20% a year. For years it did. Twenty percent became an article of faith. A moment when the cynic might have become especially suspicious was when this stock appeared in the portfolio of an excellent US investment management firm for the first time, the first non-US company which they had held in their US equity portfolios. It was a sign of too-ready acceptance, an acceptance which had spread outside the home market, that the company grew by 20% as a matter of course.

Soon after, Rentokil missed its 20% target, and it went on missing. The stock fell sharply. The same problem afflicted the largest company in the world, General Electric, which under Jack Welch chalked up 20% earnings growth year after year as regular as clockwork. The valuation reflected the confidence that this was natural and probable. Then one day it grew no longer at 20%. Disappointed expectations drove the share price down.

Tainted shares

Conversely, the greatest opportunities of all for value investors are when a stock has been tainted by a succession of exceptionally awful events. When I first began to take an interest in the stock market, at the age of 16 or 17, the shares which caught my eye were those whose prices were just a few pence. I did not know at the time that there were lots of investment clubs and newsletters devoted to this genre of investing, known as penny shares. But intuitively I felt that if a share price was just a few pence, things must be very rough. The company might go to pieces, but it might instead recover, and if it recovered then the share price might go up a good deal. There would be much more mileage in the shares of a company which recovered from near-extinction than in those of a company which did well and continued to do well, or so I reasoned, I think.

My first ever investment, at the age of 18 or so, was in a company called Britannia Arrow. I knew little about it except that it represented the remnants of Slater Walker and therefore nobody cared for it very much. It was tainted, because Slater Walker had gone bankrupt in the secondary banking crisis in the early 1970s. As it happened, I made a good profit. That set me on the road I have taken ever since, which is to prefer to invest in companies about which investors generally are unhappy and which have at least potential, sometimes disappointed, for improvement, than in companies about which the investing world is already enthusiastic.

The tendency of the stock market to taint excessively when something goes wrong is well established in behavioural psychology. Gloomy extrapolation is the other side of the coin from enthusiastic extrapolation. It springs especially from the short-termism of the markets and of most investors.

In 2002, for example, Vivendi hit the rocks. Originally a prosaic water utility, Compagnie Générale des Eaux, this company had been on an orgy of acquisition under the leadership of its charismatic, energetic chairman Jean-Marie Messier, who in that year published his autobiography entitled *J6M.com*. This was a reference, perhaps not as ironic as it should have been, to his nickname, Jean-Marie Messier, Moi-Même, Maître du Monde. The company had borrowed far too much and was in trouble with its banks.

In July 2002, Messier was ejected and replaced by Jean-René Fourtou. In the same month, Fourtou agreed a new banking facility with Vivendi's main banker, Crédit Lyonnais. This was a very encouraging sign. At the time the net assets of the company were reckoned to be in the region of €30 per share. Yet the share price was €13.

Why the extraordinary gap between share price and value? There was some criticism of Fourtou for not declaring his strategy, but he was playing a game of poker in which it was important to quickly get down the level of debt by selling assets, and it did not seem too surprising, or wrong, that he was unwilling to show his cards by making clear what he was most anxious to sell. There was also legitimate concern about Vivendi's music business, which was in rapid decline as the downloading of music took over from traditional outlets. That perhaps explained why there might not be much growth in the asset value but it still did not explain the scale of the gap between price and value.

The real explanation for the gap between price and value is that this was a classic example, always easier to identify in retrospect than at the time, of the taint in the stock market lasting longer than the justification for it. Investors extrapolate, and have an exaggerated fear that a stock whose price has been in fairly consistent nose-dive will continue its trajectory all the way to the ground. They take too much account of what is usually – not always, of course – a small probability of total disaster.

They also take too much account of the quite large probability of small, short-term disappointment. Short-termist investors were not willing to commit to Vivendi in 2002 in part because they were nervous that, if they bought and the shares did not immediately go up, they would have embarrassing meetings with clients. Scanning the list of holdings in the portfolio, a client's eye might fall all too instantly on the line bearing the word Vivendi, pregnant with scandal. Had it fallen, say, 10% from the point of purchase, the manager might feel nervously on the defensive.

Such situations provide opportunity to those who are not too concerned with the short term. Clients may show most interest in things which have gone wrong because they are eye-catchers, even if they have been bought after going wrong. For eight months or so shortly before publication of this book we held for our clients shares in General Motors, metaphorically consigning them to a part of the portfolio which we call Toxic Corner. In Toxic Corner there are serious risks, but potentially big rewards. We bought General Motors after the share price had fallen dramatically. The single holding about which we have had most questions from clients and prospective clients has been this company, because it was tainted. Those managers, therefore, who are nervous of their clients' eyes being attracted to the company in the news and in difficulties, and who are concerned themselves about the immediate short term, will tend to avoid such a company.

If a valuation is very low, there may have been some utterly extraordinary reason. A price-earnings ratio may be exceptionally low simply because the company recorded an exceptional capital gain in its earnings for the previous year. This needs to be discounted. But if, once such exceptionals are excluded, the valuation, in terms of price-earnings ratio, or price-cash flow ratio, or price to assets, remains very low, then the market is saying something gloomy about the prospects of the company. The market is predicting that, whatever the conditions were which resulted in the level of earnings most recently recorded, they are not going to last. The market may well be right, and often is. But, pushed by the short-termists so that both gloom and enthusiasm become exaggerated, it is frequently wrong.

Investment trusts at a discount

Investment trusts and, in markets other than the UK, similar quoted companies whose business is to own a portfolio of shares in quoted companies, frequently provide surprisingly good opportunities.

A visiting Martian, told how investment trusts work, would think that the investment trust's share price would correspond pretty closely with the value per share of the portfolio owned by the trust. The wide aberrations from these values reflect the fact that the share price of an investment trust, like any other price of a share dealt in on markets, is a function of the force of buying interest compared with the force of selling interest. There is at the end always a buyer for every seller – otherwise there cannot be a transaction – but the enthusiasm of the buyer compared with the enthusiasm of the seller determines whether a share price rises or falls.

At times when investors are gloomy, the share prices of investment trusts tend to fall quite far below the net asset values of the portfolios which the trusts own. These times coincide, naturally enough, with times at which the net asset values of the portfolios themselves have fallen because markets have been weak.

Investment trusts can therefore provide a double-whammy: at a time when the market itself is cheap, an investment trust can provide an excellent means for the investor to get exposure to the market because the trust's share price may be much lower than the portfolio asset value. This route is not open to very large investors because most investment trusts are not themselves large enough to allow millions of pounds worth of shares to be bought or sold easily. But it is a useful route for the investor with a few hundred thousand pounds, or less, to follow.

An extreme example of these vagaries was in 1987, after the crash. Within a few weeks, investment trusts were selling far below asset values. The large and highly regarded investment management firm Templeton had several global funds trading as investment trusts or their equivalent. Their UK global fund went quickly to a 25% discount, a bargain. But in Australia, where the crash was even more severe – share prices fell in a few days by close to 40% – their equivalent Templeton Global Fund, traded on the Sydney stock exchange, went to a 40% discount. Yet the underlying portfolio of global shares was the same in each case. This was a double-bargain.

On the other hand, a good rule of thumb is never to buy an investment trust at a premium to the value of its net assets. There have been times when certain types of investment trust have gone to a premium. In 1990, after the fall of the Berlin wall, US investors were ecstatic about prospects for Germany. Closed-end funds (the US equivalent of UK investment trusts) specialising in Germany went to a 40% premium. There was no justification for this. The investor could easily have bought German shares direct rather than through the medium of the closed-end fund, without paying the 40% extra. Within a couple of years that premium had vanished.

Just as a large discount on an investment trust is often a double-opportunity – the underlying assets may be of a type which is particularly unpopular, so that they may go up in value a lot and the discount may narrow a lot – so a large premium is a double-danger. The premium is likely to come down and to disappear altogether (as it did in the case of the Germany funds); and that will probably be against a background in which the fad comes to a sticky end.

Value traps

Some managers are prepared to invest only when they see some catalyst which is likely to make the value more readily appreciated in the market price. The problem with this is that a catalyst is visible to all, and tends immediately to be discounted, so that as soon as it appears the share price rises too far to be taken advantage of.

Concern about a catalyst is essentially a short-termist concern. If the company involved is essentially sound, with scope for improvement, but an unduly low valuation, then in time the value is likely to be realised. But it requires patience. Recognition may take a month, a year, several years, and sometimes – the value trap – it never happens at all.

There may sometimes be obstacles in the way of value recognition that are not likely to be overcome. Some companies are dominated by family shareholders who are more concerned with handing on the family silver intact to the next generation, or even more altruistically in looking after employees, than in ensuring shareholders at large get a decent return.

There used to be an antique furniture dealer in Bond Street where the value of the freehold on the premises of the company was a large part of the share price. I went to have a look. Three elegant women sat behind a reception desk. The son of the chairman appeared at my elbow. All wanted to know how they could help. There was no one else in the building. I said that I had come to browse. The chairman's son accompanied me, switching on a light in each room in turn, and as soon as I had finished in it switching it off again. The share price was never likely to reflect the underlying value as long as the family had a majority interest.

Sometimes, where the value investor sees tremendous value, it certainly does not work out. The cheap stock gets cheaper. The value investor may buy more at a lower price. It gets cheaper and cheaper, and more and more good reasons emerge for the price fall. That was the case with, for instance, Yukos. But as a generalisation the principle of buying shares whose valuations are low, quite often because there have been some serious disappointments in the immediate past of the companies concerned, is beneficial.

If two individuals are given by the fairies the same dose of discernment, and one sets about being a value manager committed to buying cheap stocks and the other sets about being a growth manager, the first will tend to do better.

FOURTEEN

Heuristics

HEURISTICS is a fancy word for rules of thumb. All investors have their own lists of heuristics gained from experience, painful and happy. They are not foolproof, because there are always exceptions, but they are reliable enough to make it sensible to stick to them most of the time. When I have not stuck to them I have usually regretted it.

If you don't keep the score, you are just practising.

Forecasts are no good, but are essential for planning purposes.

If something looks too good to be true, it probably is.

A share whose price has gone down is prima facie more interesting than before it went down.

Keep your distance.

Valuation matters.

And finally: Harold Macmillan, as Prime Minister, stuck a note to the door of the private secretaries' room which read:

"Careful calm reflection disentangles every knot."

His principal private secretary, John Wyndham, added a second line:

"And if you find it doesn't, you'll probably be shot."

Both of these sentiments are apt for the working life of a fund manager.

*The author (with clients) after a period of
careful calm reflection*

AFTERWORD AND
ACKNOWLEDGEMENTS –
FIRST EDITION

I have written this book because I like writing, and because I thought it worthwhile to try to express in plainish words what has often been rendered mysterious, dull, and inaccessible by jargon and spin. I have the luck of having had a career in which I have been on both sides of the fence, poacher and gamekeeper: an investment manager for nearly 30 years, but for ten years also in the business of seeing, evaluating and appointing other managers. As this experience is at the root of the book, I should say something about it.

I joined S.G. Warburg & Co. as a graduate in 1977. I was very lucky to get the job. At Oxford one of my special subjects in history was British foreign policy before the Second World War, and Lord (Bob) Boothby came up to Oxford to talk to the group taking this course. I happened to be driving to London afterwards, and offered him a lift. On the way he asked me what I was planning to do when I left Oxford. I said that I was applying to various merchant banks. At the mention of Warburgs, he growled: "Siegmund Warburg is one of my oldest friends. Mention my name and every door will be thrown open to you."

I would willingly have mentioned his name but did not know quite how to go about it. However, when I arrived at Warburgs for interview, I found that all three interviewers had a copy of a letter which Boothby, in typically generous and excessive terms, had written to Sir Siegmund – based purely on the fact that I had managed to get him to London in one piece. I think I only scraped in, but the in rather than the scraping is what mattered.

I set out on the two-year graduate trainee programme which involved time in every department of the bank. Within a couple of weeks I was in the international investment department. It was short-staffed, consisting then of only half a dozen people. After my allotted couple of months I was asked to stay, and did, in a sense forever after.

There was not much international investment about. In the UK, investing overseas was difficult. Although the British had a long history of international investment, the so-called dollar premium made it more expensive to buy an overseas share than a UK share. In 1979, one of Mrs Thatcher's first acts – as important a first step in office as Gordon Brown's transfer to the Bank of England of the right to move interest rates – was to abolish exchange controls and thereby remove this dollar premium.

In the US, no one bothered about abroad. The US was biggest and best. Andrew Smithers, then head of the investment side of Warburgs, a man who always saw the big picture, thought that international investment would become important to US institutions. In 1979, I was sent to New York for two years to represent Warburgs' international investment department in trying to persuade US pension funds to invest outside the US. When I returned to London in 1981, I joined the US equity team. The timing was perfect. In August 1982, the hugely influential Dr Gloom, Dr Henry Kaufman of Salomon Brothers, opined that interest rates, then 14%, were about to fall and the US bull market started. Like a pied piper it led all other markets. The bull market lasted for 18 years, with the odd blip (including the crash of 1987 which in retrospect was no more than a particularly severe blip, though that is not how it felt at the time).

Warburgs was a wonderful place to be in order to learn about merchant banking and investment – even though Sir Siegmund, responsible for the strong Warburgs ethos which long survived his death in 1982, was not himself much interested in investment. He used, before my time, to pop his head around the door of the investment room and ask, "What is going on in the casino today?" When he appointed Peter Stormonth Darling chairman of the investment management subsidiary, his first instruction was to "get rid of it". Having avoided doing this, Stormonth Darling presided over its growth from something profitless and almost worthless to a tremendous jewel. In 1997 Mercury Asset Management (as the Warburgs investment division had become) was bought by Merrill Lynch for over £3bn.

In 1996, having headed the US equity and global equity teams at Mercury, I moved to the private investment office of the Hans Rausing family. The job included the running of a global equity portfolio, with freedom from the cumbersome processes which are inevitable in a large firm with many people involved. But the main part of the job was to advise trustees on the appointment of other investment management firms.

During the nine years in which I was at this family office I saw hundreds of managers, of quoted equity portfolios, private (unquoted) equity funds, hedge funds, bond portfolios, and property. Seeing what so many others did, and what made some of them so successful, was an incomparable education.

I am grateful, therefore, to the two employers – and clients – who provided this education and experience in the world of investment: the Warburg group and Mercury Asset Management; and the Rausing family's investment office, Alta Advisers. I would like to thank especially Peter Stormonth Darling, former chairman of Mercury and among many other things later chairman of Alta; and Lisbet Rausing. Each kindly read this book in manuscript, as did Lord Rothschild, but I am grateful to them all for much more than that.

Needless to say, the errors in this book are all mine and the views are far from scrupulously objective. In investment there are lots of ways of doing it successfully. Most managers have a fairly distinct style and credo about investment. Others have a view of investment life different from mine.

For their permission to reproduce respectively a song and some pearls of wisdom I thank Norman Bachop and Chris Browne, Charles Elliott, Robert H. Jeffrey and Miles Morland.

I would also like to thank Norman Bachop, John Booth, Paul Dondos, Selina Elwell, Mark Katzenellenbogen, Rob Wallace and my colleagues at Oldfield Partners for all their comments and advice; James Burgess for his cartoons, my son Christopher Oldfield for his picture on the dust jacket and finally Jessica Fulford-Dobson for acting variously, with great good humour and tenacity, as publisher, agent, photographer, and cajoler.

AFTERWORD –
SECOND EDITION

"EVENTS, dear boy, events." The last page in the original 2007 edition of *Simple But Not Easy*, which I will give the acronym *SBNE*, also quoted Harold Macmillan. There have been plenty of events since 2007, and plenty of new acronyms to mark them: the global financial crisis, or GFC, with the crash of the banks in 2008; the desperate efforts of central banks to engineer an economic recovery through quantitative easing, or QE; the culmination of those efforts in a zero interest rate policy, ZIRP; the rise of Facebook, Amazon, Apple, Netflix, Google (whose listed parent company is Alphabet) – five companies now known collectively as the FAANGs which have become utterly dominant in their fields; the importance of environmental, social and governance issues, or ESG; the huge growth in passive, or indexed, investing through exchange-traded funds (ETFs); special purpose acquisition companies, or SPACs; and Covid-19.

The elephants in the *SBNE* room in the last decade or so have been disruption, a word which did not figure in *SBNE*; the supremacy of passive over active investment, and of growth over value.

There have been enough surprises in this extraordinary period to require a bit of re-evaluation of the main messages of *SBNE*, which boil down to half a dozen: have faith in equities; stay invested; keep a cushion of comfort; diversify; beware of hedge funds; keep your distance; valuations matter.

Have faith in equities

SBNE opened with a host of howlers from my past. In the last 14 years, the howlers have bred like amoebae. One of my mantras has been to have faith in equities. Enthusiasm for equities in a year like 2008 looks like a howler. The best performing major market in that year was the UK, with a fall of 30% in local currency terms; but for anyone outside the UK it was much worse because of the fall of sterling – in US dollar terms the UK market nearly halved. The MSCI World Index for equities fell by 19% in sterling terms and 41% in US dollar terms in 2008. The MSCI Emerging Markets Index fell by 36% in sterling and 53% in dollars.

All the same, equities have got over this debacle. The total return of the MSCI World Index from 1 January 2007 to 30 June 2021 was 8% per annum in US dollar terms and 10% in sterling terms, even though in the first two years of this period markets were pummelled by the crisis – at one point the World index had fallen by more than 50% (in sterling terms) from its high – and in 2020 it fell 25% in three weeks. Over the long term, equities have continued to provide good returns, between 4 and 6% per annum more than the rate of inflation for most markets.

Equity investors are optimists. The years since 2007, choppy though they have been, have justified this optimism. Equity investors believe that there is an upward path for share prices over the long term as profits grow, and this runs in parallel with things generally getting better: not just in raw economic terms, and in inventiveness, but in humanitarian terms – longer life expectancy with fewer deaths in war, less pollution, better healthcare and less poverty. Covid has been both a reminder that progress is fragile and uneven, and a reassurance about the speed of medical and scientific development.

In his book *The Rational Optimist* (Fourth Estate, 2010), Matt Ridley describes progress in terms of food availability, income and lifespan – all up; and disease, child mortality and violence – all down. The Ridley thesis of optimism (which survived his period of chairmanship of Northern Rock), a sensible backdrop to long-term equity investing, says little about what the next few years may bring. It is all very long-run stuff, nothing much to do with the state of stock markets in, say, the next five years.

On dozens of other measures, there has been progress. The number of people killed in war has fallen dramatically. Eleven per cent of the global population are estimated to have been killed during Genghis Khan's campaigns of the 13th century. The Second World War cost more lives than any other – 2.6% of the world's population were killed. In the first decade of the 21st century there were fewer battle deaths (including civilians) than in any decade since the Second World War. Pollution kills far fewer than it used to: in 1900, one person in 550 died from air pollution, now it is around one in 2,500. The probability of a child dying before his or her fifth birthday has dropped from a world average of 23% in the 1950s to 6%. Worldwide illiteracy has dropped from 70% in the 1970s to 23%.

Hans Rosling's book *Factfulness* (Sceptre, 2018) has much the same theme of general improvement, a Whiggish notion of progress; but there is an additional theme which is that any cohort of people, asked whether they think the level of literacy, or poverty, or child mortality, or hunger, or a host of other such conditions, is x or y, invariably chooses the more negative answer. We seem to be conditioned to be more negative than is justified. One of the advantages of equity investment is that things tend to be better – not always, but most of the time – than we think they are.

The long-term optimism which is the necessary backdrop to equity investing may be wrong. There are always plenty of Armageddonists around. Early in 2011 Harold Camping, an evangelist broadcasting on the US radio station Family Radio, forecast that the world would end on 21 May that year. When it did not, he sensibly did what Keynes advocated: "When the facts change, I change my mind. What do you do, sir?" Mr Camping's revised forecast was that the world would end on 21 October, 2011. He was reported to have retired from Family Radio on 16 October 2011, though his daughter said that he was actually working from home.

When, as occasionally happens, the optimistic view of the world is routed, as in 2008–09 and in 2020, it hurts. Both temperamentally and practically, equity investors have to be prepared for such episodes, through having enough of a protective buffer in the form of assets other than equities. Equity investment still seems likely to provide a much better return than other asset classes over time, but bumping around a good deal. The higher long-term return comes in exchange for occasional hard knocks.

Stay invested

If anyone were any good at predicting exactly when the hard knocks would occur, that would be marvellous – but, on the whole, making very sharp asset allocation shifts into and out of equities does not work because the odds are against you: the investor has to get out at the right time and get back in at the right time, with only a one-in-four chance of success. The last 14 years have given good examples of the potential cost of thinking that it makes sense to move substantially out of equities and then back in.

Investment managers too often feel a compulsion to act. In 2008, the long-serving chairman of a large family investment committee told me that he had cancelled the last two meetings because he feared that if the committee met it would want to decide to do something, and that doing anything amidst the confusion of those months had a higher chance of being wrong.

In March 2009 I saw two vivid examples of how the inclination to act could lead one astray. One of my colleagues at an investment committee had been untiringly, and rightly, negative during the whole of 2008. As markets plummeted, he became ever more vehement. His vehemence reached a peak in March 2009, when the

MSCI World Index was at half its level of 12 months earlier and the sentiment in markets was overwhelmingly negative; it was only then that he recommended getting out of equities altogether. This was within a week or two of the beginning of the bull market which has now lasted for more than 12 years. From 1 March 2009 to the end of June 2021, the MSCI World Index gave a cumulative return of 475% in sterling terms and 453% in US dollar terms, or 15% per annum.

I was a member of another investment committee where the manager told us in February 2009: "We have ranges for our asset allocation, a minimum and maximum for equities, because we find that this keeps us out of trouble: it stops us being too enthusiastic in the good times and it stops us being too gloomy in the bad times. But these times are so exceptional that we think you should have considerably less than the minimum in equities."

It was actually worse than this. This firm had a triple dosage of caution. The long-term, or strategic, weighting given to equities was low, because of an exaggerated concern about volatility; they then held less than the strategic weighting, because of their nervousness about markets; and they invested in other managers' funds which themselves had a cautious policy, with more cash than usual, because caution was all the rage. They missed out on a year or two of remarkable strength in stock markets, until they relented. It was a repeat of my own experience in 1987.

Jeremy Grantham of GMO, supremely wise as ever, said quite the opposite, heading an article in March 2009 'Reinvesting when terrified'. He emphasised that, "You absolutely must have a battle plan for reinvestment and stick to it," because otherwise enthusiasm for investment will fall with the market. "You must get them to agree now – quickly before rigor mortis sets in – for we are entering the zone as I write."

The turbulence of 2020 provided a vivid example of the risk of wrong timing. The MSCI World Index rose over the year by around 14%. Anyone who missed the five strongest days would have had a return of minus 14%. The famous banker J. P. Morgan was sceptical about trying to time such moves. Typically enigmatic, when asked eagerly what advice he would give to someone just setting out in the world, he replied: "Young man, never smoke in bed." His answer to someone else wondering what he thought the stock market would do was: "It will fluctuate." He, like the rest of us, knew that stock markets go up and down, but getting the ups and downs in the right order is tough.

Staying invested is what I would call constructive indolence – remaining more or less fully invested, not because of a Panglossian optimism but because of realistic scepticism about anyone's ability to time properly big asset allocation moves. According to the *Journal of Economic Psychology*, goalkeepers facing a penalty who do nothing, diving neither left nor right, have a much better rate of saving the goal than those who dive one way or the other. Yet only 6% of the time do goalkeepers stay in the middle rather than dive. The reason is that goalkeepers feel worse about a goal scored when it follows from not moving – staying in the middle of the goalmouth – than they do about letting in a goal by jumping in the wrong direction.

A study in the investment weekly *Barron's* shows the cost of overactive goalkeeping. In the 20 years ending in 2008, the average investor in equity mutual funds in the US made a return of only 1.9% per annum, even though the average equity mutual fund had a return of 8.4%. The average investor's cumulative return was 46% while the cumulative return of the average fund was over 400%. Investors did so much worse than the things in which they invested because of consistently poor buy and sell decisions, according to *Barron's*. "Do nothing," Peter Stormonth Darling's frequent injunction, would have been a much better solution.

The story is much the same, although not quite to the same degree, among institutional investors. John West and Jason Hsu of Research Affiliates found in 2018 that fund managers who had been sacked by pension funds outperformed those newly hired by the same funds by an average of 1.4% per annum for the next three years. The pension funds would have done better to have done nothing.

Gloom and enthusiasm become excessive. It is natural to tend to go with the flow, especially when the gloom or the enthusiasm reaches its peak, just before what will retrospectively be recognised as a major turning point. My first task when I joined Warburgs in 1977 was to conduct a study of the 1973–74 bear market in the UK, the roughest on record. Over Christmas 1974 at Sandringham, the stockbroker Peter Wilmot-Sitwell told the Queen Mother how dire it all was. The UK stock market had fallen by 55% that year. Everyone was miserable. Emerging from church, the Queen Mother confided in Wilmot-Sitwell that she had prayed for the stock market. Over the next three months it doubled.

Doing this work was a useful introduction, for a new kid on the block, to the vagaries of stock markets. To go against the grain with big changes in asset allocation, from equities to cash or bonds and back again, is extremely difficult because, as *SBNE* says, by the time you are in a state of such acute misery or euphoria that you are ready to make a wholesale move, the markets will have moved a long way and the crowd will have moved too, bit by bit, to an extreme position.

Instead, investors in a position to be patient, whether institutional or individual, should keep most of their financial assets in equities as the asset most likely to provide a good after-inflation return in the long term. If they have a sufficient cushion of comfort, outside equities, when it goes wrong the pain can be borne without panic-stricken sales at depressed prices. In terms of an active policy of allocation, they may choose occasionally to push on the accelerator or the brake without the level of angst and emotion a large-scale move would involve. Now may be a time for more use of the brake than most, but not to get out of the car and walk.

More forecasting folly

The reason that it is so difficult to make large asset allocation changes successfully is, of course, that it is so difficult to forecast. There has been ample new evidence of the folly of forecasting since *SBNE*. At the beginning of 2008 the IMF and OECD forecast world economic growth for 2009 at around 2.5 to 3%. The actual result was a minus number. In early 2020 the IMF and the World Bank expected world GDP growth of 3.3% and 2.5% respectively; the actual result was minus 3.3%, and it was hardly their fault that they were wrong.

The broad sweep of history is only clear in retrospect. Tsar Nicholas II wrote in his diary a hundred-odd years ago that 1916 had been an awful year and 1917 was sure to be better. Things so often do not turn out quite as they seem likely to. I lived in New York in 1979–81 at the time of President Carter's presidency, when America was down on its luck. Inflation and interest rates were in the mid-teens. US hostages were taken in the Tehran embassy, and helicopters crashed in the desert trying unsuccessfully to rescue them. US self-esteem was about as low as it could be. The bookstands in airports were full of books about how America needed to copy Japan. Yet ten years later, after the fall of the Iron Curtain, the US was supreme. It had discovered, in President Reagan's words, how to walk tall again. Few predicted anything like it.

The fallibility of forecasts is just as true of the particular as of the general. The 1997 annual report of Amazon, recalled by Howard Marks of Oaktree in a 2017 memo, had this to say about some individual companies: "We established long-term relationships with many important strategic partners, including America Online, Yahoo!, Excite, Netscape, GeoCities, Altavista, @Home, and Prodigy." Marks points out that the relationships turned out to be not so long-term, since the number of these important strategic partners that still exist is zero (apart from Yahoo in another form). The future was unpredictable. It still is.

The assumption that equities will do their job over the long term, and the recognition that it is hard to tell what they will do over the short term, are the justifications for staying as fully invested in equities as the investor's personal cushion of comfort allows. To do this the investor risks, as Keynes wrote, coming in for "criticism, wherever investment funds are managed by committees or boards or banks. For it is in the essence of his behaviour that he should be eccentric, unconventional and rash in the eyes of average opinion." To paraphrase Keynes, it is easier to be gloomy about markets conventionally than to be optimistic unconventionally. Gloom, leading often to the holding of large amounts of cash rather than equities, always seems so prudent and unobjectionable. Yet on the whole, purely in terms of the relative returns of equities and cash, it is wrong.

Another justification for remaining fully invested is that there are always opportunities somewhere. One of the investors whom I most admire, Peter Cundill, had a book written about him by Christopher Risso-Gill called *There's Always Something to Do* (McGill-Queen's University Press, 2011). The excesses of enthusiasm and gloom in markets and in different bits of markets ensure that something is always cheap, something is always expensive, even if sometimes the barrel needs a thorough scraping to find what is wanted.

In the cold light of day, the volatility of equities is worth enduring in exchange for the good returns that come from a long-term view, if the investor can take it. In the past couple of decades I think that wealth managers have sacrificed a good deal of return by giving too much emphasis to the importance of controlling volatility. Many of their clients have circumstances, objectively, which would allow them to live quite happily with equity-type volatility from the great majority of their assets. They have enough cushion in the form of other, non-volatile assets.

Rule number one is, as in *SBNE*, to have faith in equities. Rule number two is that valuations matter, and excessive gloom or enthusiasm in markets matters: when valuations are high and sentiment overblown, apply a little brake, and when valuations are low and sentiment dismal, apply the accelerator. Rule number three is, when in doubt as to whether to use the brake or the accelerator, remember rule number one.

Keep a cushion of comfort

There are people who do not need to cushion the blows that equity markets sometimes deliver. People who have plenty of income, no need for liquidity from their invested assets, and a long-term horizon could plan to be always in equities because they are likely to provide better returns than other asset classes, and timing when to be in or out is too difficult. But as Mike Tyson said, "Everyone has a plan until they get punched in the mouth." Even those who think themselves most hardened to volatility and most confident about the long-term potential of equities may find their plan does not survive contact with the enemy. In the depths of the 2008–09 crisis I talked to a friend who worked at a US investment bank. Nearly all his financial assets took the form of shares in his employer. These shares had fallen 88% from their peak in 2007. Every $100 had become $12. He told me that he was going to sell his shares. "I know it will be wrong," he said, "but I just have to be sure that it doesn't get any worse." He was wrong. What was worth $100 in 2007 and $12 in 2009 was worth $124 in June 2021. His was a classic example of excessive gloom and insufficient cushion: if he had had enough in non-equity assets, he would not have felt this overpowering compulsion to convert volatile shares into non-volatile cash at the worst moment.

A cushion has become more desirable because the way in which markets have developed has made sharp down moves more likely. One of the ugly features of stock market volatility is that the moves down always seem to be sharper than the moves up. Rather like reputations, which are built up over many years and can be lost in a trice, markets seem to stagger determinedly though haphazardly up an infinite staircase and to throw themselves precipitously down a flight or two from time to time – never more precipitously than in 2020, though the speed at which they afterwards climbed the staircase has been exceptional.

The risk of a precipitous down move, the sort of thing that we saw in 1987, in 2008, and in 2020, and each time thought we would never see again, is magnified by the way in which investors are now clumped together in funds that allow daily dealing and are invested in shares which could not possibly all be sold in a short time.

Money has poured into open-ended funds. The percentage of US household wealth held in open-ended funds has risen from just 3% in 1980 to 23% in 2020. Worldwide, the total net assets of funds have risen to well over \$40trn, almost a quarter of the value of all equity and debt securities. Most of these funds have open-ended structures which allow the investor to sell easily, usually daily.

All these funds with daily dealing have given the illusion of liquidity – the idea that investors can get their hands on their money at a moment's notice. The illusion has begun to be exposed. In the financial crisis of 2008–09 there were dozens of examples where investors thought they could get their money out in a day and found that they could not. In many cases the funds were gated, with the managers bringing in emergency measures, found in the small print of prospectuses, so that no purchases or sales were allowed for a period.

Most of the examples from the financial crisis were in obscure corners of the markets, mainly derivatives, of the sort which *SBNE* urges people to avoid. Some of the examples were of property funds set up to allow investors to put their money in and take it out with very short notice. But most investors understood that actually property is not very liquid. For quick access to cash suddenly to be denied was not all that surprising. So the furore about investors getting access to their money was temporary, focussed on problems during a year or so in which things had got out of hand; once the crisis was over, attention to this nagging and persistently worsening problem of liquidity subsided.

In the last few years there have been some incidents that could be canaries in the coal mine. When a fixed income manager at the asset manager GAM left in a hurry in 2018, many of his loyal investors took their money out. The firm found that, once the most liquid investments had been sold, the fund they were left with was not balanced in the way they wanted it to be. This could not easily be put right because of the illiquidity of many of the surviving investments. As a result, the firm decided to close the fund, accepting no purchases or sales for a period, and then liquidated it and handed back all the money to investors. This attracted a lot of attention, but nothing compared with the downfall of Woodford Asset Management.

Neil Woodford had a highly successful 26-year career at Invesco Perpetual. In 2014 he left, and launched Woodford Asset Management.

Money poured in, based on his track record. He invested a small but increasing part of his funds in unquoted stocks in the expectation that they would eventually become quoted, and in small quoted companies, especially in the biomedical sector. As the *Financial Times* said, "This was a big departure from the unloved blue chip companies on which he had built his stockpicking reputation." At Invesco, he not only had compliance staff all around "to keep his more adventurous instincts in check," but also the redoubtable, understated, Bob Yerbury as chief investment officer.

What Neil Woodford had not prepared for was the possibility of underperformance, which would cause, as it always does, some investors to make for the door. The underperformance came; the investors duly went. As the size of his funds fell with these investors' redemptions, the proportion of the fund in unquoted shares, which could not be sold, rose above the permitted maximum of 10%. Some of the unlisted companies arranged listings in the Channel Islands. This meant that they technically fell outside the unlisted category, but it did nothing for their actual saleability.

In 2019 Kent County Council decided to withdraw from Woodford's equity income fund. Suddenly the game was up. Just about everybody wanted out. In crisis, the fund was gated – no purchases or sales – and prepared for liquidation.

For decades the regulators have been pushing management firms to make their funds ostensibly more liquid by allowing those who buy and sell units in the funds to be able to do so daily; ironically, and belatedly, the regulators have now realised that this has been quite the opposite of beneficial to investors. Regulators can now be expected to row in the opposite direction, obliging funds to move to perhaps monthly dealing.

Lord Myners, former chief executive of the fund management firm Gartmore, and later a minister responsible for City affairs, made the point in a letter to the *Financial Times* that equity investment funds, "can't be treated as an alternative to an ATM. Daily dealing is not appropriate for anything other than the most liquid large cap portfolios." The idea that the ability to trade frequently is a public good is a myth. Mark Carney, governor of the Bank of England, put it even more strongly: "These funds are built on a lie, which is that you can have daily liquidity for assets that fundamentally aren't liquid."

Large funds invested in equities, unless in the largest and most liquid companies, need to be allowed to demand from investors a long enough notice period for redemptions: investors who want to get out of a fund should be required to give, say, 15 days' notice before the sale takes place, to give fund managers time to sell the shares the fund holds in an orderly way.

Until the regulators get around to changing the current regulations, and fund managers get around to changing the current practice, the contradiction talked about by Mark Carney is dangerous. In any major sell-off in markets, the apparent liquidity of funds and the actual illiquidity of much that they hold will have a magnifying effect, providing the potential for one of those black swan crashes that are supposed to happen only once in a blue moon.

The downfall of Woodford was seen as a blow for active management; it certainly demonstrated the risk that someone who invests with a portfolio utterly different from the relevant index may underperform for some years, a point emphasised in *SBNE* – there was no news here. The real significance of Woodford is twofold: first, the micro point that when a manager changes his or her style of investing it is a signal to be extremely cautious; second, the macro point about illusory liquidity.

That is why I feel, though an unreformed equity enthusiast, that a cushion – a chunk of assets in something other than equities – is important for investors' safety and comfort, as they say on planes and trains. How much should be in that cushion is still as much a decision based on temperament as on objective circumstances, but whatever the answer for any individual, it might be a bit more than in 2007. Some people – really long-term in outlook, with income from elsewhere and no need for liquidity, and with the temperament to weather storms – will be prepared to have 100% of their financial assets in quoted equities. Most will not. They want some diversification from equities in order to lower the risk of being hit by one of those all-encompassing bear markets which happen ineluctably from time to time.

Diversify

In *SBNE* I talked about various means of diversification, including bonds, private equity, hedge funds, and gold. Diversification was much easier in 2007 than it is in 2021. Old-fashioned diversification did the trick: bonds. New-fangled diversification, using so-called alternatives so fashionable that there was nothing alternative about them, did not work. Private equity and, with some glaring exceptions, hedge funds did not provide the lack of correlation with equity markets which people often expected of them.

Private equity

On the whole, though, private equity has done well. For the 10 years to the end of 2019, according to Bain & Co., the average private equity fund has given about the same return as the public markets: around 15% per annum.

Private equity has become increasingly popular. According to a McKinsey study the net asset value of private equity funds has grown sevenfold since 2002, twice as fast as public equity funds. Private equity funds have had huge commitments from institutional investors so that the amount of money they have sitting on the sidelines, available for investment but already committed, has doubled in the last ten years to well over $2bn.

An Ernst & Young report in 2019 found that between 2005 and 2017, 47% of the gross return of private equity funds came from strategic and operational improvement. Private equity has the attraction that the managers may make decisions that will benefit the operating performance of the companies concerned.

SBNE was cautious about investors using private equity, perhaps too cautious given that even the average fund has done well. All the same, private equity remains problematic for the ordinary investor because of the big range of returns, or 'dispersion'. Such has been the appetite for private equity that those regarded as good are already bagged by investors who have been with them for a while, with no room for new investors in their new funds. In venture capital in particular, new funds being raised by established and successful venture capital managers are generally available only to investors who have been backing those firms for some time.

In addition, research needs to be painstakingly thorough in this complex area. David Swensen was chief investment officer at Yale University until his premature death in 2021. Under his inspiring leadership Yale has done superbly in private equity. But because of the complexity and the clubbishness, he advised those contemplating embarking on a private equity programme: "don't."

The dispersion of returns means that selecting just a few private equity managers is high risk; on the other hand, appointing a manager of private equity managers, while reducing the risk, results in another layer of fees. The fees are enormous anyway: the typical 2% management fee and 20% of profit results in the portion of the investment cake available to the owner of the money being reduced very significantly. Ludovic Phalippou of the Saïd Business School, Oxford, has estimated that, over the long term, fees in private equity funds have been around 7% per annum.

Even if these obstacles could be overcome, I would be at least as cautious in 2020 about private equity as *SBNE* was in 2007. Private equity (other than venture capital) uses leverage – borrowing – to a much greater extent than quoted equity. Just as leverage can lead to outsize returns, it can also lead to disaster as in private equity incursions into the retail and restaurant businesses – in part accounting for the wide dispersion of returns. In several ways the private equity market now appears to be overegged. Leverage being used is higher than in 2007.

Valuations are very high. In leveraged private equity or 'buy-outs', valuations are as high as in 2007. In venture capital, the last few years have been a golden phase. Venture capital funding has exploded, from

$50bn a year in around 2013 to $150bn currently. Investors have had an apparently limitless appetite for financing of newish companies with new ideas and very large losses, not just initially but in a series of follow-up investments. This has never happened on such a scale before.

Bonds

Old-fashioned diversification worked beautifully in the crisis of 2008–09 and has worked beautifully since then. A portfolio denominated in US dollars with 50% in world equities and 50% in world government bonds would have provided a return of -14% in 2008; pretty awful but not half as bad as many purportedly diversified portfolios. Because of the collapse of sterling, the same portfolio, but denominated in sterling, would have given a return of +17% in 2008.

Things look a little different in 2021. Interest rates have fallen for 40 years. The last phase of the fall has been remarkable: since 2008, because of the financial crisis and Covid and the effort to recover in the form of quantitative easing, interest rates have fallen to zero and in some cases less than zero.

It is hard to justify using bonds as the counterweight to equities when they now yield almost nothing. The German government is issuing 30-year bonds with a yield of less than 0.3%. The 10-year bonds issued by the Greek government have a yield of less than 1%. If investors hold these bonds until they mature they can be absolutely certain of receiving a return per annum of near zero.

We used to think it impossible for interest rates to be so low. If you deposit money with a Swiss bank, it is the bank that receives interest: you pay for the privilege. If you want a mortgage in Denmark, the bank will pay interest to you on the amount you borrow. In June 2021 there were $13trn of bonds around the world yielding less than zero. The appearance in recent years of seriously negative yields is a 3,000-year first, according to Richard Sylla, co-author of *A History of Interest Rates, 2000 BC to the Present* (Wiley, 2005).

Near-zero interest rates mean that bonds are not much good for someone looking for assets that will provide both diversification and a decent return. If interest rates go up in the next ten years or so, then bonds bought now will show capital losses – no cushion of comfort here. Diversification into something in the throes of a bubble is diworsification.

Merryn Somerset Webb in her column in the *Financial Times* in August 2019 summed up the present position commonsensically. Negative interest rates are "the world's most bizarre financial experiment." Since we have never seen anything like it before, we cannot know what it all portends. "It makes it impossible to have any sense of certainty about what to do…The key thing to hold on to in our era of surprises is doubt."

Alan Greenspan, former chairman of the Fed, was asked by *Barron's* if investors should regard bonds as safe. He responded that some "believe there are people on Mars."

Cash and gold

If bonds are not, for the time being, a good means of diversification, if hedge funds never were, and if private equity, for all its merits, has problems, then little is left as a source of diversification to balance the risk that quoted equities have.

There are times when investors have to rummage pretty deeply in the barrel of potential investments. In the 1960s Warburgs, my old employer, appointed eminent former diplomats and civil servants as non-executive directors, who then entertained their contacts at lunch, often inviting one or two young executives at the same time. At one such lunch the British ambassador to Ethiopia was being entertained. After engaging in high-level diplomatic gossip for most of the meal, the host became aware of his two young protégés sitting silently at the end of the table. "So," he exclaimed, casting wildly around for something to bring them into the conversation, "the Ethiopian markets. Which is it to be, equities or convertible bonds?"

No need to search for diversification in the Ethiopian convertible bond market. Cash is the obvious risk reducer. Cash is the best cushion of comfort. Investors need enough of it to make them relaxed about their equities. But the trouble with cash is that it does not protect against inflation.

Then there is gold. Ben Bernanke said, when he was chairman of the Federal Reserve Board in the US: "Nobody really understands gold prices, and I don't pretend to understand them either." Warren Buffett has no time for gold, dug out of the ground, melted, and hidden away somewhere under heavy guard. But to J.P. Morgan, "Gold is money, everything else is credit."

If it is money – and generation after generation for thousands of years have treated it as such – then one of its attributes is that there is a fixed amount of it, and not that much, either. All the gold in the world could fit into the space at the bottom of the Eiffel Tower, or in a cube the length of a cricket pitch. As Jim Slater put it, "The case for gold is not so much what it is, as what it isn't. It's not the dollar. It's not Greek debt. It's not lots of other things. It's an immutable asset that has stood the test of time."

Gold is useful as an insurance policy because it tends to work well when markets are knocked off course. Since *SBNE*, gold has done its job, the price per ounce rising from $636 at the beginning of 2007 to just under $1800 in June 2021. At various points it has proved its worth by doing something very different to equities. I remain as much an enthusiast as in 2007, though the gold price is much higher than it was then – and despite the fact that holding shares in the gold mining company Barrick Gold for much of the last 14 years has been a big blunder.

Bitcoin and cryptocurrencies

Bitcoin and other cryptocurrencies have been invented since *SBNE* was published. There is a generational divide: younger people understand it and often invest in it. Older people do not understand it. I am one of the older people. Bitcoin was created out of nothing. My instinct is that nothing will come of nothing. There are visionaries such as Elon Musk who think differently.

In May 2021 a survey of a hundred hedge funds showed that they expected to hold an average of 7.2% of their assets in cryptocurrencies by 2026. To someone who does not understand cryptocurrencies this is baffling. By then perhaps other countries will follow the lead of El Salvador, the first country in the world to make Bitcoin legal tender. The US, Europe and the UK do not seem likely to be among them without a change of cast: the US Treasury Secretary has considered curtailing the use of cryptocurrencies, which are 'mainly' used for illegal activities; Christine Lagarde, president of the European Central Bank, described Bitcoin as, "a highly speculative asset which has conducted some funny business and some interesting and totally reprehensible money-laundering activity," and the governor of the Bank of England, Andrew Bailey, said that cryptocurrencies "have no intrinsic value... Buy them only if you're prepared to lose all your money." On the other hand, Jack Dorsey, the founder of Twitter, said that "Bitcoin changes everything... for the better," and Antony Scaramucci (Director of Communications at the White House for 11 days in July 2017, and principal of an investment firm which started a cryptocurrency hedge fund in January 2021) has declared "this is happening... You either get it or you don't get it."

One person who simultaneously appears to have got it and not got it is James Howells, a cryptocurrency trader who accidentally threw a hard drive containing the key to his Bitcoins into a rubbish tip operated by Newport City Council. In March 2021 Howells's Bitcoins were worth over £300m. A German programmer with a pile of Bitcoins, Stefan Thomas, has a similar problem: he has forgotten his password. The Australian computer scientist Craig Wright, who lives in Surrey, claims that he is Satoshi Nakamoto, the pseudonymous founder of Bitcoin. In May 2021 his lawyers said that he was bringing a claim relating to the theft of his electronic key, which is preventing him getting access to Bitcoin funds worth £4bn. As a store of value, Bitcoin has its drawbacks.

The name of Craig Wright's company is Tulip Trading. Bitcoin, like tulips, would undoubtedly provide diversification to an investment portfolio.

Caution, confidence and Coppock

Whatever diversification the investor goes for, equities are likely to remain at the heart of most long-term investors' portfolios. After ten years of very strong markets many are nervous. Some equities seem unusually expensive. But others do not.

Thirteen years on from the financial crash, there seem again to be masses of risks. The rise of China has been a boon to the world economy but is also a threat to the western world, politically and economically. There are plenty of other geopolitical risks. The main financial risk is that interest rates, having gone down for 40 years, cannot go down any further, and could go up to levels at which they are higher than the rate of inflation. Partly because of interest rates, things may have been too good and investors may have become too confident.

The bond and equity markets have been very different beasts over the past 40 years during the decline of interest rates. The performance of equities has been more episodic than that of bonds, with sharp but temporary downturns in 1987, 2000, 2008, 2018 and 2020 – which, given that equities are supposed to be volatile, is as it should be.

The US has been especially strong. The US reaction to the global financial crisis in 2008 was much quicker and more decisive than elsewhere, and at least as fast as anywhere else in 2020. In 2008–09 banks wrote off their bad debts more ruthlessly, and could start with a cleanish sheet. The traditional entrepreneurialism and innovativeness of the US shone through – Silicon Valley blossomed and flourished.

The US equity market rose between 2009 and 2020 every year but one. Only twice since 1900 – from 1947–56 and from 1991–99 – did it get any better than that. But outside the US the picture differs. Non-US equities do not sit at unusually high levels. The MSCI index for developed markets outside North America gave a return, including dividends, of only 4% per annum in US dollar terms between 2007 and 2020. Generally there is no euphoric overconfidence. Some investors have never quite recovered their sangfroid after the damage done in 2008.

Apart from the Investors Intelligence Survey of Advisors Sentiment which I mention in *SBNE*, the technical indicator to which I have paid attention for the last 30 years is Coppock. Edwin Coppock was asked for help with investment by his Episcopalian church in Texas. He observed how long it took to recover from the trauma of bereavement, divorce and so on and applied these observations to the stock market. Coppock buy indicators say nothing about the very short term, but are remarkably reliable in the long term.

My firm looked at the success rate of Coppock indicators for various markets – the US from 1930, Japan from 1970, and gold shares from 1980. Taking five-year returns from the point at which a buy signal was given, there were no false readings at all. In other words, the return was always positive after a buy signal – in all 26 instances in the US, all 18 in Japan, and all 15 for gold shares. 10 years after the buy signal, the average annual return was in high double figures for each of the three markets.

Counterintuitively, given how strong markets had been already since 2009, there were Coppock buy signals in various markets in 2019: the US, Hong Kong, Korea, Japan, the UK, Austria and Mexico all in September 2019. From then until June 2021 the MSCI World Index return has been 44%. Amidst all the many reasons to be cautious, Coppock (on which the *Investors Chronicle* reports) should stop investors from being too defensive.

Wary of prediction as I am, I would echo that of Ben Graham in 1974:

"I think the future of equities will be roughly the same as their past; in particular, common stock purchases will prove satisfactory when made at appropriate price levels. It may be objected that it is far too cursory and superficial a conclusion; that it fails to take into account the new factors and problems that have entered the economic picture in recent years – especially those of… the movement towards less consumption and zero growth. Perhaps I should add to my list the widespread public mistrust of Wall Street."

Plus ça change. The starting point in terms of immediate past returns and the current level of valuations matters. Since returns have been high and valuations are high, returns in the decade or so ahead may well be somewhat lower. There are, as always, risks. Inflation may come back, the world economy may be weaker than expected. There is too much debt. But equities are long-term investments and in the long term I see no reason to expect that equities will cease to provide a return well above inflation.

Beware of hedge funds

While private equity has glittered in the last decade, the performance of hedge funds, by contrast, has done nothing to make them more appealing, and I stand by the conclusion in *SBNE* that the average hedge fund is likely to provide a meagre return.

In 2011, three US academics: Christopher Clifford, Adam Aiken and Jesse Ellis, wrote a paper, 'Out of the dark: hedge fund reporting biases and commercial databases', in which they suggested that the average alpha – or the return above that of market indices, adjusted for risk taken by the managers – of hedge funds in the period 2004–09 was close to zero.

On average, hedge funds have given very little return. From January 2007 to the end of 2020 the average hedge fund's return was 0.6% per annum in US dollars. The average equity hedge fund's return was just above zero, during a period when the MSCI World Index return was 7%. *SBNE* argued that structurally there is little reason why the average hedge fund should give a decent return, and anything approaching decency is sharply reduced by excessive fees.

It has become much more commonplace to complain about the standard fees of hedge funds. Terry Smith, after a distinguished career as a fearless financial analyst and broker, set up his own asset management company, FundSmith, in 2010. He calculated then that an investor in Berkshire Hathaway, Warren Buffett's company, would have earned 20.5% per annum over the 45 years to 2009. $100 invested in Berkshire Hathaway in 1965 was worth $430,000 at the end of 2009. But if a fund had invested in Berkshire Hathaway and the fund manager had charged a management fee of 2% and a performance fee of 20%, and had reinvested all its fees in Berkshire Hathaway stock, then the investment of $100 in 1965 would have become $65,000 and the rest of the $430,000 would have been in the pocket of the manager.

In his book *The Hedge Fund Mirage* (Wiley, 2012), Simon Lack looked at the profits made by hedge fund investors and managers from 1998 to 2010. He reckoned that hedge fund managers made $441bn for themselves in those 13 years. What they made for their investors in those hedge funds was only $9bn more than the investors could have got from investing in short-term government bonds.

As in *SBNE*, I hasten to add that there are some excellent hedge fund managers who, hired today, will turn out to be worth their fees; but it is very hard to tell, in advance, who they are. The US retailer John Wanamaker said: "Half the money I spend on advertising is wasted. The trouble is, I don't know which half." Habitual hedge fund investors could say that 90% of the money they spend on hedge funds is wasted; the trouble is, they don't know which 90%.

In choosing a manager, the investor is always trying to roll a stone uphill because active managers on average underperform; with a hedge fund manager charging hedge fund fees the gradient of the hill makes the task impossible to all but a Hercules. Because of past performance and compelling presentational skills there are people who may look like Hercules, talk like Hercules, walk like Hercules, but not be Hercules.

Keep your distance

Many of the worst investment mistakes, our own and others', are made because the investor gets too close to the investment, and loses the perspective of distance. Those who invested with Bernie Madoff were captivated by his fund's record, notching up 1%, give or take a bit, every single month; they forgot to stand back and ask how. Often they were persuaded to invest because their friends, or institutions they respected, had already done so.

One of my worst mistakes in the last 14 years has come from keeping insufficient distance. We bought Tesco shares in April 2011, a month after Terry Leahy retired after 15 years as chief executive. During this time Tesco had grown tremendously, triumphing over its main rivals, Sainsbury's and Asda, and reaching a market share of nearly one third of total UK grocery sales.

Supermarkets used to be regarded as steady and reliable businesses, the main chains fighting it out at the top while sharing in secure profit margins. The game changed with the arrival of new entrants in the form of the two German private companies, Aldi and Lidl, buying sites and opening shops aggressively and thereby taking market share from the leaders. There was also the threat of online newcomers such as Ocado.

After Leahy's departure profit margins for all the supermarket chains, including Tesco, fell. In the 1960s heyday of Marks & Spencer, its chairman Simon Marks used to complain if profit margins were too high. It meant, he said, that costs were being driven down or prices being pushed up, and that meant that either the service to customers was not good enough or that they were being charged too much. What Marks warned about often happens towards the end of a long-standing and revered chief executive's time in office: in the last years the company is driven just a little too hard. It happened, for example, at Hewlett-Packard under Mark Hurd, and at General Electric under Jack Welch.

We met Phil Clarke, Terry Leahy's successor, and were sympathetic to him as he grappled with the problem of falling margins. Clarke insisted that this was temporary and that margins would return to a particular level, 5.2%. Even though in our own workings, based on assumptions about revenues and costs, we found it difficult to come up with a number as high as this, we accepted it. Into the spreadsheets it went. "More fiction has been written in Microsoft Excel than in Microsoft Word," goes the anonymous gag. The result was a glowingly attractive valuation of Tesco's shares with all the authority that spreadsheets give. Tesco had businesses in the US (nearly always a mistake for UK retailers), Europe and the Far East, and a bank. Once these were taken into account, we reckoned that the share price attributed a derisory value to the core business in the UK.

It got worse. Aldi and Lidl continued to take market share from Tesco. Tesco's trading margins in the UK fell to almost nothing. Clarke left and was replaced by Dave Lewis. Within days of his appointment, Tesco discovered accounting irregularities. When the details emerged, it was clear that large promotional payments for new products were being taken upfront as revenues. This made sense of something that Lewis had noted at his very first public meeting and that was deeply puzzling: the number of different products on sale had grown by more than 30% in a single year. For a business as large as Tesco's, this was an astonishing figure. The accounting scandal made sense of it: revenues were being boosted by what appeared to be a policy of maximising upfront payments from suppliers.

Another point to emerge was that staffing in stores had been squeezed. This was happening with all the supermarkets as automated tills came in, but at Tesco the squeeze was particularly aggressive. The number of staff per thousand square feet fell from more than six to fewer than four. Simon Marks had been right: the quality of service was suffering. At a store in Suffolk I asked to see the store manager to point out that the cereal section was in a terrible state: lots of packages torn open or crushed. "It's not us, it's the customers," the beleaguered manager exclaimed.

At one stage we had lost 65% of the value of our original investment. Lewis lowered prices and increased staffing. In the short term this would do nothing for trading margins – quite the opposite – but in the long term we felt that it was right, in order to improve the quality of service and hold on to market share before margins in due course stabilised, helped by a sharp reduction in the number of products. I visited the Suffolk store again a year later. The cereal section was impeccable. My teenage son retreated embarrassed to the car when I asked to see the store manager (a new one) to compliment her on this. The shares recovered to achieve post-howler status, becoming a respectable investment.

SBNE talked about visitee bias, the danger that by meeting management, even cursorily, investors feel that they have got under the bonnet of a company, know it better than other investors, and like it more than other companies. Our Tesco experience showed this danger. Chief executives are mortal: they do not know the future. Phil Clarke had a difficult task but he had no good reason to be confident about a return to a trading margin of 5.2% and we had no good reason to believe him.

Warren Buffett – who was himself an investor in Tesco before giving up in 2014 – famously said that if a business is bad and a management is good it is the reputation of the business that survives. In 2008 he talked to *Outstanding Investor Digest* about his investment in PetroChina and about the importance of being far from the frenzy of Wall Street:

> "The annual report came out in the spring – and I read it. And that's the only thing I ever did. I never contacted management, I never got a brokerage report, and I never asked for anybody's opinion... What's the sense of talking to management? If you talk to the management of almost any company, they'll say they think their stock is a wonderful buy... There are... overriding considerations that are enormously important. The rest is trivia that doesn't much matter... If we don't know in five minutes, we won't know in five months. The good big decisions, they don't take any time at all. If they take time, you're in trouble."

We took endless trouble about Tesco, agonising over it more than about almost anything else. Managements can only do so much and the lesson of Tesco was not to be credulous about the optimistic noises that a determinedly cheerful management makes. Managements should be judged by what they do rather than what they promise. Businesses need analysing, the issues need understanding, but investors should not kid themselves that by proximity and by intensity of research they will know all there is to know. Perfect understanding is an unattainable ideal.

Henry Kissinger said that people have absolute confidence in something about which they know nothing or something about which they know everything. To know everything is impossible. Investors should have a grip on the basic business of the company in which they invest and of the major issues that will bring success or failure. It is tempting, particularly when investors are engaging with managements to try to persuade them to do this or that, to become too involved. Stay engaged, avoid marriage. To keep some distance is a virtue. Investors ought to make sure that they stand back far enough to see the wood for the trees.

Valuations matter

Value investing, in its strictest definition, means investing in companies with low valuations – low price-earnings ratios, price-cash flow ratios, price-book value ratios, price-sales ratios. Value investing can be defined more broadly, and with the underperformance of companies with low valuation ratios over the last decade there has been a tendency for those who class themselves as value investors to push out the boundaries to include higher valuation ratios of businesses thought likely to grow strongly. As I said in *SBNE*, there are many ways to skin the investment cat, but what I was concerned with there was the narrower definition, both because it is what is in my blood and because it is an approach which, over the long term, appears to have an advantage.

There is ample evidence from the past about the long-term outperformance of value and the relationship between valuations (in the form of what is called the Graham and Dodd price-earnings ratio or in slightly different form the Shiller price-earnings ratio – today's share prices in aggregate divided by average post-tax profits per share over the previous 10 years) and returns over the ensuing decade.

What these statistics show is the all-powerful, simple, empirical truth that, based on market performance since 1880, if investors pay high price-earnings ratios then on average they get low returns and if they pay low price-earnings ratios, on average they get high returns.

Ben Graham regarded the tendency of the market "to overvalue common stocks which have been showing excellent growth or are glamorous... [and to] undervalue – relatively, at least – companies that are out of favour because of unsatisfactory developments of a temporary nature" as "a fundamental law."

But the fundamental law, and the evidence, are easy to forget when problems abound with companies having low valuations, and there is masses of enthusiasm for those with high valuations which are apparently on a roll. In the short term, returns from shares and markets with low valuations may be rotten. By their very nature, the companies and markets that have low valuations are those that have problems.

This is what deters the majority of investors and provides the minority with opportunity, if they can wear it. Sometimes there is a long wait. A whole decade can feel like forever. And occasionally there are exceptions to the general rule: 10-year periods in which low valuations have not produced the goods.

The period from 2007 to 2020 has been one of those in which shares of companies with high valuations have done very much better than those with low valuations. Returns from the value end of the market have been respectable: up to the end of 2020, the MSCI World Value Index has given a return of 9.4% per annum from 2009 and 7.6% from 2011; even from before the global financial crisis, the return has been 4.4%: no disaster. But growth has hugely outperformed. The degree of underperformance of value compared with growth over the last 14 years has outmatched all previous such episodes, even 1999-2000, the peak of the tech bubble. The Growth Index has done better than the Value Index by a remarkable 5% per annum over the 14 years to the end of 2020 – more a story of growth doing remarkably well than of value doing badly.

Anyone, like me, who is innately attracted to value investment has to wonder why. Part of the explanation, so easy to see and to say now with the benefit of 2021 hindsight, is that the world economy was first pulverised by the financial crash and then, in recovery, has stuttered and spluttered uncertainly, with a much lower growth rate than is typical for recoveries. This is not good, relatively, for value: industrial companies, cyclically sensitive, typically occupy value investing territory, having low valuations. The other part of the explanation, the major part, is disruption.

The eruption of disruption

When *SBNE* was published, disruption was something that happened in classrooms. It has since come to be a major theme, in fact the major theme, in stock markets.

In *One-Upmanship* (London; Hart Davis, 1952), Stephen Potter wrote that the surefire rejoinder to someone saying something knowledgeable about India was, "Yes, but not in the south." The riposte to the investment case for a dozen industries these days is, "Yes, but what about disruption?" Many companies in traditional industries with what appear at first sight to be unreasonably low valuations may be the victims of technology, changing everything so that nothing traditional can be relied on. The new sweeps away the old.

Not everything that seems new is new. Forty-five years ago I worked in the food department at Harrods. There was a method of online order then: it was called the telephone. Lady Something would ring to place an order and ask that it be delivered to Kensington Mansions. But the food department was still packed with people because they wanted to look at and smell the fresh food they bought.

A few years later I spent six months in the offices of Aetna Life & Casualty in Hartford, Connecticut, where I met my first robot. It made stately progress along the sprawling corridors, beep-beep-beeping and stopping from time to time so that people could collect tea and coffee from it.

Disruption itself is not new. Wood for energy was succeeded by coal, coal by oil and gas; tanks displaced cavalry, guns displaced bows, trains displaced horses. Some of these disruptions are astoundingly quick. In 1910 there were 128,000 horses at work in Manhattan. The Ford Motor Company was incorporated in 1903. The wholesale move from horse to car took roughly 25 years.

There are always disruption-deniers. In 1876 William Preece, chief engineer at the British Post Office, declared: "The Americans have need of the telephone, but we do not. We have plenty of messenger boys." Similarly, Daimler, early in the 20th century, thought that there would be need for no more than 10,000 cars because there would not be enough chauffeurs to drive them.

Nowadays robots do more than make the tea. They make TVs (Panasonic has a multi-acre site staffed by just 15 people) and cars; they trade shares; they can do language translations; they hand out money and look after checkout tills; they perform surgical operations without getting the shakes; they are test-driving cars, at the moment with a human beside them occasionally intervening; robots even make robots.

If a company can be said to be 'Ubered' when its core business is completely upended by the arrival of new technology, there is a lot of Ubering about. Taxi drivers around the world are in revolt against the incursions of Uber itself. Advertisers know all about Ubering. Music producers have been Ubered as the original method of distribution has changed half a dozen times – from gramophone records to tapes to CDs to digital to streaming. Car insurance may be Ubered by the arrival of driverless cars and a dramatic fall in accident rates. The car industry may be Ubered if we all buy electric cars. Retail has been Ubered by online. Online retailing has wrought havoc in high streets and shopping malls. The chief executive of the German pharmaceutical company Merck worries that healthcare may be Uberised by personalised treatments, medicines specific to the individual. Offices and airlines have been Ubered by Zoom during lockdown.

Stephen Hawking alluded to the most extreme form of Ubering, of humanity itself, when he suggested the possibility that progress in artificial intelligence might lead to robots taking over from humans and fighting each other.

There is a second order of disruption in the way in which the disruptors are financed. In the old days investors did not long tolerate companies which could not produce a profit. The last decade saw an enormous expansion of Silicon Valley confidence. Huge sums of money could be raised, apparently *ad infinitum*, for wave after wave of financings of companies which needed new money in order to grow and whose business model relied on a land grab, leading (after an extraordinarily long period of unprofitability) to a pot of gold at the end of the rainbow.

Disruption has seemed to have it all its own way, obliterating anything in its path. It is a truism that the pace of change is very fast, and the most important point about truisms is that they are true. But it is not quite the one-stop explanation, the Stephen Potter silencer, that markets recently have seen it to be. Disruptive changes in many areas have been accelerated by Covid and lockdown. Online retail sales have grown from less than 20% of all sales before Covid to 36% in June 2021. In other areas disruption does not proceed in a straight line and its course is not easy to predict. Changes have unforeseen consequences – the biggest beneficiary of WiFi is Starbucks.

There can occasionally be a sort of retro-disruption. Kindle sales have fallen in the last few years, and sales of physical books have increased. The founder of Facebook, Mark Zuckerberg, naming 2014 the Year of the Book, found "reading books very intellectually fulfilling. Books allow you to fully explore a topic and immerse yourself in a deeper way than most media today."

George Orwell, writing in 1936 in *Keep the Aspidistra Flying*, thought that cinema was the "art destined to replace literature." The death notices for cinema have been written several times with the arrivals of TV, DVDs, and streaming. The number of cinemagoers has fallen, but 2019 was the third-best year ever for US box office revenues. It remains to be seen what the future of cinema is post-Covid.

Retail is now in turmoil. There may eventually be a point at which the devastation of bricks-and-mortar retailing stops because, as in the food hall at Harrods, people still like to go shopping. We used to be told in the 1980s and 1990s that shopping is a leisure activity, and at Bicester, Bluewater and Westfield, vast English shopping centres, it still is. Just now, to say that physical retailing is not dead may provoke only a hollow laugh; but things change.

This is not to deny the reality of disruption. *Tempora mutantur, et nos mutamur in illis* – times change, and we change with them – was the first tweet of Jacob Rees-Mogg, the founder of Somerset Capital Management. On the same note the research firm 13D quoted Charles F. Kettering, head of research at General Motors between 1920 and 1947: "If you're doing something the same way you have been doing it for 10 years, the chances are you are doing it wrong." There are plenty of sectors suffering acutely and possibly terminally from disruption by new technology.

But it was the tendency for markets to assume, when they spot a trend, that events will move from point A to point Z without anything much in between, that created the tech bubble in 1999–2000, with talk of the new era sweeping aside the old economy. It led to a tremendous bubble in valuations of technology stocks. In fact, many of the technological developments that the market was latching onto did indeed happen. They happened very quickly but, as *SBNE* discussed, not quite as quickly as market pricing implied.

Disruption in the car sector

The car sector has been a paradigm for disruption: Mary Barra, chief executive of General Motors, has said: "I believe the auto industry will change more in the next five to 10 years than it has in the last 50." The *Financial Times* suggested that individual cars could go the way of the horse and cart. Apart from the ordinary to-and-fro of economic cycles there are three technological threats to the traditional car industry: electric vehicles, autonomous or driverless cars, and car sharing.

The traditional companies have a good chance of competing in electric vehicles. General Motors' electric car, the Bolt, has a 200-mile-plus range, costing about the same as Tesla's Model 3 with roughly the same range. Tesla and others may well make huge inroads into the electric vehicle market but there is no obvious reason why the traditional carmakers should not be successful with electric cars. Tesla's market capitalisation was $650bn, more than twice that of General Motors, Ford and Volkswagen combined. Tesla produced half a million vehicles in 2020; General Motors and Ford, between them, produced about 5m in the US alone, and Volkswagen about 9m.

In 2019 an Oxford professor in artificial intelligence told a group that the challenge of driverless vehicles had been cracked. I queried this. He explained that what he meant was that the technological problem had been solved; what was left was a problem of execution. It would be 30 years before any of us could wander into a car showroom and buy a car with no windscreen.

In the US, the National Transportation Safety Board, in a public hearing to determine the cause of a fatal accident in March 2018 when a self-driving car killed a pedestrian as she crossed the street with a bicycle, was scathingly critical of the National Highway Traffic Safety Administration for putting "technology advancement... before saving lives." A board member of the NTSB said that the NHTSA's guidelines, 'Automated Driving Systems, a Vision for Safety', was "laughable" and should be renamed 'a Vision for Lax Safety.'

The last few per cent of minutely accurate mapping is essential. There are also the moral quandaries to be dealt with: if someone with a pram steps off the kerb without looking, at just the same moment that a child on a bicycle is veering across the middle of the road, which should the car avoid? A driverless car will have to be programmed to deal with such dilemmas, though they do not happen in real life very often.

The impact of the eventual move to autonomous vehicles could be that there will be more demand, not less. If it becomes possible to do work or play games in the car, tolerance for trips, and for long trips, may actually go up rather than down. The efficiency in traffic of autonomous cars may, other things being equal, reduce congestion, but the reduction in congestion may draw other cars, autonomous or not, onto the roads until the mysterious saturation point at which people's tolerance is exhausted.

This is the opinion of a Brussels-based cleaner transport lobby group, Transport and Environment, who worry that, "Automated vehicles with no driver could become so cheap to run that they would encourage people, or even cars without people in them, to travel more and for longer." They warn of "a rush hour that lasts all day."

Car-sharing poses more of a threat to car-makers. Owning a car is not as important to young people as it used to be. A University of Michigan study in 2016 found that 69% of 19-year-olds in the US had driving licences in 2014, compared with 87% in 1983. In a car-sharing age, the second car in a two-car household may seem truly redundant when in any case it spends 95% of its time idle. However, the other 5% tends to be very much the same for everyone: it is the time of day when people are driving to the station or to work, or taking their children to school.

The threat of car-sharing would be greater if there were true car-sharing: not sharing with an Uber driver or, for that matter, a robot, but sharing with other passengers. Yet all experience suggests that people prefer not to share cars with strangers. In emerging markets as they develop, the proclivity to share with other passengers reduces. In India and other emerging economies, we are used to seeing taxis packed with passengers dropped off at different destinations. In developed markets, on the contrary, we see, in the worst traffic jams, cars with only one occupant.

In the early 1980s, when there were lots of train strikes, I used to drive from Kent up the A2 until I reached traffic at a standstill, usually around Greenwich, and then park, get my bike out of the boot and cycle the rest of the way to the City, sweeping smugly past lines of cars – each of which had only one occupant: the driver. It was a lesson that tolerance for traffic jams is enormous. It seems unlikely that the tolerance for jams tomorrow will be any less than the tolerance for jams today. In spite of the jams, people simply like driving. If people wanted to share cars with other passengers they would already be doing so.

Like Stephen Potter on India, just to breathe the word 'disruption' has seemed enough to pulverise the arguments for traditional companies. The car sector is not untypical: disruption undoubtedly applies, but in myriad ways with effects that are nuanced, and not uniformly disastrous for the car companies. Moreover, the spectre of disruption reduces valuations to levels at which they may more than adequately take account of disruptive effects.

Valuation vertigo

Much of the performance of markets in the last decade has been the work of the stars of disruption, especially the five companies that make up the FAANGs. A handful of new age companies have stolen the show, while much else has been part of a bedraggled chorus, limping wearily into the wings as the stars continue to dazzle. They have earned their star status, having shown remarkable growth in earnings. The problem is that these outstanding companies are very difficult to identify before it becomes obvious to everyone, and that so many other companies now have valuations suggesting they are the next FAANGs.

In the last year or so there has been a rather *fin de siècle* atmosphere, as much in the surroundings of stock markets as actually in them. There is Bitcoin. There is the yield on junk bonds. There is Uber and Lyft and WeWork. J.K. Galbraith said that in times of euphoria, "past experience… is dismissed as the primitive refuge of those who do not have the insight to appreciate the incredible wonders of the present." Present wonders are reflected especially by exuberance in many technology companies' share prices, and pockets of complacency after too much of a good thing.

The Victorian economist and political guru, Walter Bagehot, opined that low interest rates incite speculation and the taking on of too much debt, and "thereby store up trouble." He continued:

> "John Bull can stand many things, but he cannot stand 2%… Instead, people invest their capital savings in something impossible – a canal to Kamchatka, a railway to Watchet, a plan for animating the Dead Sea, a corporation for shipping skates to the Torrid Zone."

We will see over the next several years whether there have been too many canals to Kamchatka. In 2000 all the talk was of a new era, and those who had seen the light told those who saw clouds that, "You just don't get it." In terms of valuation, there is nothing new under the sun. The conviction that everything is a victim of disruption has led to the triumph of the disruptors in markets.

Recent parallels with 1999–2000 are evident. I was far too early in pointing out these parallels years ago, but the parallels have got even more parallel than they used to be. At the end of 2018 the amount of venture capital investment into tech companies surpassed the dot-com bubble peak for the first time.

In June 2021 there were more than 700 unicorns – start-up companies valued in the private market at more than \$1bn. A billion dollars is a lot for a start-up. 80% of US listed initial public offerings in 2018 involved companies that lost money in the preceding 12 months. According to *Financial News*, "the previous high-water mark was 2000, when 81% of companies going public were unprofitable."

The flotation of Lyft in 2019, with losses of nearly \$1bn, followed soon after by that of Uber, with nearly \$2bn of losses, had an end-of-cycle flavour. WeWork, a property company owned by private equity funds, achieved \$1.9bn of losses with \$1.8bn of revenue. In 2018 it got through cash of \$2.3bn. Its occupancy rate was 80%. WeWork was to have had an initial public offering. Only months before the due date in 2019 it had been valued at \$47bn. After the offering was cancelled, another transaction valued it at \$8bn. WeWork's business was to own and let office space, providing lots of trendy shared services beyond the obvious and traditional. This made it a disruptor. The founder, Adam Neumann, described its mission as being, "to elevate the world's consciousness," and the accounts included an item described as, "socially adjusted earnings before interest, tax, depreciation and amortisation." It is a property company.

The prospectus in 2019 for the cancelled WeWork offering had 383 pages. As Brett Wallace wrote in the *Financial Times*, "WeWork's business model isn't complicated." Uber's initial public offering document was 431 pages long. (By contrast, that of Microsoft in 1986 was 52 pages.) Its stated mission is, "to ignite opportunity by setting the world in motion." Uber is a taxi service with an extra facility, so one might expect an Uber ride to cost more than an ordinary taxi ride. It does not, because its drivers are paid badly and because customers have been subsidised by the company's losses, in turn subsidised by the appetite of private equity for companies such as this engaged in a long-term land grab. There is not enough land for all the land-grabbers to be successful.

There has been no sign of shortage of supply of equity. For the last 10 years private equity funds have been willing providers of money. The bursting of the bubble depends on an attack of valuation vertigo, the sort of thing that can happen at any point when absurd heights are reached, but which is unpredictable. A resounding finale to the outperformance of growth over value could come in the form of an end, sudden or gradual, to the splurge of private equity financing of businesses making large losses, at interest rates of close to zero. When that happens it will bring into sharp relief the contrasting merits of moderate valuations of businesses that may be humdrum, growing slightly if at all, but at least have the advantage of producing profits and free cash flow.

As in 1999, many traditional companies are at valuations below their traditional levels, and these are exactly the sort of companies to which favourable attention turned in March 2000 when the tech bubble burst: most of them went up when the market went down. In the auction houses, contemporary art has been all the rage, while for decades brown furniture has been scoffed at and prices have fallen. In today's markets, the shares of many large, well-known, companies worldwide are the brown furniture of the investment world, partially overlooked by investors searching for the more exotic.

No one can predict exactly when the turning point in this unusual trend will come. Railing about the continuing outperformance of growth has been akin to the caricature of King Canute telling the sea to go back. It kept on coming, and so did growth. The tide will turn, but when? In the words of the economist Alec Cairncross:

"A trend is a trend is a trend.
But the question is, will it bend?
Will it alter its course
Through some unforeseen force
And come to a premature end?"

I thought the turn had come in February 2016, three months after the first rise in US interest rates. There is a strong association between a rise in interest rates and outperformance of value; logical since a higher discount rate damages the valuation of companies where it is necessary to look forward several years to anticipated earnings in order to justify investment. After the initial rises in interest rates in 2017 and 2018, the Fed retreated.

Then came Covid. Around the world central banks poured money into the economy. Ironically, the global financial crisis of 2008–09 provided the solution to the economic crisis caused by Covid and lockdown: it was the global financial crisis that had produced near zero interest rates and the rediscovery and embellishment of quantitative easing. Governments spent by borrowing in the bond markets, and central banks bought the bonds. In what is termed modern monetary theory there is no obvious limit to how much can be borrowed and spent. Central bankers blusteringly dismiss modern monetary theory, but it seems to be one of those things that does not work in theory but (in the exceptional circumstances in which everyone is doing it at the same time) can work in practice, at least for a while.

The trouble is that, once the magic money tree has been discovered, it is hard to stop using it. If the vast increase in money supply finds its way into the real economy, prices will rise much more than they have done during the past decade (and more) of extremely low inflation. Eventually interest rates will rise from their present unnaturally low level.

Value managers tend to have an innate bias towards buying what is cheap. In 2007, even with foresight about the effects of QE over the next ten years, I would have found it difficult to escape from a bias towards value. I think pretty much now as I did in 2007 about value investing.

I learned a lesson or two in 2008 and put a greater emphasis on the unpredictability caused by a stretched balance sheet. But in essence I believe in the same things as I did then: concentrated portfolios managed with individual accountability and no 'committeeitis', and consisting of shares held patiently in companies with basically sound businesses which are at low valuations because of the vagaries of fashion or because something has gone temporarily wrong.

Priced for perfection

Stock markets have cycles. In the 1970s and early 1980s, a time of high government debt, government spending, and inflation, investors wanted companies with real assets, for example commodity producers. In 1980, energy constituted almost one third of the MSCI World Index, and six of the world's top ten companies. Even in 2010 five of the top ten were energy companies. By 2021 none of the top ten was an energy company.

In 1990, eight of the biggest ten companies in the world were Japanese, and six of those were banks. Japan was thought supreme in economic and corporate management, and everyone else wanted to copy the Japanese. But in fact 1990 was the peak and it has been downhill ever since. The consensus about energy in 1980, and the consensus about Japan in 1990, were dislodged by the events of the following years. In 2000, the new economy was the rage, and advocates of old economy stocks were has-beens.

US equity markets constitute 56% of world markets, and the consensus is that the US knows how to do things better. The Shiller price-earnings ratio for the US is now higher than more than 95% of readings since 1871. All may turn out wonderfully, but what this suggests is that the return of US equities over the next 10 years will probably be much lower than the long-term average after-inflation return of about 6% per annum.

One symptom of over-exuberance is the enthusiasm of retail investors who have never previously been anywhere near the stock market and whose trading is now facilitated by online platforms such as Robinhood. Another is the fashion for special purpose acquisition companies, 'SPACs'. These are companies which have initial public offerings before they have any activities. They can then spend up to two years looking for targets to buy, providing private companies with a potentially easy path to a public listing, avoiding a prospectus. By June 2021 more than $200bn had been raised in SPACs. A typical filing stated that: "Our founders have expertise and experience investing across virtually all industries and sectors and we may pursue an acquisition in any business industry." They may do very well, but SPACs are reminiscent of the mythical South Sea Bubble company, which was formed "for carrying out an undertaking of great advantage, nobody to know what it is." Such excesses are the result of a combination of FOMO-meets-KATRINA: fear of missing out, and keep asset-buying, there really is no alternative.

In the US, now looks like a time for a foot on the brake. Markets outside the US have much more attractive valuations so that their chances of decent returns over the next 10 years are much higher.

Green and good

With disruption everywhere, it is certainly not safe to assume, in whatever industry one happens to be looking at, that things will continue much as they are. The oil industry has been the latest victim of bouleversement. The idea of stranded assets – reserves that may never be used because of the switch to alternative sources of energy – has been around for a while. The acknowledgement of climate change is now almost universal.

There are so many people at sustainability conferences that comparison could be made with new paradigm views at 2000 technology conferences. At one of these sustainability conferences, in New York, I sat next to a man who had taken part in a panel discussion. In the year before, he had flown 75,000 miles. He felt that the impact he had on his various audiences meant that nonetheless he was producing a net benefit to emissions.

It is possible to regard any fossil fuel assets as being in part stranded, but coal leads the way. In 1882 the UK became the first major country to use coal for electricity, and it has been the first to promise to phase it out (by 2025). The link between environmental impact and asset values was first made in around 1989, about the time that Margaret Thatcher was in the vanguard of politicians warning about climate change. Attention to stranded assets took off in 2011–12.

A Stanford University study has suggested that wind, water and sun could provide all electricity by 2050. Lower demand for fossil fuels could come from more efficient use and also from substitution, with rapid progress being made in electric and hydrogen-fuelled cars. Storage and battery prices will come down hugely, not in a straight line of improvement but exponentially. The government policy pushback against climate change is going to continue relentlessly. Policy will incentivise development of renewables and less use of conventional energy sources if markets, research and innovation are not moving fast enough on their own.

We used to worry that the world would run out of oil, but that is no longer the main cause for concern. As Sheikh Yamani, the former head of OPEC, once observed, the Stone Age did not come to an end because the world ran out of stone. New technologies push out the old.

On the other hand, more than 40% of oil produced worldwide is currently used to fuel transport. Gas-guzzling SUVs are more popular than electric vehicles, economies grow, and fossil fuels, which now account for 85% of all energy, might account for a lower proportion but an even larger quantity in 2050.

Divestment and demonisation

The ESG lobby – to persuade large institutional funds to sell their holdings in fossil fuel companies – adds pressure. The momentum behind this pressure is enormous. People who cast doubt on policies that deal with climate change are reviled as climate change deniers. Failing to participate fully in the demonisation of fossil fuel companies is regarded as *ipso facto* wrong, whatever the activities of the fossil fuel companies may be.

Universities, pressurised by students, are getting rid of some of their fossil fuel investments. By early 2021 just over half of the UK's 154 universities had committed to some fossil fuel divestment, as had the Church of England. For most, the divestment is very limited – it applies to companies for which coal mining or tar sands oil extraction form a major part of their portfolio. The Church of England found that adopting its new policy meant it had to sell only £12m of assets from its £8bn of funds.

Global assets with an ESG mandate (a broad description) have risen from nothing at the turn of the century to about $38trn. The lobby group Sustainable Investment Alliance forecasts that this will rise to $150trn by 2036 – more than the market capitalisation of all equity markets now, and a striking example of extrapolation.

Divestment is a simple step to take, but deciding what to divest is not easy. Superficially obvious answers turn out to be suspect. Some people take a very strong line about genetically modified foods. Others regard GM as essential to dealing with the prospect of food shortage. Some dislike parts of the press so much that they recoil from investment in media companies. Others think the balancing advantage of a free press is overwhelming. Some dislike the practices of pharmaceutical companies, and others the practices of social media companies – both their abuse of privacy and conversely their provision of anonymity, which fuels the most unpleasant Hobbesian instincts.

A friend once took me to task for investing in easyJet, because short-haul flights are disproportionately polluting and carbon-heavy. The aviation industry is responsible for approximately 3% of (human-induced) carbon emissions. This compares, for example, with 40% from electricity and heat production, 25% from industrial, 11% from passenger road vehicles, 7% from road freight vehicles, and 1% from rail. I am a user of easyJet. I would regard it as hypocritical and inconsistent to take any kind of prohibitive view about investment in easyJet, other airlines, or air travel in general when I do all these terrible things myself. So does my friend. EasyJet will be the world's first major international airline to offset carbon emissions on all flights. EasyJet also operates one of the most fuel-efficient fleets, more so in the future with the introduction of the latest version of the Airbus A320. It is working with Airbus to develop electric and hybrid electric planes for short-haul European flights and with Wright Electric, a US company which is developing electric planes.

It is for elected governments to decide on policy and if a government should decide that it is in the public interest to put more tax on, or otherwise penalise, short-haul flights I will have no complaint about their right to do so. Warren Buffett talked about the difficulty of investors imposing these ethical judgements: "It's very hard to do. If you give me the 20 largest companies, I don't know which of the 20 behaves best, really... I like to eat candy. Is candy good for me or not?"

Judgements about dilemmas in behaviour are subjective. Different people may take different views about the consistency of using a company's − or an industry's − products or services on the one hand while prohibiting investment in such companies or industries on the other. Clients may prohibit this or that. It makes sense for charities to prohibit investment in companies whose activities are inimical to their charitable objectives. I was a trustee of the Royal Marsden Cancer Charity for nine years. We prohibited investment in tobacco, naturally and logically. But the logic of most prohibitions is not so clear-cut.

For institutions like pension funds and charities that hire managers, applying personal prejudices or ethical judgements is more questionable, given the inconclusiveness of most of the debates. To ban sectors or companies can even be self-indulgent or shallow − virtue-signalling or greenwashing.

The same is true of managers. Rather than demanding that they ban investments in particular companies or sectors, investors might instead expect managers to show that they think about these things. Consideration of environmental − as well as social and governance − concerns should be part of every investment manager's process and they should be able to show how they take these concerns into account. They should avoid companies where they have serious concerns about governance or about business being conducted unethically, and should be prepared to talk to managements to keep up the pressure to reduce environmental impact – not least because in the long run companies with bad practices are unlikely to do well.

Companies are usually neither saints nor sinners. Those most castigated for their environmental damage are frequently making the most effort to redress the damage they have done or reduce the damage they are doing now – BP and Royal Dutch Shell, for example. Shell is planning to invest $2–3bn a year in wind, solar and other green energy. Steel is needed in wind and solar farms, and to make steel coal is needed. Attempting to suffocate these companies by making their shares untouchable or starving them of borrowings is a short-sighted, and indeed counter-productive, policy since they need capital to make the changes.

There are now plenty of ESG funds that exclude companies and sectors such as tobacco, defence, and fossil fuels. Investors may well feel more comfortable with these sorts of exclusions. But there is a better objective argument for engaging with companies in these areas, choosing companies that have the best practices or are reforming their practices fastest, are trying hardest to reduce their environmental impact, and are at the forefront of innovation with environmentally friendly products.

The pre-eminence of passive

The battle between passive and active has been another key theme in recent years. There has been hugely increased popularity of exchange-traded funds (ETFs), which are a form of index funds, or 'passive' funds.

The passive world has evolved: initially, passive meant investing in line with a particular well-established market index such as the S&P 500 or the MSCI World Index. ETFs have become the most-used form of passive investment. These allow the investor to hold a single security, in some cases the security of a fund that itself holds the components of a market index and in other cases a security for which an intermediary, in the form of an investment bank, commits to provide the return that the market index would provide. At the end of November 2019, the total value of index-tracking investment vehicles was $11.4trn, compared with $2.4trn in index funds ten years ago.

Many such ETFs take the traditional approach, replicating the return of an index; many others are increasingly sophisticated subsets of indices. The investor can choose, for example, an ETF which gives exposure to US technology companies, or to European steel companies, or to global small cap value or global small cap growth. An ETF is available in 120 companies which are relatively immune to an international trade war. Some degree of active decision-making is inevitable: even if a robot makes every decision after the first, the first decision regarding asset allocation cannot be made by a robot.

The fees on such specialised funds are sometimes close to those of active managers (0.81% in the case of the Trade War ETF, compared with 0.095% charged by State Street for their ETF based on the S&P 500, SPY, which has a total value of $250bn).

A portfolio constructed of index funds or ETFs can be quite simple in having a small number of holdings, and can also be much cheaper than wholly active alternatives. Passive has the great virtue that, in a sense, it cannot be wrong: there will be no underperformance. Given the range of choice in passive, its cheapness and its apparent simplicity, it is natural to ask, "What is the point of active?" There can be only one point, and that is the potential for outperformance, a potential which ultimately has to be realised for it to be worthwhile. The investor has to believe, first, that there are active managers who more likely than not will, against the odds for active managers overall, outperform; second, that it is possible for some people to choose such outperforming managers; and third, that the investor is one of those people.

I think that it is possible to choose a group of active managers the majority of whom will outperform for the majority of the time. To succeed in this it is necessary to avoid the temptation, which so many committees fall into, of lurching – sacking the manager who has just underperformed and appointing the manager who has just outperformed for other clients. This tail-chasing temptation tends to lead to underperformance, as described elsewhere.

I would not put the argument for choosing active managers more strongly than that. As *SBNE* described, active has an uphill struggle: since markets are dominated by professional investors who are active managers, in the long term the average active manager will underperform the market (and therefore passive funds representing the market) by at least the extent of their fees and the cost of transactions. Moreover, all active managers, however successful over the long term, have patches of poor performance.

Investors who think that they can appoint active managers who will all consistently outperform would be better advised not to try. Equally, investors who doubt that they can choose active managers who will mostly outperform in the long run should not try, and should settle for going passive. It is far better to accept the market return that passive will give than to attempt something to which the investor is not committed and incur the risk of self-damaging reactions at the wrong moments. Investors using active managers need to be sure that they will not be lurchers, and that means basing decisions about managers on judgements about the people, their approach and process, and the environment in which they work; not on immediate past performance.

The last decade has been marvellously good for passive, index-tracking, funds. But it has been dangerously bad for index-huggers who purport to be active managers but in fact stick very closely to the relevant index. In November 2019, Janus Henderson was fined £1.9m by the Financial Conduct Authority in the UK for 'closet tracking'. Janus Henderson had told its institutional customers when they changed the policy of two funds so that they followed the indices more closely, but had not told its retail clients. The FCA ruled that, "the fees charged… were inappropriate, given the diminished level of active management." In 2016 the European Securities and Markets Authority found that up to a sixth of actively managed equity funds were potential closet-trackers.

SBNE makes the case for investment managers who have portfolios radically different from any index (very different from these index-huggers). For most such managers, the period since *SBNE* has been tough. As *SBNE* says, the average active manager should be expected to underperform the benchmark indices. But in the last decade that underperformance has been immense. Only 19% of global equity managers outperformed the index in the ten years to June 2020. Something funny has been going on.

In one sense the mass migration to passive funds is perfectly sensible because the odds are against the active manager and the person trying to identify an active manager who will outperform. It is what investors who do not think they can outperform, or pick managers who will outperform, should do. But in another sense it is one of the waves of enthusiasm that move markets, which in time will reverse.

This one is due for reversal. An article in the *Financial Times* in January 2020 was headed: 'Next decade will not be kind to active managers' and included the prediction that the next ten years for asset managers would be, "probably much the same as the past ten years." I would bet on exactly the opposite: that the next ten years could, on the contrary, be a golden decade for active managers because the trend away from them has been too strong and is due for a large dose of reversion to the mean.

The top five stocks, by market capitalisation, now account for 22% of the Standard & Poor's 500 in the US. This figure has almost never been higher. The average active manager, holding between 60 and 100 stocks, does not hold as much as 22% in five stocks. So the effect of the move from active managers to indexing is to produce buying pressure for the very large companies that have outsized weightings in the S&P, and to drive up their prices.

Critics may well question why this should not continue. But just suppose there is a period in which Facebook, Apple, Amazon, Netflix and Google do not do so well, and the actions of disappointed active managers are sufficient to push their prices down: the effect on the S&P will be greater than the effect on the average active manager, because of the relative weightings in these companies.

If this were to go on for a year or two, indexers would notice that their index funds were now underperforming active managers disproportionately. Some of them might then hurry back to active management. This would magnify the underperformance of index funds; the hurrying of a few could become the hurtling of a herd. There might then be a sustained period in which active management was vindicated.

Ultimately, the nature of markets means that the average active manager must underperform over the long term; but for quite some time the boot might be on the active foot. This seems to me, full of the folly of forecasting, a reasonable expectation.

Patience, patience, patience

A truly active policy, with a portfolio quite different from any index, requires great patience because, even if investors are able to make the leap of faith in their ability to choose active managers who will outperform in the long term, they can be quite sure that every manager will disappoint for a period, and maybe a long period.

Peter Cundill provided a vivid example of the necessity of patience if a manager and its clients are committed to a truly active policy with a portfolio that differs radically from the composition of the relevant market index.

By the time Peter Cundill died in 2011 he had a glittering track record. $100 invested with him when he started in 1975 had turned into $10,173 by the end of 2010, while $100 invested in the MSCI World Index would have turned into $3,531. But had the music stopped at the end of 1999 it would have been a different story. In the four years from 1995 to 1998 Peter Cundill's Value Fund performed very poorly, as a result of which for the whole period from inception in 1975 to 1998 there was underperformance: $100 invested at inception would have turned into $3,716 by the end of 1998, compared with $4,006 if invested in the MSCI World Index (without fees).

What changed everything was the bursting of the bubble in

early 2000 and the superb performance of the shares of companies with ultra-low valuations which he owned from 2000 onwards. He needed, and had, an iron constitution to bear the underperformance of the late 1990s. It was all worth it in the end. As he put it during those painful years, "I will have the last laugh but I may miss a lot of jokes on the way." The investor Jason Zweig, who writes about the business of investing, describes the necessity of a condition known as ataraxia – the state of not being bothered by the things that bother other people. Peter Cundill had plenty of ataraxia.

Appropriately, one of Peter Cundill's mantras was: patience, patience, patience. As *SBNE* pointed out, the Latin word from which patience is derived is also the root of the word passion, and the biblical meaning of passion is suffering. Unfortunately, investors concentrating on apparently deeply undervalued shares have to have a great capacity for suffering, because there will be many periods in which the thing that they are patiently waiting for takes an awfully long time to happen, and they may suffer a great deal while it is not happening, and have to be pretty passionate about it.

Still simple, still not easy

In films based on fact, before the credits roll, we are often told what happened afterwards to the protagonists. I should try to summarise, in closing, what has happened to the themes and thoughts of *SBNE* in the 14 years since its publication.

Rip van Winkle Asset Management, whose chief investment officer spends long periods, sometimes decades, asleep, has been doing fine. If he wakes up soon, he will be satisfied by the cumulative return in US dollars of global equities since 2007 of 197%, 7.8% per annum, or 5.7% in real terms. In sterling, this was equivalent to 321% cumulatively, or 10.4% per annum, or 8.3% in real terms. In the long run, equities have continued to provide a better after-inflation return than just about anything else. We need not tell Rip about the 2008–09 debacle: being absent during those two years meant he avoided the temptation to get too gloomy during the crisis, temptation to which many succumbed and which is still reflected in cautious investment policies a decade later. He slumbered also through 2020. It will be evident to him, looking at the state of markets, that the world must have been an unusually stable place while he was asleep.

"Bonds are death; equities life" has been an overstatement. Around the time that *SBNE* was published I chaired a meeting of a particular investment committee for the first time. Someone suggested that government bonds were a hopeless investment and all of us nodded away – the perils of consensus – with the honourable exception of the brave consultant from Cambridge Associates who said that one could never be quite sure and that the diversification that bonds provided could be useful. We decided to have no government bonds. From 2007 to June 2021 the FTSE World Government Bond Index has given a return of 3.7% per annum in US dollar terms, 6.4% per annum in sterling terms: not glittering, but not a bad diversification over the whole period and particularly useful in a shock year like 2008.

Hedge funds in aggregate have been dismal. In *SBNE* I suggested that if equities gave a return of 6% per annum then the average equity hedge fund could be expected to give about 2.3% per annum. In fact, equities have given a return of 7.8% in US dollars since 2007 and the average equity hedge fund gave a return slightly above zero.

'Value managers outperform' and 'Why Value goes on working' are the headings of two sections in chapter 13 of *SBNE*, fragile claims since 2007 when the leitmotif has been the underperformance of value – if that means investing in companies with low valuation ratios. Disruption (unmentioned, like Brexit, in *SBNE*), near-zero interest rates, and slow economies have been a fearsome trio, conspiring to produce value traps by the barrel-load. In relative performance value slightly lagged growth in 2007–11, and in 2012–20 was trounced spectacularly by growth.

Fees have mattered, and been seen to matter. Index-clingers have been under closer scrutiny: why cling to the clumsy clone if you can have the real thing for less cost? Index funds, on the other hand, have had the time of their lives.

Forecasting has been as erratic as ever, especially during the crisis in 2009 when there were excesses of first complacency and then of gloom. The record of forecasters is still worse than a dart-throwing monkey could manage: in September 2018 there was complete unanimity among economists that interest rates were set to rise, and the consensus, both of the economists and of members of the Fed in the US, was that there would be three interest rate rises in the US during 2019. By the middle of 2019 there was complete unanimity in the opposite direction. And that was before the *deus ex machina* event of Covid.

The jargon of those in the investment profession has not improved. "We maintain a positive view of Ford's improving optionality regarding further asset structure optimisation." Or, as it might be put, if the company wants to sell assets it has plenty of choices.

The messages of *SBNE*, with a flesh wound here, a flesh wound there, survive. *Simple but not easy* is a paradox, and investment, like life, is full of paradox. Ralph Waldo Emerson said that "A foolish consistency is the hobgoblin of small minds." Successful investing means juggling with paradoxes. There is nothing new under the sun, but times change and we must change with them. The behaviour of markets is the behaviour of crowds, and we have always seen it all some place before; and yet… *plus c'est la même chose, plus ça change.*

ACKNOWLEDGEMENTS – SECOND EDITION

In addition to all those I thanked for their help with *SBNE* in 2007, I am grateful to Harriman House for suggesting that they publish this new edition, and to Christopher Parker, Tracy Bundey and Lucy Vincent for their invaluable part in getting it done; and to Wilf Craigie, Richard and Rachel Garstang, Jacob Laursen, Arul Nathaniel, and Christoph Ohm for their help and comments.

INDEX